CHELTENHAM
IN THE
GREAT WAR

CHELTENHAM
IN THE
GREAT WAR

NEELA MANN

In Association with Cheltenham Local History Society

The
History
Press

This book is dedicated to

Alfred Mann (1855–1929),
Cheltenham Town Councillor for Middle Ward 1908–1928,
Alderman 1928–1929, known as 'the working man's
Conservative'; and to his great-great-grandsons Henry Mann,
born 22 August 2015, and Jason Mann, born 10 March 2010,
who have a history to be proud of and a future to look forward to.

First published 2016

The History Press
The Mill, Brimscombe Port
Stroud, Gloucestershire, GL5 2QG
www.thehistorypress.co.uk

British Library Cataloguing in Publication Data.
A catalogue record for this book is available from the British Library.

ISBN 978 0 7509 6415 9

Typesetting and origination by The History Press
Printed in Malta by Melita Press

Front cover images: The Municipal Offices, Cheltenham and
group of people (Neela Mann). Sopwith Camel (THP)

Contents

Acknowledgements

Firstly, thanks to Sir Henry Elwes of Colesbourne Park, a member of Cheltenham Local History Society, who contributed the foreword to this book. Sir Henry's grandparents gave Leckhampton Court to the Red Cross to be used as a hospital during the war.

The research for this book was carried out with the help of knowledgeable experts. One such was Christopher Rainey from Cheltenham Local and Family History Centre. Christopher's help was invaluable in answering a multitude of diverse queries and discovering material such as a dusty volume of newspaper cuttings, entitled *Food 1917* – a resource that may not have seen the light of day for nigh on 100 years. Dr Steven Blake gave much help and unearthed important material at The Wilson. Vicky Thorpe at Gloucestershire Archives and Jimmy James of www.remembering. org.uk provided important background information. David Read of the Soldiers of Gloucestershire Museum supplied regimental information and images and David Drinkwater gave willingly of his important research on Cheltenham's soldiers – some of David's research can be read on the county archive website. Thanks also go to Albert Hands, whose love of Cheltenham and prolific contributions on the Facebook forum 'Days Gone By In Cheltenham', have been a source of such fascinating information.

Members of Cheltenham Local History Society contributed initial research for the exhibition, which provided the basis for this book. In particular thanks go to Sue Robbins, whose extracted information from letters in the *Gloucestershire Echo* has been so important for the book, Kath Boothman for information on Cheltenham Ladies' College and Heather Atkinson for the use of her notes on food rationing. Joyce Cummings and Vic Cole were both a mine of information and thanks must go to the committee of Cheltenham Local History Society, chairman David Scriven and, in particular, Gwyneth Rattle for supporting the project.

Particular thanks to my wonderful sister-in-law and good friend Julia Manning who read the draft of the book and gave solid, constructive advice and encouragement, as has Jill Waller who, with her vast knowledge of local history, was also the verifier of obscure information.

Thanks to the caring nursing staff of Bay C, Ward B3, Gloucester Royal Hospital who made it possible for me to finish the book when I broke my ankle two weeks before the deadline.

Last, but certainly not least, my heartfelt thanks to my husband Nicholas Mann, whom I have taken within a whisker of total exasperation and without whose patience and sufferance this book could not have come to fruition.

Thanks also go to:

Bob Allard; Barry Attoe, Post Office Museum London; Norman Baker of Prestbury Local History Society; Adrian Barlow; Jill Barlow of Cheltenham College; Derek Benson; Chris Bentall; Dr Robert Billings; James Brazier; Alwyn Burton; Paul Evans and John Putley of Gloucestershire Archives; Wayne Finch; David Hanks ('Cheltenham Past and Present' on Facebook); Ann-Rachael Harwood at The Wilson Art Gallery and Museum; Marion Hearfield of Stroud Local History Society; Helene Hewlett of The Suffolk Anthology Independent Book Shop, No. 17 Suffolk Parade, Cheltenham; Jerry Holmes and Rebecca Sillence (Cheltenham Local and Family History Centre); the late Jerry Jenkinson and Caroline Meller of Gloucester Local History Society; Anne Jones; Dr Anthea Jones; Richard King (Billings family); Mick Kippin; Eric Miller of Leckhampton Local History Society; Geoff North; Karen Radford, Cheltenham Borough Council; Rachel Roberts of Cheltenham Ladies' College Archive; Sue Rowbotham; Professor Peter Simkins; John Whitaker; Bob Wilson.

Foreword

Little has formally been recorded about life in Cheltenham during the First World War and indeed one writer, Simona Pakenham, even recorded that 'Cheltenham in the 20th century marked time until 1919'! I am sure this view was not shared by the many hundreds of families who made a significant contribution to the war effort both on the various fronts and at home.

The Promenade war memorial is testament to the enormous sacrifices made by so many Cheltenham families and this has been brought into true perspective throughout 2014, the 100th anniversary of the start of the war. We must also not forget the many hundreds of families who kept the war effort going from home by building aeroplanes, billeting troops, running hospitals for the wounded, knitting warm clothes for the soldiers and even collecting chestnuts for the manufacture of explosives. Few, if any, families were untouched by the Great War.

Many of these family experiences, never mentioned on war memorials, are now recorded in Neela Mann's well-researched work and demonstrate that Cheltenham has as proud a record of service as any other town in England. How good that it is now here for all to see.

Sir Henry Elwes KCVO
Former Lord Lieutenant of Gloucestershire and Pro-Chancellor
of the University of Gloucestershire
August 2015

Introduction

Published material on Cheltenham has neglected the town's history during the First World War. Simona Pakenham in *Cheltenham: A Biography* writes '… the twentieth (century) does not really start till the end of the First World War. In the first nineteen years Cheltenham marked time …' This book shows that Cheltenham and its people did much more than mark time during 1914–18. In fact, the town contributed richly to the war effort. It tells of a town coping with enormous and unprecedented change. Many of the stories have never been told before – it is a book that had to be written. But it is just a glimpse of life during the Great War in Cheltenham – a walk through what Cheltenham was like for those left behind.

The book came to fruition from research into the subject for Cheltenham Local History Society's biennial history day exhibition on 19 July 2014. The main part of the research was carried out by piecing together information from the local newspapers of the day, scouring the town council minutes, searching the Gloucestershire Archives and the Cheltenham Local and Family History Centre. An enthusiastic team of researchers from Cheltenham Local History Society gathered information for the exhibition.

There was one exceptional resource from the Gloucestershire Archives – the letters of Maynard Colchester-Wemyss to the young King of Siam, Rama VI. Quotes from the letters appear throughout the book. During the war Colchester-Wemyss wrote 221 handwritten letters, which provided a unique weekly snapshot of current events, political comment and opinion through the eyes of a remarkable man. Maynard Colchester-Wemyss was, amongst some of his wartime duties, Chairman of Gloucestershire County Council, Chairman of the War Agricultural Committee and, for a short while during 1917, based in Cheltenham as the Honorary Acting Chief Constable of Gloucestershire. As he wrote: '… perhaps, 100 years hence, someone will unearth them and read them with interest.' They did!

What was Cheltenham like in August 1914? Pakenham describes it thus:

… a retiring place for Army, Navy and Indian Civil Servants, the prosperous to the genteelly poor … Outward respectability concealed an area of distress, poverty and unemployment in slums that had arisen in Victorian times, and a degree of prostitution that would alarm visitors … By the time the war came the place was in a state of incipient decay, described as a 'Town to Let'.

Two of these factors – the ex-colonial, retired military population and the number of large, empty houses – became plus factors for Cheltenham. The first factor gave Cheltenham a leisured class who had time on their hands, were used to looking after their 'troops' and a class to whom voluntarism was part of their culture. The second factor was vital to Cheltenham, making it an ideal town to billet large numbers of troops and house Red Cross hospitals. In *A Century of Cheltenham* Robin Brooks claims that in 1901 there were 800 houses in Cheltenham either to let or empty. The following decade saw little change. Nationally, the state of Britain pre-1914 was that of industrial unrest, agitation by the women's suffrage movement and the problem of Ireland and the Ulster Unionists, from which some thought the country was approaching the threshold of a civil war.

The largest proportion of Cheltenham's 55,000 population was working class, mostly of the service industry which kept the people of the Regency terraces and the visitors for the spa waters functioning. There was not much of an industrial base in Cheltenham other than the Cheltenham Original Brewery and H.H. Martyn of Sunningend works. The latter company was to become significant during the war, increasing its workforce from 200 to over 800. The country's pre-war unemployment had also hit Cheltenham. The shipping lines advertised passages to Canada, Australia and South Africa in local newspapers, as did agencies offering work in these countries. Many Cheltenham men returned to England or joined the armies of their adopted nations to fight for their country. Sixty-five of these emigrant Cheltonian men died for their homeland – 4 per cent of the total from the Cheltenham area who died.

The class and political allegiances of the local newspapers were clear. Cheltenham's daily newspaper was the Conservative-leaning *Gloucestershire Echo* (referred to as the *Echo*), which claimed to 'reach all classes'. The *Echo*'s weekly compendium, the *Cheltenham Chronicle* (the *Chronicle*), had a separate weekly supplement, full of photographs, the *Cheltenham Chronicle and Gloucestershire Graphic* (the *C&G*) – the source of a majority of the photographs in this book. The weekly magazine, the *Cheltenham Looker On* (the *CLO*) described itself as 'the organ of society circles in town'.

Cheltenham experienced three distinct phases on the home front during the war. For the first few months there was a mix of panic and excitement or, as Robin Brooks described it 'jingoistic euphoria' – the young men leaving in droves each day. Out of nowhere, the spirit of voluntarism mushroomed when groups of middle- and upper-class women came to the fore. They rattled tins and sold flags for the numerous 'fund days', packed parcels and manned soldiers' welcomes, knitted and sewed together in workrooms to provide war necessities and donned aprons in the eight hospitals for wounded soldiers in Cheltenham. This was followed in 1915 and 1916 by the second phase which afforded new freedoms for women as the employment opportunities opened up – women in men's jobs for the first time, especially when conscription stripped the town of more of its male workforce. During the third phase, the last two years of the war, the battle was focussed on combating food shortages and the food economy campaigns. It was an issue that further drove a wedge in the division of the classes in Cheltenham. The food rationing and increasingly rigid state control which followed then levelled the divide, affecting as it did all classes equally.

And then the Armistice was signed, which came almost as unexpectedly fast as had the declaration of war. Cheltenham was to mourn the loss of over 1,600 dead from the 7,000 or so men, and some women, of Cheltenham who had gone to war.

What happened next? The aftermath of the war and its effects on Cheltenham were so far-reaching that it would need another book to tell that tale!

Neela Mann,
March 2016

CHAPTER 1

Fêtes and Fate

July 1914 started blazing hot but finished as 'one of the chilliest Julys in the memory of most of us'. The *Cheltenham Chronicle*'s (the *Chronicle*) 'Nature Notes' of 18 July typified the drowsy peace of a summer's day. Amongst talk of loganberries it read, 'The Summer Calm! How good it is to be able to enjoy the summer heat and stillness, lie beneath a hedge and listen to the birds …' Then there were thunderstorms, lightning and torrential rain. At the new showroom of the ladies' outfitters, Vanderplank, a sales assistant reported that lightning struck a mirror. Seven years' bad luck?

July brought the usual summer activities. Cheltenham Middle Ward Conservative Committee's annual outing, this year from Birdlip to Miserden, passed through on their way, '… the much-discussed Whiteway Colony where Russian Anarchists plant the humble potato rather than the bomb.' At tea, Councillor Alfred Mann reported that after his recent trip to Ireland in the company of other local politicians, they all agreed Home Rule for Ireland would be a tragedy. Ireland and the question of Home Rule was to take a back seat for a while. Baker Street Institute Sisterhood went in charabancs to Evesham, not forgetting parasols and wide-brimmed hats. Cavendish House held its Sports Day – the ladies ran their races in long cotton dresses.

Baker Street Institute Sisterhood, out for a summer outing, went in charabancs to Evesham. (*Cheltenham Chronicle and Gloucestershire Graphic*, 1 August 1914)

The commemoration of Dr Edward Wilson was in the news with the unveiling on 9 July 1914 of the familiar bronze statue in the Promenade, sculpted by Lady Katherine Scott, widow of Captain Scott, leader of the Antarctic expedition. One of the initial suggestions to commemorate the explorer was for two bronze medallions to be cast and placed in the entrance lobby to the Town Hall; one to Scott and the other to Wilson. Wilson's widow, Oriana, objected. Her husband had a horror of

Unveiling of the memorial to Dr Edward Wilson on 9 July 1914 by Sir Clements Markham, President of the Royal Geographical Society. (*Cheltenham Chronicle and Gloucestershire Graphic*, 11 July 1914)

being closed up indoors and would have wanted an outdoor memorial. The 400 subscribers to the memorial had been invited onto the cordoned-off area around the statue. The Promenade was thronged with people one hour before the ceremony and the band of the 5th Battalion Gloucestershire Regiment played patriotic airs.

Archduke Franz Ferdinand had been assassinated in Sarajevo on 28 June, less than two weeks before the unveiling. Was there, amongst this worldly-wise group, a sense of what might be unfolding in Europe, beyond the imminent possibility of civil war in Ireland? Was there an understanding of the implications of the assassination and a foreboding that a war was a dreaded possibility? The drama in a faraway place called Bosnia remained distant until it was all too late.

One month later, on 28 July, the War Office ordered Special Service Sections of the Territorial Force units, as a precautionary measure for a period of time, to proceed to their stations on the coast – probably the east coast – of England. Three days later the *Echo* asked the question: with Belgrade in flames and chances of peace perceptibly dwindled, will Europe be dragged in?

THE GREAT UNIONIST AUGUST BANK HOLIDAY FÊTE

On the first day of August, in Leckhampton Road, a runaway cart ran into the back of tramcar 16 at 5.30 p.m. opposite Moorend Road. The driver told the passengers to jump and then jumped from the tram himself, but the conductor stayed on board and stopped the tram. He described it as '… an unusual and thrilling experience'. Readers more interested in the international situation would have read – and would have been right to be alarmed – 'At the present moment all Europe is an armed camp … As we go to press, news comes that Germany has been declared under martial law.'

In Dover on 3 August, Field-Marshal Earl Horatio Kitchener of Khartoum, formerly Commander-in-Chief in India but presently Consul General in Egypt, having been home on leave, was preparing to return to Egypt. Herbert Asquith, the Prime Minister of England, recalled Kitchener from Dover, not wanting him to be out of reach. Great Britain, on the eve of war, needed a dedicated Secretary of State for War.

Bank Holiday Monday, 3 August, the major event of the weekend which had been billed as the biggest, brightest and best fête ever held in Cheltenham, was the Great Unionist August Bank Holiday Fête at Stonewall Fields – three adjoining fields on the south side of Prestbury Road. The turnout certainly exceeded whatever had been seen before as 15,000 people attended the event. Was it because train excursions had been cancelled suddenly, due to troop movements, or was it the need to have one last bit of fun before God knows what would happen?

The cost for the day was sixpence (6*d*) for adults or thruppence (3*d*) for children. The weather was perfect. The day, planned with military precision by Major Percy Shewell, who was later to become the recruiting officer for Cheltenham, consisted of '… a programme that was one continual round of merriment'.

At 11.15 a.m. the Cabinet was meeting in London. At The Oval Cricket Ground, Surrey was playing Nottinghamshire and at noon Jack Hobbs went in to bat.

In Cheltenham, crowds were gathering for the procession that commenced at midday. Tradesmen's turnouts, decorated cars and costumed competitors flowed through the town from Imperial Square, via the Promenade, High Street, Winchcombe Street and thence to Prestbury Road. At Stonewall Fields there were morris dancers, aerial gymnasts, hand balancers, comedy boxers, sports races – including the 100-yard handicap race for married women. The confetti battle was hotly waged all over the field. There were equestrian competitions for jumping, trotting and driving. Or for those who favoured more static equines, there were painted horse rides at Mr Marshall Hill's funfair.

Four o'clock and time for cooling bottles of beer for the crowd in Cheltenham. At the same time, Gloucestershire Yeomanry officers at the Agricultural Show in Monmouth were recalled by telegram and left at once. Jack Hobbs was still batting at The Oval, having notched up his second century. In London, Sir Edward Grey, the Foreign Secretary, rose to deliver his statement to the House of Commons and afterwards admitted that this would be the war that might shatter civilisation as we knew it. 'I hate war,' he said. Hobbs was out on 226 runs at 5.30 p.m. just when the trotting competition was starting at Stonewall Fields.

The acrobatic platform was cleared at 6.30 p.m. for the speeches – speech making that was very different in subject and tone from that which had been contemplated when planning the fête. At the start, an announcement, loaded with foreboding, was made. 'Owing to an urgent summons to Parliament, the Borough Member [MP Mr Agg-Gardner] is unable to be present.' Cheltenham's political parties agreed that, in view of the national crisis, party politics were wholly taboo in their speeches today. It was just as well; within the month, the party agents for the two principal parties – Mr Tom Packer of the Conservatives and Mr John Allcott of the Liberals – had to collaborate as the town's joint army recruiting agents. The principal guest speaker, Will Dyson, otherwise known as 'Will Workman – the popular voice of the people', spoke as one who was aware of the gravity of the hour, having two sons in the regular army and two sons in the Territorial Force: '… we are meeting on the eve of what would probably be the most momentous crisis in the world's history.'

At the Foreign Office in London, telegrams were sent out at 9 p.m. warning every British diplomatic and consular mission throughout the world that war was imminent.

The grand illumination of the Stonewall Fields commenced at 9.45 p.m. – a magnificent bonfire and display of fireworks concluding with the huge fire portrait of the absent local MP. The fête closed with thousands of voices singing rousing patriotic anthems – 'Rule Britannia' and 'God Save The King'.

In London, at 10 p.m. 20,000 people gathered outside Buckingham Palace were rewarded with an appearance on the balcony of the palace of the King and Queen, accompanied by the Prince of Wales.

Were the revellers a little subdued, but at the same time a little excited, wending their way home, as country and town waited for the impending result of the ultimatum issued to the Kaiser? The Kaiser's reply had been requested by midnight that day. What would the next day, 4 August 1918, bring? If there was to be a war, everyone said it would be over by Christmas.

'THE LAMPS ARE GOING OUT'

Whilst the merriment continued at Stonewall Fields, E and F companies of the 5th Battalion of the Gloucestershire Territorial Regiment were away on their annual summer camp. Having left on Sunday, they had only been away twenty-four hours when an order was received from the government: break up the summer camps and entrain for destinations, not divulged at the time. Eighteen hours before war was declared, Territorial Force platoons were in place guarding vital railway lines on which the British Expeditionary Force would travel to France. Army manoeuvres, which were fixed to take place in parts of Gloucestershire, Worcestershire and Herefordshire during the latter part of August and the beginning of September, comprising over 50,000 troops, were abandoned.

Page 6 of the *Echo* of 3 August included headlines such as 'Hands off Belgium – Reply Requested by Midnight – Our ultimatum to Germany'. Sir Edward Grey, in his speech to Cabinet the day before, insisted that this country had a duty to Belgium and that if Germany attacked Belgium a full-scale war was inevitable. That evening, on the eve of the First World War, Grey, on looking out of his window at the Foreign Office, spoke the words: 'The lamps are going out all over Europe, we shall not see them lit again in our life-time.'

CHELTENHAM IS AT WAR

The day after the fête, Tuesday, 4 August, was a day like no other. Headlines on the front page of the *Echo* said it all: 'An important statement by Sir Edward Grey – The Peace of Europe Could Not Be Preserved.' War had come to Great Britain, Gloucestershire and Cheltenham. As Jeremy Paxman in his book *Great Britain's Great War* wrote, '… a decent man had failed.'

On page 2 of the *Echo* there was a detailed report of the Bank Holiday Fête. On page 5, Mr Harry Jones's ball at Oddfellows Hall the day before was declared a great success amongst the 150 who danced from 9 p.m. until 2.30 a.m. Alongside was a report that the Territorials were to be embodied and the government had mobilised the entire British Army. The Reserves were to be called out and the Territorials would be summoned to undergo six months' training to prepare them for active service. And at cricket, Gloucestershire had won their first victory in the County Championship after an exciting finish, defeating Somerset by 1 wicket on the county ground in Bristol. Our local county cricketer, Alfred Dipper, was caught out on 5 runs. Six weeks later Dipper left Cheltenham, having enlisted for the Gloucestershire Yeomanry, and survived the war. At The Oval, during the last day of the Surrey vs Nottinghamshire cricket match, signs appeared on the gates. The Oval was to be commandeered for military purposes at the close of the match. Jack Hobbs, who had scored 226 runs the day before at The Oval, later served with the Royal Flying Corps.

Throughout Tuesday, 4 August, the Cheltenham headquarters of E and F companies of the 5th Battalion Gloucestershire Regiment at the Drill Hall in North Street had been besieged with enquirers wanting to know when the men were likely to be called away. Just before 7 p.m. the notification of the embodiment was posted on the Drill Hall's double doors. The police posted similar notices in different parts of town and in all post offices. Messages were flashed onto cinema screens. The Territorials were told they must assemble at 10 a.m. on Wednesday, 5 August. At 9 p.m. Tuesday night, Major J. Frederick Tarrant, Secretary to the Council of Cheltenham Ladies' College, but now in command of the Cheltenham Territorials, had been called to Gloucester. Tarrant travelled there on his motorcycle, to receive orders. He assured his troops that he would meet up with them soon. There was no indication then of their destination.

Patriotic demonstrations took place around Cheltenham that Tuesday night of 4 August. At the Conservative Club at midnight, the assembled members '… lustily rendered "God Save The King" and other songs'. In the streets of Cheltenham could be heard singing. 'The Lads in Navy Blue' and 'Three Cheers for the Red, White and Blue' alternated with the national anthem and 'Rule Britannia'. At 10.30 p.m. a special edition of the *Echo* was issued containing a report announcing the loss of a navy minelayer. The *Echo* paperboys found themselves pocketing halfpennies faster than they could hand out the copies of the paper. Headlines read: 'Five Nations at War – Invasion of France – Demolition of Belgrade.'

On 5 August 1914 the *Echo*'s leader ran with these words:

> WAR! The die is cast. Great Britain having heard that the reply to her demand for the preservation of the neutrality of Belgium was the declaration of war by Germany on Belgium, replied last evening by throwing down the gauntlet to Germany … What is needed is a heaven-born organiser of our home forces … All England calls with one voice for Lord Kitchener's appointment as Secretary of State for War.

How right it was – Kitchener was appointed that evening. Not entirely enthusiastic to have appointed Kitchener, the prime minister said, 'It is a hazardous experiment, but the best in the circumstances, I think.' Kitchener was one of the few to foresee a long war and said, 'The conflict will plumb the depths of manpower to the last million.'

The front page of the Wednesday, 5 August newspaper was dominated by an explanation of the meaning of 'embodiment of the Territorials'. Territorials were, strictly speaking, a home-based defence force and were not obliged to serve abroad. However, Lord Kitchener had asked the men of the Territorials nationally to volunteer for overseas service. Whilst the national uptake had been around 50 per cent, in Cheltenham it was far higher at 86 per cent. Once their numbers had been made up to full strength, these units would fight alongside regular army battalions as the second line in the battle. Then reserve units would be used to release those on the front line.

The Yeomanry and the National Reservists were the next to be called up. Thirty of the Cheltenham Corps of Reservists left for Horfield Barracks, Bristol, on 6 August – most of these thirty were engineers. The National Reserve was a pool of men who had previously served in some capacity in the army and who had registered their names as willing to re-enlist in an emergency. That emergency was now.

For the first time, a new column appeared in the *Echo* – 'War Items', all too soon to be followed in the days to come by 'List of Casualties'.

CHELTENHAM'S TERRITORIALS LEAVE

The news that the Territorials, our citizen soldiers, were to leave Cheltenham for the second time within three days, spread like wildfire through the town. By 9 a.m. Wednesday, 5 August people were congregating in great masses at the junction of North Street and the High Street and surrounding the Drill Hall. The *Echo* stated: 'There were many anxious faces in the great crowd. Fathers and mothers, big, strong brothers and sweethearts, not to mention little brothers and sisters assembled in the great crowd to watch their boys and daddies march out to the aid of Britain in her hour of need.' News had leaked out, somehow, that after meeting up in Gloucester with the other companies of the battalion from all parts of the county, the Territorials would be heading for the Isle of Wight.

In the absence of the Territorial's commanding officer, Major J.F. Tarrant, who had travelled ahead to Gloucester the night before to take orders, it fell to Captain Noel Huxley Waller, son of Gloucester Cathedral's architect and himself an architect, to be in command of the combined E and F companies, numbering around 200 soldiers. The companies also included six out of seventeen members of the Cyclist section and the Band. Inside the Drill Hall, the reporter recounts that he saw, 'a sturdy sergeant, obviously moved as he kissed his mother "Goodbye"'. The report continues: 'In spite of the popular enthusiasm there is something extremely touching in the departure of these citizen soldiers, even if they never leave our shores and never get under fire.' However, these Territorials, 1/5th Battalion Gloucestershire Regiment, did leave our shores, arriving in France on 29 March 1915 and serving in France, Belgium and Italy, including battles at the Somme, Ypres and Cambrai.

The two Maxim guns and the baggage, loaded onto drays, had been sent on ahead of the men. The crowd had built up as the time to leave approached. Captain Waller addressed his men at the last minute: 'All we ask you to do is to go forward with your work quietly, work in the same manner as you did Monday morning.'

To the strains of the band playing 'Get out and get under' the men marched out into North Street. Cheer after cheer was raised along the route. At 10 a.m. the platform at St James station was closed to all but those with a valid railway ticket.

Those determined to be as close as possible to the men on the platform bought third-class single tickets to Churchdown. People climbed on every available vantage point – on the high walls round the station and the roof of the lamp sheds – anywhere they could to see the departure of the train. Crowds even lined the railway tracks as the troops moved out at 11 a.m. It was reported that 'The tears of the sweethearts and the wives who are left behind were mingled with the cheering'. That evening the soldiers entrained from Gloucester for the Isle of Wight.

Marching off to war, down Clarence Street, past the Clarence Lamp, soon to be the scene of many recruitment meetings. The first soldiers to leave Cheltenham on 5 August 1914 were E and F companies of the 5th Battalion Gloucestershire Regiment. (*Cheltenham Chronicle and Gloucestershire Graphic*, 8 August 1914)

'The Famous', men's and boys' outfitters of the High Street, in its usual front page advertisement on Thursday, 6 August, trumpeted 'England Expects Every Man To Do His Duty! Peace Prices During War'. The *Echo* announced that to preserve paper stock it would be reduced to four pages from this date.

Kitchener's first 'Call to Arms' advertisement was sent out to newspapers. Page 4 of the *Echo* carried the advertisement on Thursday, 13 August. It read 'Your King and Country Need You' – and asked for 100,000 men aged 19–30 years. Cheltenham lads were to go to the National Reserve Headquarters next to Alstone Baths, Great Western Road, where the recruiting office had been hastily opened, or any post office or military depot.

On 7 August the *Echo* reported that the British cruiser HMS *Amphion* had been sunk by a German mine in the North Sea with the loss of 131 lives. Five Gloucestershire lads were on board; two died. Amongst the survivors was Leading Seaman William Miller of No. 23 Dunalley Parade, Cheltenham. More people from Cheltenham were being involved in the war.

Saturday, 8 August saw the publication of the first issue of the *Chronicle* since the outbreak of war. The front page showed no indication of war. More prominent were details of the will of Cheltenham's former borough surveyor, Joseph Hall, designer of the Neptune's Fountain in the Promenade. He died in Bombay where he had been borough engineer, after moving from Torquay to establish Cheltenham as 'a garden town' to rival Royal Leamington Spa. War had been relegated to page 2, alongside the announcement of the notable visitors to the town staying in the more prestigious hotels. Mr and Mrs H. Gordon Selfridge, Miss Selfridge and Madame Selfridge of Selfridges department store, London, were staying at The Queen's Hotel; Lady Blanche and maid at Tate's Hotel, the Promenade; and at Malvern View Hotel on Cleeve Hill, General Sir Charles Tucker – veteran of the Boer War.

Page 4 was full of newsy reports from around the county of army movements. Snippets of interest from the country included news that Gwilym Lloyd George, second son of the Chancellor of the Exchequer, David Lloyd George, had enlisted with the Territorials of the Royal Welsh Fusiliers. German spies had been reported on the Isle of Wight, consequently those hanging around military establishments were liable to be shot.

The *CLO* on the same day rallied its readers:

> Local patriotism is on fire … We who are left behind can show our patriotism in as forceful a manner as those who shoulder the rifles … In a few days there will be battles, the like of which have never been seen. The death toll will be enormous … Our time of trial is not yet come …

The paper reinforced the news that had been given out on Monday. Great Western Railway announced that all tourist, excursion, weekend and reduced tickets were suspended. In the very month that people looked forward to trips out during their days off, war intervened. The country urgently needed its trains to move the troops around.

The Revd Dwelly held a Service of Intercession on Sunday, 9 August at St Matthew's church in Clarence Street. At the service his impassioned prayer included these words: 'O Cheltenham, the loved home of so many who are today waiting to answer the call. Cheltenham, the adopted home of so many of England's heroes … England hath need of Cheltenham; Cheltenham hath need of each one of us … Young men, "To the Front" is the call today.' As Robin Brooks writes of this occasion '… a bulging congregation … prayed for victory and, as God was undoubtedly on the allies' side, expected it sooner, rather than later.'

CHAPTER 2

The Boys Leave:
Kitchener to Conscription

RECRUITING

Recruiting seems to have been started in a somewhat disorganised fashion in Cheltenham. The *CLO* of 22 February 1919 read: 'The recruiting work of 1914 was hurried and comparatively unorganized ... the first 40 days were days of popular hope and alternating despair, of agony and suspense ...' After Kitchener's initial appeal, notices had been put up around town urging men to enlist. Photos taken on 11 August, outside the new recruiting station at Alstone Baths, were captioned that recruiting had been 'extraordinarily busy since Lord Kitchener asked for another army. There was a crush to get into the enlisting office.' The first photos of recruits in this week's paper included ten drivers from Cheltenham Blue Taxis who had enlisted for motor transport service. The army advertisement appearing in the *Echo* on Friday, 21 August included the additional line 'Note:- Old soldiers can enlist for one year or duration of war between the ages of 30 and 43.'

AEROPLANE MESSAGES

What must have been more alarming to Cheltenham residents
was the notice in the paper on 21 August 1914:

The attention of the public is called to the possibility of messages being dropped from aeroplanes. The messages will be enclosed in a weighted canvas bag, fastened with two spring clips, attached to which are two streamers of blue, red, and yellow cloth, each 4ft long. Any person finding or seeing such a bag dropped from an aeroplane should at once open it and take steps to forward the enclosed message to the person for whom it is intended.

MONS AND A FURTHER 100,000 NEEDED

The disaster, expensive in manpower, that was the Battle of Mons, hit the headlines on 25 August. Peter Simkins, in his book *Kitchener's Army: The Raising of the New Armies 1914–1916*, says, 'Reports of the battle … had an immediate impact on the recruiting figures. The mood of the nation altered perceptibly, and people everywhere were roused to fresh heights of patriotic energy.' This day at Mons, Albert Butler was the first Cheltonian to be killed in action. On the same day, in his maiden speech as a Minister of the Crown, Kitchener informed the House of Lords that he needed a further 100,000 recruits.

By 27 August Cheltenham recruiting staff had had 'an exceptionally busy time'. So far, 291 men had enlisted, whilst others were 'only waiting to settle up their private affairs before joining'. On the same day it was reported that Captain Blythe (Adjutant of the National Reserve) in a speech to 160 Cheltenham National Reservists at the Drill Hall, informed them that he would be raising money to buy a few thousand rounds of ammunition for practise at Seven Springs Rifle Range. He appealed to the townspeople of Cheltenham to give money, lend cars to transport the Reservists to the rifle range and to employers to allow their workers time off for an hour or two during the daytime, in order to practise firing their rifles.

Major Percy Shewell, valuable as an able organiser recruiting for the army in Cheltenham, was appointed as recruiting officer for North East Gloucestershire on 29 August. Shewell, ex-Indian Army Staff Corps, was the ideal person for this post. Here was the man responsible for heading the organisation of the largest Grand Fête ever held in Cheltenham on Bank Holiday Monday: could he rally more troops for King and Country?

CHELTENHAM CRICKETERS

W.G. Grace, Gloucestershire player, was perhaps the most universally known cricketer of all time. It was said, when he played on the Cheltenham College Ground, that he had one eye on the clock in the pavilion when batting one end of the wicket and one eye on the main hospital entrance batting the other end – he was aiming to hit sixes at each. Grace wrote a letter to local papers on 29 August 1914, in response to the high casualties at Mons, calling for the cessation of county cricket owing to the war. He wrote, 'It is not fitting that able-bodied men should be at play day after day and pleasure seekers look on. I would like to see all first-class cricketers set a good example.'

The same issue of the *Echo* announced that Gloucestershire County Cricket Club was in 'grave danger of collapse … a monotonous list of defeats … nothing can save the club from extinction … the professional players have been informed

DEAR DORA, OR THE DEFENCE OF THE REALM ACT

This extraordinarily wide-ranging Act, first passed 13 August 1914, was added to throughout the war, as and when necessary. Lord Riddell, influential newspaper proprietor, referred to DORA, as it was known, as 'A law which wipes out Magna Carta in a few lines.' It gave the government unprecedented powers to bring in laws without the necessity to go through Parliament. Restrictions included making it illegal to ring church bells, for civilians to buy binoculars, to speak on the phone in any language other than English, whistle under railway bridges, fly kites, keep pigeons, feed flour biscuits to dogs or throw rice at weddings.

Unlikely but true, in 1914, Harrods was offering its customers 'A welcome present for friends at the Front' containing cocaine, heroin and syringes. But it wasn't until May 1916 that the sale of psychoactive drugs to soldiers was forbidden without a prescription, under DORA, after numerous reports that drugs were being sold by prostitutes to soldiers in army camps. It was also an offence under DORA for a woman suffering from venereal disease to infect a soldier, even if that soldier was her husband and he was the person to infect her.

---

that there would be no winter pay for them at the end of the present season.' By December 1914, ten players from the Gloucestershire team had enlisted. One of the principal Gloucestershire players of the time, Major Cyril Sewell, was with the 83rd Provisional Battalion of the South Midland Brigade (including some of the 5th Battalion of the Gloucesters) guarding 20 miles of seafront on the south-east coast of England, keeping a look out for Zeppelins. Sewell set up his own cricket team, mainly of Cheltenham men, although he refused to be a playing member! It is said that W.G. Grace used to shake his fist at Zeppelins flying over his house in London, saying, 'I could see fast bowlers but I can't see these beggars'.

MORE MEN LEAVE

Notices displayed around the town on Wednesday, 26 August appealed for an additional 250 men to make up the 5th Battalion Gloucesters Regiment (Territorials) to active service strength, 86 per cent of the rank and file having volunteered for foreign service. By Saturday, 29 August, eighty-four Cheltonians had signed up at the Drill Hall, home of the Territorials. Of those not able to find a place in the 5th Gloucesters, a further nineteen signed up to form the nucleus of the new 8th Battalion of the Gloucesters. Within nine days they had recruited all that was needed.

Monday, 31 August through to Thursday, 3 September saw recruits being sent off from the station each day. On Monday, eighty recruits set out from the Drill Hall and were met at the railway station by the mayor who shook hands with them all and gave each one a box of twenty-five cigarettes. It is noticeable that the local paper gave the names and addresses of each one of these recruits, which included the sporting sub-editor, the articled pupil and a member of the office staff of the *Echo*. At later dates, this list was reduced to name only and eventually just the number of men leaving was given.

In the adjacent column the report told that at 4 p.m. the same Monday another batch of recruits for Kitchener's second 100,000 men left by train for Bristol from Alstone Recruitment Centre. This time the *Echo*'s editor and another two more members of staff were amongst those departing, five others were already serving and two more were to leave the next day. Eventually, twenty-three former members of the *Echo* staff were to serve. Three of them, brothers Jack, Dick and Joe Mason, died within an eighteen-month period between August 1916 and November 1917. The editor of the *Echo* was 33-year-old Edwin Willoughby, an old Cheltonian (ex-Cheltenham College), Oxford graduate and a barrister. He was considered to be the tallest and heaviest man to enlist in Cheltenham at the time. Willoughby refused to take a commission in the army, feeling that his place was in the ranks. As the need for more officers became urgent, Willoughby was gazetted in November 1914 as a lieutenant and a captain in January 1915. He was to give up his life for his country, leading his men into action in Gallipoli, on 8 August 1915.

The next day, 1 September, Major Shewell sent off eighty-six volunteers, described in the *Echo* as 'socially a mixed band, gentlemen's sons and labourers' sons and many of intermediate degrees, all starting equal in the race to help the Motherland.' Shewell left them in no doubt of what was expected of them: 'We are in a bit of a tight pinch and you men will do all you can to get us out. Do your very best. You can't do any more … but don't come back if you don't do your duty!'

Saying goodbye to the Territorials
at the station. (*Cheltenham Chronicle and
Gloucestershire Graphic*, 8 August 1914)

One Cheltenham father did the opposite of encouraging his son to enlist.
He told the lad if he enlisted he would be cut off with only a shilling,
It's not known what the son decided to do.

On Wednesday, 2 September, ninety-four paraded from Alstone Baths Recruitment Office amid '… hearty but subdued manifestations of public enthusiasm'. This time the recruiting agents had chosen a new route – New Street, High Street, Promenade, and into Queen's Road to Lansdown station – the idea being to stimulate '… zeal and interest in the recruitment movement'. It would appear that the enthusiasm was waning. Thursday, 3 September the batch of eighty-four was considered to be '… the most enthusiastic of the week … entirely free from the "mafficking element".' Amongst them was an older recruit – a veteran of the Boer War – 34-year-old Ernest Artus, a plasterer who worked for A.C. Billings the local builder. He would lose his life at Loos in France on 25 September 1915.

Hearing that there was little provision for the recruits at the Bristol end of the journey, such was the number of recruits pouring into Horfield Barracks, the Scouts of the 12th Cheltenham Company distributed many baskets of ripe pears and gave each man a bottle of ginger beer, most welcome as the afternoon was 'boiling', according to the report. Mr F. Brandt, a local JP, had also heard of the recruits' plight and, feeling that cigarettes were not much good to sustain the potential troops, had sent eighty-four boxes, one for each recruit leaving Cheltenham on 2 September. The boxes contained ½lb of cheese, ½lb of bread and ¼lb of tea. Mr Brandt's son, a captain in command of HMS *Monmouth*, went down with his ship barely four weeks later on 1 November. The ship was sunk off the coast of Chile, in a gallant attempt to help HMS *Good Hope*, which was on fire and sinking – 1,600 sailors were lost on these two ships. What Captain Brandt could not have known was there were twin sons of a well-known Cheltenham chimneysweep on board the HMS *Good Hope* that day who also lost their lives – Edward and Henry Turner, navy reservists.

Appeals for recruits came from all quarters. Willie Holt of Burnley, Lancashire, the billiard table company, paid for advertisements in local papers to encourage enlistment. An advert appeared in the *Echo* on Saturday, 29 August aimed at men who used the billiard club at the King's Hall in North Street, directly next to the Drill Hall of the Territorials. In the form of a letter it was headed 'To every employee and friend of the Willie Holt Co., Wherever He May Be. Dear Brother Briton … ' The appeal asks that every man will do his duty to his country – and spend more money so that trade doesn't suffer! This seemingly patriotic advert had an ulterior motive; most of Willie Holts' customers would be going to the front.

TOO YOUNG

Although the minimum age for volunteers was 19 years of age, there were those who managed to slip under the age limit. One such was 16-year-old Joseph Sidney King who lived with his parents at No. 6 Brunswick Place, Upper Bath Street and worked on the WHSmith bookstall at the Midland Railway station. Joseph was born in July 1899 so when he enlisted in December 1914 he was 15 years old. His family included three older brothers serving in the army. Joseph was wounded in the Battle of Loos with the 10th Battalion Gloucesters and died at Netley Hospital in Sheffield of wounds on 8 October 1915 but his death certificate had to state he was 19 years old. It was reported in 1918 that one Cheltenham lad who had signed on at the age of 14 years had already served four years, been wounded twice, and was now of the right age for the army so there was no point in sending him home.

KITCHENER'S SECOND APPEAL

'Another 100,000 Men Wanted' appeared in a large advertisement on page 3 of the *Echo* of 31 August. It seems that nationally, apart from the rush the previous week in the light of the losses at Mons, overall recruiting had begun to slow down. This time the age limits were raised to 35 years of age for new volunteers. After Kitchener's first appeal, Simkins writes, many thought that 100,000 was the total number needed and once that quota had been filled that would be it: 'People had not fully understood the nature or the magnitude of the task facing the country. It was not indifference but ignorance of the consequences of defeat.' Little did people realise that over 2 million men would eventually be asked for.

The government now wanted more local autonomy in army recruitment. As local political agents were best qualified in knowing how to motivate support for the purposes of voting in their local areas so, it was considered, they would be perfectly placed to recruit for the army. Thus, in Cheltenham, Messrs Tom Packer and John Allcott laid aside their political differences and joined forces for the good of the country and Cheltenham, as honorary local recruiting agents. Up to this point Major Shewell had recruited 526 volunteers from Cheltenham, now it was up to Packer and Allcott.

The first of the new, locally organised recruitment drives appeared in the *Echo* on 31 August – the same issue as Kitchener's appeal for a further 100,000 men. Events consisted of a series of open-air meetings to be held at local gathering points in town over a period of seven days – Wednesday, 2 September at the central lamp in Clarence Street; Thursday the Gas Lamp; Friday near the Norwood Arms; Monday at Hewlett Lamp. Prior to each meeting, Mr James's band played national and

Recruits marching with the mayor at the head, past The Rotunda to Lansdown station, on their way to Horfield Barracks, Bristol, on 10 September. Most of these men were destined for the 10th Battalion Gloucestershire Regiment. Note the decorative lamp, which is now the Tivoli Lamp. The Drew Fountain wasn't erected until October 1914. (*Cheltenham Chronicle and Gloucestershire Graphic*, 19 September 1914)

patriotic music from 7 p.m. until 8 p.m. when the meetings commenced. Those meetings at the central lamp in Clarence Street had additional means of persuasion – war pictures were shown on a sheet hung on the walls of the abutting premises of Messrs Engall, Cox & Co. At each meeting there were facilities for the enlistment of recruits and at one meeting a heckler wanted to know 'why aren't the middle classes doing their bit?' These open-air meetings alone resulted in around 200 new recruits.

WHERE TO PUT ALL THE RECRUITS?

Owing to the pressure at Horfield Barracks, there was some delay in sending the men off. So much so that the Mayor of Cheltenham needed to ask the newspapers to reassure the new recruits through their columns that they would still be paid sixpence per day subsistence allowance. Simkins explains that in many cases men had expected to go to depots straight away on enlistment but were sent home on deferred enlistment, as there was no way to deal with such a large influx: 'Many men had not realised and had given up jobs and were unable to exist on 6*d* per day.' As a consequence, in September 1914, the allowance had to be raised to 3*s* a day. Recruiting had been going on at a faster rate than the processes of military assimilation. Horfield in Bristol, where most of the recruits were headed, had proven unequal to the digestion of so much material for Kitchener's Army.

The National Reserve, it had been suggested early in September 1914, might provide at Cheltenham a temporary training camp for 500 or so recruits as a means of regulating the flow, whilst they were awaiting despatch to Horfield or elsewhere. A scheme was proposed for the Alstone Baths to be boarded over and used for sleeping accommodation and the use of Pittville Pump Room. This never came to fruition but 120 of the local National Reserves trained in Cheltenham for three weeks and thirty-four of these men from Gloucester and Cirencester were billeted in Cheltenham. These men left Cheltenham on 4 November 1914 for guard duties on the railways around the Swindon district

The following week, on Thursday, 10 September, another 120 recruits, the largest batch yet to be sent, were escorted by the mayor and the Boys' Brigade Bugle Band. Within their number were members of the Cotswold Hills Golf Club including their scratch player, Donald Bailey. Bailey was a lieutenant in the Gloucester Regiment. He and his brother-in-law, L.K. Barnett, who were inseparable golf companions at the club, were both killed in 1917.

Recruits marched down the Promenade from the new recruiting station, opened on 4 September at the Imperial Rooms, behind Neptune's Fountain, through Clarence Street, and back to the Promenade via The Colonnade. An immense crowd watched the start and at the station the assemblage was of huge proportions. The Scouts from Gloucester Road School sang 'The Marseillaise' but they were hardly heard above the cheers. Four Scouts of the 12th Cheltenham Troop were amongst those leaving – Ashfield, Bridgman, Gainer and Gapper. None of them came back. One wrote to his mother two weeks later from Horfield Barracks to say, 'You won't know us when we come back; we are military men now!' The men were given a parcel of bread and cheese and cocoa and every man received a tiny copy of the Gospel according to St John, bound in khaki. The train left amidst much blowing of bugles, cheers, and firing of fog signals.

The next afternoon, Friday, 11 September, another batch left. This time there were even more in the party – 162 men. Amongst them was William Jennings who worked for Coole's Bakery in the Bath Road. His account in Nick Christian's *In the Shadow of Lone Tree* reads:

> One day I was delivering bread in Cheltenham when an aristocratic lady stopped me and said 'Young man you really ought to be in France.' That evening I was out with friends, we had all drunk a fair bit of cider and decided to go to the recruiting centre near the Norwood Arms …

Jennings must have attended the open-air meeting on Friday, 4 September near the Norwood Arms. He survived the war, having been invalided home after the Battle of Loos where he lost his left thumb and forefinger.

The council minutes of 12 September recorded that St Paul's Rugby Club, one of the oldest and strongest clubs in the town, would no longer be using the Agg-Gardner Recreation Ground. All sixteen of their playing members were now serving in the army and fixtures had to be cancelled. On Tuesday, 15 September another fifty recruits departed from Cheltenham for the Reserve of the 5th Gloucesters (Territorial) Battalion '… being a smart, athletic lot, evidently from the commercial and clerical classes', remarked the *Chronicle*. There were three Dodwells who left that day, William – later to be a prisoner of war – Samuel A. and T. Dodwell.

CAVENDISH HOUSE AND THE 'FIGHTING 30'

One wonders if Cheltenham traders grasped the true impact that war was to have on the town, as seen by this report from the Traders' Association on 26 August: 'Trade in Cheltenham is better than might be expected … If trade were not so good the recruiting officers might have more to do, in fact they expect to have a much busier time when the harvest is in, if by that time the war is not over.' And yet, on the same day, a report pointed out that few establishments of its kind had had so many enlistments from their

Boys of the 'Fighting 30' leaving on 11 September. They were gathered from the furnishing and drapery businesses of Cheltenham, mainly Cavendish House.
(*Cheltenham Chronicle and Gloucestershire Graphic*, 19 September 1914)

staff in proportion to the number of employees as Cavendish House: two men were called up with the Territorials, seven had been accepted for the Royal Engineers, three porters and four out of six staff in the gentlemen's department had enlisted, up to this point. By March 1915, forty-two members of Cavendish House staff had enlisted.

In early September 1914, Mr A.J. White – 'a popular Cavendish House man' – formed a group called the 'Fighting 30'. This group was made up of young men drawn mostly from the furnishing and drapery businesses of the town. Mr White was promoted to lance-corporal in the morning and put in charge of the squad of thirty. Although others had already gone from these trades, it was hoped that these thirty could stay together as recruits during the war. It is not known, but highly unlikely, that they stayed together or were even in the same regiments as they were sent on different days to Horfield Depot to be drafted into various regiments. The last four of the 'Fighting 30' left the town on Wednesday, 16 September 1914, including Mr White.

THE FIRST MILITARY FUNERAL IN CHELTENHAM

The grim reality of war was brought home to Cheltenham on Wednesday, 16 September with the first semi-military funeral in the town. Driver Albert Preston of the 16th Battery Royal Field Artillery had been wounded at the Battle of Mons and died at the Cambridge Hospital, Aldershot. He was the sixth Cheltenham man to die. The coffin was accompanied to the cemetery by the only military body left in Cheltenham at the time, the National Reserves, and the Boy Scouts. It didn't take long for Dicks & Sons to advertise mourning wear in the *Echo*, starting on 26 August 1914. However, there were few military funerals in Cheltenham as the countries agreed it would be out of the question to bring the bodies back from the battlefields.

ENLISTMENT SLOWING DOWN

Up to this point, well over 1,000 recruits had left Cheltenham in the four weeks since war was declared. During the next four weeks the number had only risen to 1,400. Recruitment drives took on a very different slant after the initial rush. Those recruiting for the 11th Battalion of the Gloucesters took a bizarre line when advertising in the local paper by listing a typical daily menu the recruits could expect and ending the advertisement 'Join Today and Be Happy'. Packer and Allcott were ever more ingenuous in devising events. There were smoking concerts (ladies were only allowed on the balconies of the Town Hall for these), marathon races, sports days, lectures and free concerts by regimental bands. Gone was the rush to enlist buoyed merely by patriotic fervour. More enticing means were necessary.

CHELTENHAM CAN DO IT!
YES!
CHELTENHAM CAN DO IT!

52 SO FAR (Monday, Tuesday, Wednesday)

HOW MANY TO-DAY?

ONLY 150 MORE
Cheltonians Wanted to complete a Grand Total of
3,000
BRITISH VOLUNTEERS
FOR THE NEW ARMIES
FROM THE GARDEN TOWN

NOW'S YOUR CHANCE!

LET CAPTAIN BALDWIN HAVE

150 MORE THIS WEEK.
DON'T DISAPPOINT HIM.

Back Up the Gallant Gloucesters!

KEEP SMILING! WORK WILL WIN!

STICK TO IT, CHELTENHAM!

Please Cut Out this Advertisement and post it in a prominent position.
Look for Results day by day in the "Echo," and work away.

1	38	76	113
2	39	77	114
3	40	78	115
4	41	79	116
5	42	80	117
6	43	81	118
7	44	82	119
8	45	83	120
9	46	84	121
10	47	85	122
11	48	86	123
12	49	87	124
13	50	88	125
14	51	89	126
15	52	90	127
16	53	91	128
17	54	92	129
18	55	93	130
19	56	94	131
20	57	95	132
21	58	96	133
22	59	97	134
23	60	98	135
24	61	99	136
25	62	100	137
26	63	101	138
27	64	102	139
28	65	103	140
29	66	104	141
30	67	105	142
31	68	106	143
32	69	107	144
33	70	108	145
34	71	109	146
35	72	110	147
36	73	111	148
37	74	112	149
—	75	—	150

This most persuasive advert appeared on the front page of the *Echo* on 19 August 1914.
Some 3,000 recruits had enlisted by May 1915. (*Gloucestershire Echo*, 19 August 1914)

By 16 July 1915, inducements to find volunteers had resulted in an advertisement in the *Echo* headed 'Important Notice to Soldiers on Furlough'. It offered soldiers an extra day's leave for every approved recruit they brought in. As an incentive, the new recruit could join any corps and be posted to any battalion they wanted in order to be with their friends, similar to the Pals battalions. The students of St Paul's Training College waited until the end of the Christmas term before signing up – thirty-two of them enlisted together.

PROPAGANDA

War events were milked for the purposes of propaganda, to elicit a fevered response, stoking up a patriotic desire to 'Save the Motherland'. Two such events were the sinking of the *Lusitania* in May 1915 with the loss of 1,200 civilians and the murder of Nurse Edith Cavell. But the most worrying must have been the shelling and bombing on the east coast of England and the Zeppelin raids, affecting those both home and abroad. The raids lowered the morale of the men in the trenches – they were fighting away from a home which was being attacked and vulnerable. They didn't know if their families were safe. Should they, they were asking themselves, be fighting in France or protecting their homes and families? On the other hand it brought home to slow enlisters the potential threat of their own homes being invaded, their own families being killed. As the poster said, 'It is far better to face the bullets than be killed at home by a bomb'. It was reckoned that for every bomb dropped on British soil another fifty recruits signed up.

THE RECRUITMENT DRIVE HOTS UP

An advertisement on 13 October 1914 announced: 'Men of Cheltenham … Your Country Still Needs You. Attend in your thousands at the Great Town Hall Recruiting Meeting.' The 'big guns' had certainly been wheeled out for this meeting. It was chaired by Earl Bathurst and on the platform on the stage were the MP, the mayor, three reverends, two colonels, an admiral, a lieutenant general, Sir Henry Winterbotham, the principals of Cheltenham College and Dean Close, four aldermen, fourteen councillors, local businessmen including H.W. Bennett of the Cheltenham Newspaper Company and A.C. Billings, prominent local builder. In the front row of the seating was a selection of the Belgian refugees living in Cheltenham. After the playing of the Belgian national anthem, three hearty cheers were given for 'brave little Belgium'.

One speaker extorted: 'You have no right, if you are young enough and fit enough, to leave those 1,300 Cheltonians to fight the battle. Your place is by their side.' But the stirring speech by the local MP must have gone over the heads of most of the audience when he said, 'We are fighting to avert the thraldom of Prussian despotism.' Nevertheless, 100 men signed up after the meeting at a special recruiting office opened in the small drawing room of the Town Hall. One wonders how much more the relentless recruiters could do to entice the reluctant recruit to sign up – until April 1915.

THE GREAT RECRUITING CAMPAIGN

During Easter week April 1915, the biggest and most impressive of all of the recruitment drives was held. Sacker and Devereux's remarkable account of the plight of soldiers of Cheltenham, *Leaving Behind All That Was Dear*, described it as 'an unusually elaborate propaganda exercise … ever carried out'. The campaign started with open-air meetings each night of the week and culminated in a military procession on Saturday, 10 April. The procession was headed by the mayor in full mayoral regalia, on horseback, flanked by mounted police, followed by two brigadier generals on horses and their mounted staff officers. Following them, with a variety of military and civilian bands, were the 9th and 10th Battalion Gloucestershire

The great Easter Recruitment Drive week of April 1915 ended with this enormous procession, part of which, pictured here, shows the mounted staff officers. It is seen from Marlborough House, looking down on the Gordon Lamp at the top of Lansdown Road. (*Cheltenham Chronicle and Gloucestershire Graphic*, 15 April 1915)

Regiment and the 175th and 176th Company, 12th Division of the Army Service Company, billeted in Cheltenham at the time, the Royal Gloucestershire Hussars Yeomanry and the 2/1st Division Cycling Corps. These soldiers totalled around 3,500 men. Behind them came the only ladies in the procession, the newly formed Cheltenham Women's Volunteer Reserve of around thirty women and fifty of the Red Cross contingent. There were the two local Volunteer Corps, the Cheltenham Rifle Association, comprising 120 men carrying an assortment of weapons, a much depleted fire brigade, 300 Scouts from twenty-one Cheltenham troops, fifty-one Gordon Boys, 120 Boys' Brigade and fifty-six Church Lads and their bands.

Assembling at the Gordon Lamp, this procession stretched back to the railway bridge by the Lansdown Castle, where Gloucester Road meets Lansdown Road. Filtering into the procession when it moved off at 2.30 p.m. was a line of groups stretched down the length of Queen's Road. The procession, 1 mile long, took thirty minutes to pass a spectator and one and a half hours to pass around town on its route to the Athletic Ground, arriving at 4 p.m. The report said, 'In mere length of procession it is the most impressive on record.'

At the Athletic Ground there were rousing speeches but the recruitment was far from impressive, being described as 'undoubtedly poor'. The reason suspected was that 'the willing man had already enlisted'. Only one man had publicly come forward after the speeches, although several others gave their names to the recruiting officer. The previous month 102 recruits had volunteered in Cheltenham in four weeks. For all this effort the massive recruitment drive produced only twenty-six recruits. Many considered that it was now time for men to be conscripted into the army.

NATIONAL REGISTRATION AND DERBYITES

The National Registration Scheme, announced in July 1915, required every person aged 15–65 years of age to be registered, except for men discharged from military service. The government needed to compile a register of national resources, i.e. to know how many people were in what employment, what skills were available and resources needed. Underlying this was also a need to know how many men were of military age. In Cheltenham district, on Sunday, 15 August 1915, 36,000 homes received forms, hand delivered by eighty-three voluntary enumerators under the council's supervision. The Cheltenham volunteer enumerators comprised fifty-two private residents, fourteen ladies, fourteen school leavers and three Corporation officials. There were nine questions on the paper; one question asked how many people were dependent on the person registering. A wife was not considered to be a dependent of her husband because '… all wives have a right to be supported by their husbands' according to the government.

Nosy neighbour! Mr Smith collecting National Registration papers in the Naunton Park area on Monday, 16 August 1915. (*Cheltenham Chronicle and Gloucestershire Graphic*, 21 August 1915)

It was realised by October 1915 that with heavy losses of soldiers on the battlefields of France, the need for fighting men outweighed the waning numbers of recruits now signing up. Appointed National Director of Recruiting in October 1915, Lord Derby had devised a voluntary enlistment scheme which, it was hoped, would defer the inevitable conscription for a while longer. Under Derby's scheme, the volunteer swore an oath of allegiance to the King and received 2s 9d, being one day's pay and ration allowance. The volunteer, now referred to as a Derbyite, then returned to normal employment until called up for enlistment.

In Cheltenham, 5,000 men were canvassed to join Derby's scheme, National Registration having pinpointed who could have enlisted but hadn't. Between 8–12 December 1915, at Manchester Street (now part of Clarence Street) over 1,000 men from the area took the oath – 814 being from Cheltenham. A special ceremony was held in the Supper Room of the Town Hall on Monday, 20 December 1915 at 2 p.m. when the first official khaki armlets were handed out to 100 men. To show he had volunteered, the man wore a khaki armlet with the Sovereign's crown embroidered in red if he had signed up for the army and a navy armlet with a red anchor for the navy. Alderman C.H. Margrett (Chairman of the local Parliamentary Recruitment Committee) was to hand out the first few armlets. Six tables were laid out, behind which sat three clerks, some of them ladies, ready with bundles of the khaki armlets. Eight people received armlets from the mayor, the first one being Mr John Allcott, one of the town's two recruiting officers and the second, the youngest recruit, Joseph Williams of Jersey Cottages, being 18 years and 2 months. Mr Allcott was promoted in September 1916 to sergeant major in the 30th Gloucestershire Railway Labour Battalion, having been the first to join the battalion.

On 16 January 1916, Cheltenham was to hold the first Derbyite church parade in the country, comprising 500 new recruits. The parish church service ended with the hymn 'Hold the fort, for I am coming'. Four days later the first Derbyite recruits left, and the next day and the next day. Voluntary attestation ceased on 1 March 1916. By this time, far in excess of 3,000 men of Cheltenham were gone from the town, serving King, Country and Cheltenham.

An unusual angle on recruitment advertising. (*Cheltenham Looker On*, 10 April 1915)

CONSCRIPTION

Not enough men had attested under Lord Derby's scheme, however, and reinforcements were needed faster than could be recruited after the Battle of the Somme. The Military Service Act of January 1916 brought in conscription. Choice was no longer an option. The first part of this bill was initially known as the 'Bachelor's Bill' and referred to the first men to be conscripted – single and widowed men of 18–41 years of age, who had no dependents. Finally, on 25 May 1916 a bill was passed 'for the general and immediate compulsion of all fit males of military age not now in the Navy or Army'; universal conscription now included married men. Four months later those born in 1899 were conscripted, with the assurance that they wouldn't be called up until they were 18 years old. During some weeks of 1916, men left Cheltenham every day of the week for training camps. In the wake of conscription Cheltenham held its first military tribunals for those claiming exemption from military service by dint of having a protected employment, dependents or – the most disliked group of all – conscientious objectors, of which there were around twenty registered in Cheltenham.

Within a few months of an archduke being murdered in a far-off country, the lost summer became the final memory of a passing age. The army had taken the cream of the town's – and the country's – youth: 18–40 year olds. Few of the recruits would have ventured more than a few miles from the homes in which they were born and fewer still would have known what to expect of war. There had been no war between the Great Powers since 1871. As A.J.P. Taylor wrote, 'No man in the prime of life knew what war was like. All imagined that it would be an affair of great marches and great battles, quickly decided.' The reality of war for Cheltenham was that every three days there was the death of a Cheltenham man somewhere in the world. Whereas in normal times death was expected to be in your own bed in your own home, with the ritual of a funeral, burial wake and tombstone, this war reversed the norm. Men were not brought back from the battlefields to be buried at home. It was so much harder to mourn without the ritual or the body to bury, the tombstone to mourn by. As a consequence many had the irrational belief that when the war was over, the dead men would return. Life in Cheltenham would never be quite the same again, and neither would the people.

CHAPTER 3

Shaming Shirkers and Shoppers

Cheltenham people were to experience a dislocation of their way of life from August 1914, coping with changes that could not have been foreseen. The home front truly became a place to show patriotic spirit and to fight a different kind of war. For the traders of Cheltenham this was a precarious time – depleted staff and dwindling custom, unstable supplies and an uncertain future. For the soldiers' families life was even tougher.

HELP FOR THE SOLDIERS' FAMILIES

Within days of the declaration of war, the editor of the *Echo*, Edwin Willoughby, had set up the first of many funds and appeals by the newspaper – a Patriotic Fund to help the wives and children of Territorials, Reservists, Red Cross and St John Ambulance members who had been suddenly called up and had already gone to war. With a generous £50 donation, the first person to give was Major Percy Shewell, the recruiting officer for Cheltenham. The donors on the list included the *Echo* editor and the Cheltenham Newspaper Company, Herbert Unwin of Arle Court, the Revd R.H. Bouth and Colonel Ashburner. Unwin and Ashburner were local philanthropists whose names frequently appeared in lists of donors. However, when Colonel Francis Ashburner of 5 Lansdown Place discovered that the Cheltenham Local Patriots' Fund was to be merged with the national fund, within weeks of its inception, he withdrew his donation of 50 guineas. His donation, he said, was beyond all proportion to his income as he wished to support a fund where the help was given directly to *local* patriots.

Meanwhile, the Chairman of Gloucestershire County Council, Maynard Colchester-Wemyss, was charged with the mammoth task of setting up an umbrella organisation, a General Committee, to exercise control over all eventualities and welfare throughout Gloucestershire. The sub-committees, of which there were nineteen, one for each Gloucestershire area, needed to plan what to do to alleviate distress caused to the families of those enlisted, to ensure trade and industry kept working and to make provision for the sick and wounded who may be sent to the county. The initial meeting, called on 10 August 1914 at Shire Hall, consisted of 180 local representatives. Colchester-Wemyss writes, in a letter to the King of Siam, dated 25 August 1914:

> It required great care and caution to get every class and every interest. All sorts and conditions of men and women were there, all distinctions of class or politics or religion were forgotten. One moment I would be talking to a Duke, the next perhaps to a Trades Union Leader; then perhaps to the wife of an Earl and directly afterwards to the daughter of a butcher, then the Bishop of the Diocese, but each one was activated by the same thought – how best to take his or her share in carrying out the object that had brought us together.

The day of Mr Colchester-Wemyss's meeting, a telegram was received by Cheltenham's Town Clerk from the Local Government Board asking him to: 'Please get in touch at once with the local branch of the Soldiers' and Sailors' Families Association … and let dependents of men joining the colours apply to the "office" from tomorrow onwards.' The next day a letter appeared in the *Echo* announcing that the Soldiers' and Sailors' Families Association (SSFA) had taken an office at No. 3 Royal Well Terrace, St George's Road. The letter's purpose was twofold: to let dependents know where to come for help and to appeal for funds to support struggling families. The process of paying Reservists and Territorials had not yet been set up and families were not receiving the army separation allowance. As many of the men who had enlisted or been called up early had previously been unemployed, their families were left with no immediate means of support. The lucky families whose breadwinners worked for the Post Office, Cheltenham Corporation, the Gas Works, A.C. Billings & Co., the *Echo*, Cavendish House, Bristol Taxi Co. and Gloucestershire Cooperative Society were paid a proportion of their wages whilst the men were at war.

Five days later the Association had been contacted by 200 soldiers' families needing help. As with all funds, subscribers' lists appeared in the newspapers weekly. In the *CLO* of 5 September 1914, beneath the headline 'War and Home Life: How Cheltenham Families Fare' appeared this tear-jerking piece about the Association's work:

> Mount the winding staircase that leads to three, little, barely furnished rooms at the top of 3 Royal Well Terrace. Here … ladies are continuously interviewing the dependents. On that landing waiting room are to be found … those left on the verge of poverty by the sudden call to arms. One will not come down without leaving a donation as an expression of one's approval.

By 31 October 1914, £655 4s 4d had been raised, including £2 from Mrs Whitcombe's dog 'Denis'. On 19 December the fund had reached £1,086 6s 7d including £1 14s 2d from 'Denis'. As an interim measure the fund had served its purpose. In July 1915, due to the Naval and Military War Pensions Bill, it was expected that the government's plans would virtually sweep away the SSFA and pass the work over to mayors to administer as part of the War Relief Fund. Lieutenant-Colonel Sir Donald Robertson of the SSFA described this as 'a national catastrophe'. Robertson pointed out that he 'didn't know Mayors and Aldermen would know the difference between Horse Guards and Royal Marines'.

NO MORE CRICKET

Meanwhile, the annual festival of cricket held at Cheltenham College from 10–19 August was suffering. Attendance was poor – so poor that the combined gates for the first two days of play were £52 3s 6d whereas for the same two days in 1913 the gate had totalled £193 2s. By Wednesday it was announced, after three Festival Committee Meetings, that, contrary to the rumours, the festival was not going to be abandoned. However, by Thursday admission was reduced to 6d in the hopes of boosting numbers. Cheltenham would not see another annual cricket festival for five years. Neither would it see the Leckhampton Flower Show, the Hatherley and Reddings Horticultural Show, the Liberal's Fête or racing at Prestbury after 1915 – annual events all so much a part of town life. The great Three Choirs Festival was abandoned, not to be revived until 1920. Luckily the venue for 1914 wasn't Gloucester.

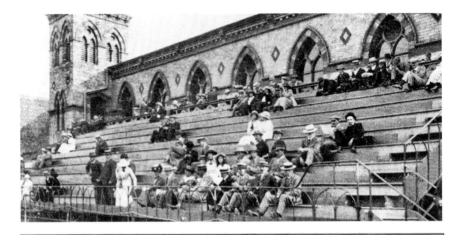

The grandstand at Cheltenham Cricket Festival on the afternoon of Monday, 18 August during the Surrey match, showing interest in cricket was killed by the war. (*Cheltenham Chronicle and Gloucestershire Graphic*, 22 August 1914)

USING WOMEN TO SHAME SHIRKERS

Propaganda during the First World War purposely targeted women as never before, using them as persuaders to encourage young men to enlist. The Order of the White Feather, started by Admiral Fitzgerald in August 1914, was aimed at getting women to hand out white feathers to any healthy young man who seemed capable of joining the army. Culture at that time put a great deal of emphasis on masculinity and to have women in particular call you a coward was highly insulting. The use of a white feather originated from an old cock-fighting belief that a cockerel with a white feather in its tail was of an inferior breed and therefore had no fighting spirit. The idea spread throughout the country with astonishing rapidity, so much so that the Home Secretary had to issue badges for civilians on war service reading 'King and Empire'. By September 1916, Silver War Badges were given to soldiers honourably discharged from the services and to women munitions workers.

The Women of England's Active Service League was formed by Baroness Orczy, author of the book *The Scarlet Pimpernel*. The 20,000 women who joined the league pledged not to be seen out with a man who had not enlisted and to 'persuade every man I know to offer his service to his country'. The baroness made an impassioned plea to the women of England in the *Daily Mail*: 'Your hour has come! … Give your country the men she wants. Give her your sweetheart, she wants him; your son, your brother, your friends. She wants them all!'

On 11 September 1914, the first item under 'Local War Notes' in the *Echo* was headed 'The White Feather'. There were occasions when the indiscriminate handing out of white feathers – or posting through the mail, as seems to have been the case in Cheltenham – reached the wrong people, many of whom had served honourably and were home recovering or discharged due to being wounded. Seaman George Samson, wearing a suit, was handed a feather on his return from having been awarded the Victoria Cross by the King. A man on a tram told the lady handing him a white feather, 'I am in civvies because my uniform is full of lice but if

I had it on I wouldn't be half as lousy as you!' A Mr Fruin wrote to the *Chronicle* of 15 September 1914 saying that he was rejected for army service for reasons of chest size but was 'yesterday pounced upon in Malvern by a foolish flapper putting a white feather in my buttonhole and wanted to catch Cheltenham young ladies should they have started a similar campaign'. He was a little too late!

The problem of those not enlisting was a vexed issue in Cheltenham. The *Echo* frequently carried letters from disgusted ex-soldiers and irate readers stating their strongly held views. At the start of the war, some of the letters were positively vitriolic, such as this one from a 70-year-old man whose letter appeared in the *Echo* on 5 September 1914. It is interesting how he used the term 'cannon fodder' in this context and how the writer sees women:

> Can nothing be done to shame into obeying their country's call the hundreds of able-bodied, well-to-do, young fellows in Cheltenham who are loafing away their days in amusement and idleness. One sees them lolling on the seats in the Promenade … while their country sorely needs their services. They do not appear to be women, though they act as such and they cannot be called 'men'. They skulk at home to save their worthless skins … Are there not a sufficient number of patriotic women in Cheltenham to drive out these lazy shirkers, or to label them 'coward' for all to see? They are fit only to be German slaves and I would like to see them all shipped off to Germany and put in front of the Kaiser's troops as 'cannon fodder'.

Young men playing tennis were referred to as 'loafers' and 'flannelled funks' by one writer and another even objected to women playing tennis, suggesting 'they should scorn tennis when there is so much for them to do!' And indeed there was so much for the ladies of Cheltenham to do and so much they did do.

'A Cheltenham Woman' appealed in her *Echo* letter to: 'Young men what are you doing in Cheltenham? Women, why are you not sending them to the front!' 'Cheltenham Mother' aimed her barb at middle-class mothers:

> The lower classes have made a fine response to the call for patriotism. The aristocracy have answered the call of sacrifice. It seems now to be the 'comfortable' classes which hold aloof. Ah, you other women whose sons have not gone. What is wrong with your sons? Have you not taught them patriotism?

Lieutenant Fitch of the 11th Gloucestershire Regiment on Monday, 6 September 1915, whilst recruiting in the town, '… urged the ladies to use their influence' in persuading young men to enlist. He added encouragement by promising those volunteering would be placed in his own company and he would assist them in every way. Twelve men signed up. This letter writer to the *Echo* believed enlistment to be the responsibility of ladies and shopkeepers! He considered bachelors who had not volunteered should be:

> … held up to public scorn for their poltroonery and by their employers giving them no choice. Every young woman should refuse to speak to these effeminate creatures who prefer to stand behind shop counters … labour employers should require 'able-bodied' bachelors to leave their service during war … It lies then to the ladies of Cheltenham and the shopkeepers to prove themselves patriots at this juncture.

Rumours abounded around the town as to the demise of reluctant enlisters. Notices were put up on lamp posts in Cheltenham telling young men that if they didn't enlist they would be sacked. A letter writer considered this was the 'unBritish methods of a few of Cheltenham's local "busybodies" and the greatest indignation exists in Cheltenham owing to the notices in question.'

A recruitment cartoon of the day. (*Gloucestershire Echo*, 30 January 1915)

CHELTENHAM'S TRADERS – BUSINESS AS USUAL?

At the start of the war there was a state of confusion as to how life was going to continue in Cheltenham, none more so than for the traders of the town. Countrywide, the message had been 'business as usual', but these were far from usual times. To top it all, customers were purposely extending credit to unacceptable lengths and demanding the same service from traders who had fewer workers to supply high standards of service.

The impact of recruitment on Cheltenham employers was apparent by this list, from figures published in the *Echo*. It shows some of the companies whose employees had enlisted by 3 September 1914, within four weeks of the start of the war:

Cheltenham Corporation	29	Cavendish House	24
Gloucestershire Police	24	Gas Works	21
H.H. Martyn	18	Brewery	16
Blue Taxis	14	Light Railway	12
Newspaper	8	Lance & Co. (Drapers)	12
George's (Caterers)	8	Collins & Godfrey	12
Webb Bros (Brickworks)	7	Post Office	6
R.E. & C. Marshall	5	Norman & Sawyer (Printers)	4

The Cheltenham Original Brewery used their advertisements to encourage enlistment by appealing directly to their wholesale customers to influence their workers. This advert appeared in local papers on 4 September 1914: 'An appeal to Hotel Proprietors, Licensed Victuallers and all other customers of the Cheltenham Original Brewery. Your country expects YOU to use all your influence to persuade young able-bodied men to come forward and enrol in Lord Kitchener's Army. Trust Kitchener.' An advert for 'The Famous', the men's outfitters, just read: 'Keep your boys but send your men!'

In May 1915, at the Cheltenham Traders' conference, it was clear the delegates' concerns hadn't been resolved. The Chairman, Mr Welstead, remarked that '… before traders are asked to release more members of their already depleted staff, the scores of young men who are seen about the streets should be rounded up!' Exasperation can be felt in the words of A.W. Bryant of 1 Colonnade when he was fined 30s for sending in an incomplete record of employees to the recruiting office after conscription. He had written on the form 'The Recruiting Officer has done his damnedest with the others'.

HOME FRONT – LOCAL PATRIOTISM OF A DIFFERENT KIND

The day after war was declared, Mr Edward J. Burrow – newspaper proprietor, entrepreneur and avid promoter of Cheltenham – wrote a heartfelt letter of appeal to the *Echo*: 'Sir, I wish to protest with all the energy I have at my command against the insane, unBritish panic that has induced so many of our townsfolk to clear the grocers and provision dealers' shops on the prospect of a slight rise in price.' He admitted later that the letter had rather offended some of his friends but he felt it had to be said.

In the first issue of the *CLO* since the outbreak of war, on 8 August 1914, the paper followed up Burrow's plea to its readers:

> The 'man in the street' is facing the situation with calmness and determination … We who are left behind can show our patriotism. We can stick together, sink all class prejudice and refrain from taking any advantage over less fortunate fellow-men. Above all else, we should refrain from hoarding money or provisions against a time of necessity. We have ample food for a few months. Don't let us therefore take a mean advantage and send up the price of food for those worse off than ourselves.

The concern over hoarding of provisions seemed to be paramount in the minds of some. Others felt there were more pressing priorities than food hoarding.

The Traders of Cheltenham have freely given
MEN AND MONEY
for National Defence and Relief. They confidently ask the inhabitants of Cheltenham to
HELP THEM
by the prompt payment of accounts, by the spending wisely which keeps trade normal, and showing their appreciation of
LOCAL PATRIOTISM
BY SHOPPING IN THE TOWN.
E. J. B. & Co., Ltd.

This advert in the *Echo* appealed for people to support their local traders. (*Gloucestershire Echo*, 26 September 1915)

On Saturday, 26 September 1914 the front pages of all local newspapers carried a notice headed, 'Official Message from the Home Office, Whitehall to All Town Councils'. This message could not be missed. It was certainly official:

> It is neither desirable or necessary in existing circumstances to dismiss any Assistants but, if economies in the carrying on of businesses are necessary, they should be met by Other Means. THE MAYOR OF CHELTENHAM asks the shopping public to make this recommendation possible by the prompt payment of accounts, spending wisely and Shopping in the Town, so that money may be more freely circulated and business establishments able to retain their employees.

Advertisements appeared in the papers reminding townspeople of responsibilities on their own home doorstep. Cheltenham Original Brewery advised, 'Spend Wisely and Purchase Goods that will find Employment for Local Labour.' Jennings, the tailor at Town Clock Corner, agreed: 'Be Patriotic … Spend your money locally for the benefit of the town.' Waite & Son, the jeweller in the High Street, ran a series of adverts throughout the war, designed to look like important news reports, but which were aimed to boost their sales of items for soldiers. Right next to the Home Office notice ran their advert: 'Behind the Man in Khaki is a nation of patriotic shopkeepers … who are doing their best to retain their staff on full pay and thus lessen the suffering and privation of the coming months … Will you help us by sending your repairs to us?'

Clearly, certain Cheltenham consumers had ignored the impassioned plea of Ed Burrows and the Home Office. Editorial in the *Echo* emphasised the message with the heading 'Prompt Payment Patriotism' and referred to the Burrows advert:

> This appeal deserves to be repeated and emphasised. Complaints have been made that the 'residential' element is not doing its duty. It is a poor patriotism which contributes to patriotic funds while leaving tradesmen's bills unpaid. Long credit is a marked weakness of Cheltenham and this is a juncture when the unfairness and dishonesty of it should be strongly reprobated.

The issue didn't end there. It stirred up a veritable can of worms. One letter claimed that a teashop in town had raised their bread prices because of the war. The managing director of George's Ltd, a prominent baker, caterer and teashop owner in the town, replied that to his knowledge no teashop in Cheltenham had inflated their prices.

Not only artificially hiked prices were a problem but, according to another letter to the *Echo* there was a '… very great evil … several tradesmen are using the war as an excuse to rob their employees by means of reducing their salaries … to variable extents from 10% to one day's pay.' Lance & Co. replied that it was not their policy to do this and none of their employees had been dismissed or had their salaries reduced.

George's shop in Clarence Street. George's was a prominent Cheltenham caterer, baker and teashop company. (*Cheltenham in old postcards* by Roger Whiting)

Dicks & Sons placed a large advert in the *Echo* on 6 January 1915 stating, in very large capital letters: 'We have not reduced the salaries of any of our sixty employees in consequence of the war and ask the support of the public to enable us to continue this policy.' Mischief-making and rumour-mongering ran rife in Cheltenham.

Matters didn't improve in the ensuing year. Councillor Silk, at the Cheltenham Traders' conference in May 1915 made a particular point that, in spite of the appeals from the mayor, there was still an extreme lack of consideration shown by many customers. The long credit system – payment of 'little bills' – was still not being settled promptly. However, of more concern was the fact that many customers thought nothing of requiring three or four deliveries of goods a day when one would suffice.

However, spending patterns and consumers were changing in Cheltenham. Maynard Colchester-Wemyss noted on 25 November 1915:

> Soldiers' wives are spending freely, the girls munitions-making are spending freely, and so the smaller shops are doing an immense trade … but the higher class shops are not doing anything like as well, because their customers are the professional and landed classes and are feeling badly the pinch of the war.

The traders of Cheltenham, through their organisation, did much to encourage tourism to the town during the war. A special meeting of the Cheltenham Chamber of Commerce was held on 25 September 1914 to address the revival of the town as a spa in view of the war. Amongst numerous measures outlined by Ed Burrows was a series of advertisements in the *Daily Mail*, the *British Medical Journal* and *The Lancet*, which proposed visiting Cheltenham as an alternative to voyaging abroad to take

A WORD OF ADVICE TO
CHELTENHAM VISITORS.
If unable to purchase the Celebrated
CHELTENHAM ALE
At your Home,
WHY NOT TAKE A HOUSE AT CHELTENHAM,
Where you can get this Delicious Beer delivered punctually?
C.O.B.

The Cheltenham Original Brewery's advertisements reflected topical news of the day. This one referred to the town's invitation to residents of east coast towns, shelled by German warships, to take a house in Cheltenham where they would be safe. (*Gloucestershire Echo*, 26 September 1916)

A SCULPTOR REFUGEE

Was it just a coincidence that Auguste Rodin rested for six weeks in Cheltenham from Paris during September 1914? The 74-year-old sculptor was persuaded to come to Cheltenham by his friend Mlle Judith Chadel, who had sisters in Cheltenham. Rodin stayed at the Sussex House Hotel, Winchcombe Street, simply, and walked to the Town Hall a few times a day, where communiqués on the progress of the war were posted. He also paid several visits to the museum where, it is said, he minutely examined the collection of flint implements, Phoenician and Roman glass vessels. Coincidentally, Lady Scott, sculptress of the Wilson statue in the Promenade, was a favourite pupil of Rodin.

the waters. The brother of Mr E.B. Wethered, former Mayor of Cheltenham, happened to be the editor of one of the journals and agreed to write an article extolling the medicinal virtues of the spa's waters. Advertisements had been placed inviting 'good-class French and Belgian refugees to come and reside in Cheltenham'. Another promotional venture was showcards to read 'Germany is closed', to be displayed in 2,000 chemists across the country, by United Chemists' Association Limited (UCAL), who had won the contract to bottle Cheltenham waters.

On 31 May 1915, the Cheltenham Traders' Association started a series of summer concerts – two in the morning and one in the afternoon – which included '... refreshments of a light character'. The reason was two-fold: firstly concerts would encourage people to partake of the spa waters and thus revive the spa's popularity and the traders' businesses. Secondly, entertainment, it was hoped, would entice visitors to spend summers in Cheltenham rather than east coast resorts, which had been shelled, or continental resorts which were not safe. Most of all, the concerts were frequented by those in the town who wished to see and be seen.

'FAIR PLAY FOR GERMAN RESIDENTS!'

We are informed that some Cheltonians have been treating with discourtesy certain Germans now in residence in the town and in one case a German who has lived and worked in Cheltenham many years, has been turned out of his lodgings for no fault – only on account of his parentage.

So read the leader in the *Echo* of Monday, 20 August 1914. It didn't take long for there to be hatred of a nation that had once been much admired by the British. Indeed, the Royal Family's surname was Saxe-Coburg-Gotha of the House of Hanover through the marriage of Queen Victoria with Prince Albert. King George V replaced the name with 'Windsor' in 1917. The King instigated the Titles Deprivation Act 1917 by asking for the names of seven German and six Austrian royals to be struck from the roll of the Most Noble Order of the Knights of the Garter – three of the British princes and dukes were serving in the German Army! All newspapers bombarded their readers with gruesome stories of German atrocities, not all of them true, to incite people's hatred and in turn stoked the jingoistic patriotism which swelled the recruitment queues.

Six days after the outbreak of war, a bureau was set up at Cheltenham Police Station under the Alien's Restriction Order, with a German-speaking deputy registrar. Those of German and Austrian nationality had to register at the police station as aliens. In Cheltenham twenty-two men and twenty-two women registered by 26 August 1914. In October 1914, fifteen Germans and Austrians were assembled at Cheltenham Police Station to be driven by taxi to GWR Malvern Road station for the concentration camp at Shrewsbury. Four of these were waiters at a 'prominent' hotel in Cheltenham – one of them came to England at the age of 3 months and had married an Englishwoman.

The manager of The Queen's Hotel, Stanley G. Holman, wrote to the *Echo*'s editor, angry at the treatment of some of his staff and the misunderstanding by the general public, whipped up by the hatred of all things 'Hun':

> Already a young Frenchman in my employ has been blackguarded as a German by an individual. The public should not be tricked into imagining the Bohemian, Slav, Czech and Prussian are all alike … shocked that one I'd employed since 1898 – a German – had taken his life because of it.

A spate of replies to Mr Holman's letter contained sentiments such as '… our visitors should not be attended by … a heterogeneous collection of undesirable aliens'; 'England for the English'; 'The foreign waiter is a modern fancy'.

Men of alien nationality, who were family breadwinners married to British women, caused a dilemma for the Cheltenham Board of Guardians. An application for 7*s* 6*d* per week Poor Relief was received from a woman whose husband, a Bavarian of military age, had been interned and therefore she had been left without any source of income. The wife had been born in Cheltenham and had three young children to feed and clothe. The Guardians considered her an irremovable pauper, i.e. she had nowhere else to go and no means of support.

Cheltenham, used to continental visitors who sojourned for the 'season' in the town, had a number of permanent inhabitants with Germanic-sounding names. Many were given short shrift by suspicious townspeople, scared of German infiltration and spies. One such trader put this notice in the *Echo* on 8 August 1914:

> Mr George W Hider (Messrs Willet and Co Bakers, Hewlett Road) asks us to refute the slander current in the neighbourhood that he is a German. He states he is a native of Somerset where he was born 4th February 1876 and his family have lived for over 200 years at the village of Seal near Sevenoaks.

Mr Hider acted as an interpreter for the Belgian refugees in Cheltenham. In December 1914, the editorial in the *CLO* felt it necessary to defend one of its principal advertisers, Mr F.J. Vanderplank, furrier and ladies' costumier: 'Amongst the many rumours connected with the war which have been circulated in the town, none is so baseless as the one which charges Mr Vanderplank with sympathy for our alien foes … the name of Vanderplank has been associated with Romney Abbey as far back as 1670.'

The Musical Director of The Hippodrome, Karl Meyder, in a letter to the *Echo* of 5 September 1914, stated: 'As there seems to be a doubt as to my real nationality, I wish it to be known that I am an Englishman by birth.' Four months later, Carl Hertz, one of the acts at The Hippodrome, had to explain before his performance that he was an American and his sympathies lay directly with the British, so much so that he was giving half of his salary to the War Relief Fund. Mr C. Wedberg went as far as taking a half-page advertisement in the *CLO* to state, in capital letters, that 'HE IS NOT A GERMAN' as so many people supposed, but Swedish. He reproduced the wording of his passport in the advertisement and invited readers to see the original at 6 Montpellier Avenue. Mr Schlenthein, former lessee of the Winter Gardens, went further and changed his name to Seaholme. He explained in the *Echo* in November 1914 that he was never a German subject but a citizen of the world.

Those on the bench at Cheltenham Police Court in October 1914 had a tricky time of figuring out what to do with 68-year-old Jacob Schuck, a German street musician of Stanhope Street. Schuck was charged under DORA that he, being an alien enemy, had unlawfully kept four homing pigeons. His son, an English subject, claimed the pigeons were his and intended for the cooking pot.

J. Lyons & Co., a national chain of grocers, cafes and tea distributors, took a large advertisement in the *Echo* on 14 September 1914 headed 'Action for Libel' to publicise the Interim Injunction they had been granted in the High Court of Justice. The company took Liptons, another national grocery chain with a shop in Cheltenham's High Street, to court for suggesting the directors of Lyons were German and that customers buying goods from Lyons would be assisting the enemy.

The Anti-German League, popular nationally, held a public meeting in Cheltenham Town Hall on 22 September 1915 entitled 'Britain for the British'. Seats were reserved for members wearing badges – the league already had sup-porters in Cheltenham. It took the town council a while to catch up. It wasn't until March 1916 that the council's General Purposes Committee passed a resolution that no contract was to be entered into with any person of German or Austrian nationality. The war highlighted what an enormous range of goods were imported into this country including glass eyes, most children's toys, carbon for public lighting and dried vegetables! England would now have to produce these for herself – and Cheltenham was part of that.

CHAPTER 4

Belgians, Bullets and Jam – A Plum Role for Cheltenham

BELGIANS

'Belgium has been struck down by barbarous hands and levelled to the earth before the astonished gaze of the civilised world ... little Belgium had offered the most remarkable defence to be found on the pages of history.' – Canon L'Estrange Fawcett (rector of Cheltenham's parish church).

An estimated 1 million Belgians had fled their country after the invasion at the beginning of August 1914 – 100,000 of them to Britain. By June 1915 there were 1,209 Belgians in Gloucestershire.

The *Echo* of 19 September directed readers to an advertisement on a previous page requesting help for refugees and recommending Miss Plumer's '... excellent scheme to give hospitality to Belgian refugees'. The advertisement suggested that a house be taken to accommodate twenty Belgians, headed by a voluntary lady superintendent, a paid housekeeper and two paid Belgian servants. The project could be funded if 100 people could be found to subscribe 2*s* per week. A lady Scout would make weekly calls to collect the money. The home, it was pointed out, 'would NOT be for the poorest classes'. Meanwhile, when the fate of Belgium was widely known, a Belgian Relief Fund was started in Cheltenham and hundreds of pounds quickly subscribed. A letter from the mayor appeared in the local papers, appealing for homes for Belgian refugees. By 23 September, a Belgian Home Office had been set up in North Street, courtesy of Sir Jesse Boot, founder of Boots the Chemist. It was open daily 10 a.m. – 1 p.m. by Miss Plumer to answer potential homeowners' questions. Three days later some thirty householders in the district had responded to the mayor's letter by offering to receive one or more refugees into their homes, including Mr Fairlie Muir of Crofton Lodge, who temporarily housed the first refugees.

Belgian refugees 'of the industrial class' with Miss Plumer (holding the dog) who organised the housing and welfare of the Belgian refugees in Cheltenham. (*Cheltenham Chronicle and Gloucestershire Graphic*, 17 October 1914)

On the evening of Wednesday, 7 October 1914, twenty Belgians – four men, five women and eleven children – arrived to be housed in Western Lodge, Western Road, lent by Mrs Seaver. The Belgians were described as being 'of middle or trading class'. These Belgians were French speaking and all Protestants whereas the second contingent of twenty people who reached Cheltenham, the next evening, to be housed at St Philips Lodge, Painswick Road, were Flemish speakers only, all Roman Catholics and 'of the peasant class'. The latter group had previously been housed in Alexandra Palace in London. Four days later, fourteen more refugees arrived, including a party consisting of a lady of 78 years old, her three sisters and a niece. There were only two Flemish speakers in Cheltenham who could act as interpreters, Mr Van Neste and Mr Hider. Mr Hider, of Willet & Co., bakers of Hewlett Street, wrote to the newspaper in August and made a point of letting it be known that he was not to be referred to as German. Later in the month, four families of Belgians from Malines, furniture makers and toolmakers, were found accommodation at Charlton Kings. Talking with the refugees through an interpreter the *Echo* reporter solemnly declared: 'We are impressed with the intolerable pathos of their position and their sterling grit.'

By 6 November 1914 there were five Belgian Homes in Cheltenham – Western Lodge, St Philips Lodge, Greenfield, Longford and Oakfield in The Park, in total housing eighty-eight refugees. The Belgians cooked for themselves and did their own housework but each home was run by a matron who received a small salary. Eventually, two of the matrons of these homes were themselves refugees. The Cheltenham Belgian Refugee Committee added another two homes in December with Painswick Lawn and Torquay Villa in Selkirk Street, lent by the local builder A.C. Billings, whose staff paid for the upkeep of these refugees. Local medical men also opened a hostel, which ran for some months. The homes were open to visitors for two hours in the afternoon to encourage people to bring supplies of fruit, vegetables, coal and clothes, or money. It was estimated that running costs were 6s per head per week but there was the advantage of a reduction of rates, taxes and water charges. The people and organisations of Cheltenham raised money, held concerts, gave clothing, made cakes, found work and, by all means possible, supported the refugees during their stay. Some of the Belgians did find work in the town. The arrival of the Belgians did not go unnoticed by the quick-witted pens of the copywriter of the men's outfitters, 'The Famous', whose advert in the *Echo* read 'Belgium makes history! We make clothing!' and Cheltenham Original Brewery's advert, 'Belgium is swarming with Bad (H)'Uns'.

Many people in Cheltenham went out of their way to support the refugees. A generous entrepreneur with an ever-vigilant eye for publicity was Cecil Gillsmith of The Hippodrome variety theatre, who invited the refugees to come to a performance at the theatre the day after their arrival. Forty-two refugees attended and, it was said, '… included so many babies!' Twenty-three householders in Burton Street started a penny a week fund for the Belgian refugees – the first payment was for 1s 11d in October 1914. For the first three months the Belgians were in Cheltenham, the children of Christ Church School brought vegetables into school for them on one day a week. These gifts from the children were divided between New Court, which opened as a hospital with fifty-five wounded Belgian soldiers on 21 October 1914 and for the refugees at Western Lodge, which was close to the school.

Some of the inhabitants of St Philip's Street showed true Christian spirit by making a large and handsome cake for one of the Belgian refugee houses at Christmas time. Ten Cheltenham doctors gave their services free of charge to look after the Belgian's health, including Grace Billings, who was the first female GP in the town. To the Belgian children schools offered places – Cheltenham Ladies' College took fifteen girls, Pate's Grammar School for Girls took seven as did the Ursuline Convent in The Park. Of the boys, five were taken free of charge at Cheltenham College, two at Dean Close, nine at the Grammar School for Boys, two at Glyngarth School and one at Mr Gurney's private school. Eight students had free admission to the School of Art and four to the technical schools.

BELGIUM MAKES HISTORY!
<u>WE</u> MAKE CLOTHING!

EVERYTHING FOR MEN

Fighting or Working.

BUSINESS AS USUAL!

PEACE PRICES.

BRITISH MADE GOODS.

"THE FAMOUS,"

350-1 HIGH STREET,
CHELTENHAM. TELEPHONE 724.
Registered and Est. 1886.

The Belgians were welcomed in Cheltenham and the advertising copywriter for 'The Famous' didn't miss the opportunity to note the invasion of their country early in the war. (*Cheltenham Chronicle and Gloucestershire Graphic*, 22 August 1914)

Major Prayon-van-Zuylen, a Belgian barrister, in a money-raising lecture at the Winter Gardens on 13 November 1914, told the audience:

> You are treating us not only as friends, not only as allies, but as brothers. You could not have done better for us even if we had been your own countrymen. From being one of the happiest and most prosperous nations 15 weeks ago, Belgium had become a land of desolation and of horror, ravaged by a relentless foe and threatened with the gaunt spectre of famine.

Two films – before and after bombardment with shells – were shown at the lecture to demonstrate the appalling devastation in Belgium.

SOUTHWOOD HOUSE – THE PRIMROSE LEAGUE

In a separate enterprise, but working with the Mayor's Relief Committee, the Cheltenham Habitation of the Primrose League had been lent Southwood House by the Revd T. Wolseley-Lewis. The house had been a college boarding house capable of housing ninety people but had lain empty for five years. To add confusion, there was also another college boarding house named Southwood House in Sandford Road at the same time and people were asked not to deliver gifts intended for the refugees to this house. The involvement of the Primrose League in the setting up of this home caused outrage in some quarters of Cheltenham. The Primrose League was an organisation for spreading Conservative principles and it had been agreed between the political parties at the outbreak of war that there would be a political truce – all parties were to work together for the common good. The strongest opponent of the Southwood House scheme was the Revd Fred Dwelly, curate of the parish church. In a letter to the paper under the heading 'Politics (?) and Charity', he called the political involvement 'thoughtless … bad taste … stupid … wicked'. The opposing political party in Cheltenham, the Liberals, referred to it as '… an insidious way to forward party ends under the guise of charity.' The reasoning behind the Conservative project was that the Primrose League wished to start a subscription list for those only able to donate small amounts of money. Consequently, the home was funded by hundreds of small subscribers whose money was collected regularly by 150 collectors of the League, who in total raised £2,500.

Southwood House was opened in early November 1914 and within three weeks was home to thirty-five refugees. By the time it closed in December 1917, some 138 refugees, disabled soldiers and Belgian soldiers on leave had passed through the doors – ninety-eight different individuals had stayed a considerable time and forty Belgian soldiers for shorter periods. When the home closed, the few remaining

Her Imperial Highness Princess Clementine Napoleon of the Belgians visited wounded Belgian soldiers in New Court Hospital on 11 February 1915. (*Cheltenham Chronicle and Gloucestershire Graphic*, 13 February 1915)

refugees were given a small house and a weekly allowance before being repatriated. By coincidence, the very morning the meeting was held to decide whether the home should close, the Committee received a letter from the Revd Wolseley-Lewis to say he had let the house and was giving them one month's notice.

All was not exactly sweetness and light with the organisation of the Belgian refugees, it transpired at a later date. The Clothes Department of the Cheltenham Belgian War Relief Committee, which took in second-hand clothing for the refugees, found they had 'some laborious work to perform as it was noted that fondness of dress was a characteristic of Belgians of all classes.' Other reports stated: '… dealing with the problem of the Belgian Refugees in Cheltenham … called for an exceptional amount of tact and in some cases, firmness.' The problems, it transpired, were that the intermingling of the Flemings and the Walloons did not always lend itself to harmony and the language question was necessarily trying. The refugees didn't sufficiently realise that their first duty was to be self-supporting and they were particularly reluctant to do any work for other refugees. By 3 May 1919 the last of the Belgians had been repatriated.

ROTHESAY HOUSE – THE FIRST OF ITS KIND IN ENGLAND

Cheltenham had one place of particular importance for Belgians – Rothesay House Hostel, Albert Road. This home, the first of its kind in England, was opened for discharged, disabled Belgian soldiers on 9 March 1915. It was to have been opened during a special royal visit of Her Imperial Highness Princess Clementine Napoleon of the Belgians on 11 February but, not being complete, the princess visited the wounded Belgian soldiers at New Court Hospital in Lansdown Road instead. Rothesay House was started by Commandant Van Weyenberg and five soldiers and during its time some forty-five soldiers passed through. Eighteen took regular work, four worked in the house and garden; two made carpets, others made leather work and embroidery; one was farming; two worked in market gardens; several worked in munitions, one was a clerk and one a tailor. There were some residents unfit for work. Although there was a garden around the house, the commandant had hired a piece of land worked by the men as a kitchen garden, growing vegetables for the home.

WESTERN COUNTIES WAR EXHIBITION

Never before had such a large event been held in Cheltenham, using the whole of the Town Hall, a large portion of the Winter Gardens and the grounds of both of the buildings, with the exception of the bowling green. The exhibition's subject matter and range of diverse exhibits had never been shown in Cheltenham then or since. Neither has it been rivalled in Cheltenham in terms of the length of time the exhibition was staged. This was the Western Counties War Exhibition held from 23 September to 20 October 1915 from 11 a.m. to 11 p.m. every day and opened by Baron C. Goffinet, Plenipotentiary Minister of HM the King of the Belgians. The purpose of the exhibition was 'to convey … a vivid and instructive idea of what modern war really means' and to raise money for the Belgian Red Cross Anglo-Belgian Committee work.

The exhibition was a continuous round of instruction or 'living interest' by means of lectures by experts, concerts and recitals by renowned artists and exhibition displays and stalls. As the exhibition publicity promised at the time: 'Never, as yet, in Cheltenham, have so many events of first class interest followed each other at such short intervals.' Internationally renowned artistes in the world of theatre, music and art contributed. One such worthy was 'the great French actress Madame Réjane'. Madame's *pièce de résistance* was to declaim Emile Cammaert's words in Elgar's famous 'Carillon', accompanied by the great Russian pianist Mark Hambourg and the Philharmonic Orchestra. Madam Réjane's third performance of this work had been at the Promenade concerts at the Albert Hall in May 1915 which was described by *The Times* as '… an even more lurid reading than those which she has given before.' Illustrated lectures were given by experts such as Mr 'Fred' T. Janes (of *Jane's Fighting Ships*, an annual review of the world's ships, which is still published) who gave a thirteen-point lecture ending 'The reason why "Trust the Admiralty" is the only motto for the British public'.

On entry to the southern transept of the Winter Gardens, the visitor was assaulted by a panoramic mural around the walls – all 14,000 square foot of it – of 'Hun-ridden Belgium', painted by Signor G.P. Tondi. Whilst walking though the hall amidst pictured ruins of devastated Belgium, visitors would have heard the strains of music coming from the Cinema Orchestra of Mr Field's Picture House (which was resident in the Winter Gardens), where special film plays were being shown throughout the day. Five hundred trophies of war were exhibited – shells, hand gre-nades, bayonets, German helmets and numerous articles curiously constructed out of the oddments of shells and cartridges. There were war photos of the Dardanelles, Egypt, Russia, Italy and France. Cheltenham's well-known philanthropist, Colonel Ashburner had lent his collection of remarkable relief maps of war zones.

The Winter Gardens, Imperial Square, home of exhibitions and fund-raising concerts, was used in part as an aeroplane factory. It was considered to be a white elephant, costing the council too much to maintain. Those living in the square complained they could hear the music from concerts and, when it rained, concert-goers complained they couldn't hear the music because of the rain on the roof. (Author's collection)

Corporal Moinet, one of the first injured Belgian soldiers to arrive at New Court Hospital, Lansdown, left a young wife behind in war-torn Brussels. His recovery was not helped by the fact he had heard nothing from his wife since he left for the fighting. In December 1914, whilst sitting in the lounge at the hospital, in walked Mrs Moinet. Having heard that her husband was in hospital in Cheltenham, she had decided, come hell or high water, to see him. Having no passport, she had to travel at night-time, crossing the Dutch border and travelling onwards as best she could. Mrs Moinet was later found accommodation at Western Lodge refugee home.

The fine art section showed the works of art smuggled out of Belgium. Visitors could not but be full of admiration for the method of saving the pictures. The canvasses had been cut out of their frames and wrapped in clothing, to get them passed through enemy lines undetected, as the pictures' owners were fleeing Belgium. The pictures were to be sold for the benefit of the Belgian artists ruined by war. Amongst the finer trophies of war was stained glass from a ruined church at Laventie and a portion of a gas bracket from Ypres Cathedral.

The vast extent and range of the exhibition can be imagined from the descriptions of some of the diverse exhibits. Outside, using the tennis court, was a section on the Science of Aviation. This display was of a number of aeroplanes recently used at Hendon Aerodrome (now the RAF Museum) and a selection of propellers. Included was a propeller which had been used on a plane being flown by the late Colonel Samuel F. Cody, in one of his remarkable flights, which landed on a cow as the plane was coming in to land. Cody was a famous Wild West showman who had travelled extensively around England but more seriously was a kite developer and aviator and died on 7 August 1913 when his plane broke up over Ball Hill, Farnborough. He had made the first powered, controlled flight in the UK, albeit for only 30 seconds, 16ft above the ground. On the grass more commonly used for strolling to the Winter Gardens, were constructed realistic representations of actual war trenches with dugouts, shelters, peep-holes, periscopes, parapets and parados. The trenches were set up with miniature rifles where people could practise firing at German trenches placed at practically the same range as between the hostile trenches in Europe.

Inside the halls and rooms of the Town Hall and the Winter Gardens were a range of exhibits that would make visitors gasp at their ingenuity. A miniature sea could be marvelled at with a fleet of naval working models from a super-Dreadnought to a submarine. There were demonstrations on munitions making from a model munitions factory, electrically driven, with fifty to sixty working lathes and machines used in shell making. A model of a complete Red Cross train showed how the injured soldiers travelled from the front to one of Cheltenham's eight Voluntary Aid hospitals.

During 1914 Cheltenham Borough Council had been actively trying to entice a manufacturer to set up a jam factory in the town, similar to the 'Golden Shred' new model factory at Brislington in Bristol. On the council's behalf, Ed Burrows had been advertising Cheltenham as an ideal venue in national newspapers. The council members' reactions were mixed. In July 1914 Alderman Baker 'felt it would help the public industries … provide sadly needed employment and … needs no unsightly chimneys' whilst the *CLO* editorial asked, 'Why do the Corporation fritter away the ratepayer's money in fatuous schemes like this?' Another comment epitomised Cheltenham townspeople's attitude to industry: 'Hands go up in holy horror when the idea of starting any kind of factory in Cheltenham is mooted as though a factory was a blasphemy or something in the nature of the "abomination of desolation standing in a holy place".' On 12 September 1914 Cheltenham Borough Council made its report. Due to the commencement of the war, the council had decided to 'defend our country first and then go back to the question of jam!'

Armies needed vast quantities of jam. Fruit and vegetables needed preserving. In 1917, the government's Food Department set up twenty fruit pulping and canning factories in towns throughout the country. Cheltenham was not one of those towns. Cheltenham Market Gardeners' Association appealed against the decision and persuaded the government to change its mind by offering to guarantee a supply of as much fruit and vegetables as the factory needed. The government, in return, agreed to install all the plant and manage the pulped and dried foodstuffs once processed. The scheme would be for the duration of the war and for six months afterwards.

Carrying baskets of plums weighing 24lb ready for pulping at the new Cheltenham Fruit and Vegetable Factory housed in buildings (formerly Stibb's Brewery) at the corner of Albion Street and Sherborne Place. (*Cheltenham Chronicle and Gloucestershire Graphic*, 18 August 1917)

Guaranteeing supply was no mean feat for the Association – the factory used 30 tons of fruit a week in season and 80 to 100 tons of vegetables and it was expected that 400 tons of fruit would be processed during the first season. Why was it that the Association approached the government and not the council? This explanation was given by 'The Chatterer' in the *Chronicle*:

> It seems the outcome of the opposition of the Council to the wishes of the Market Gardeners' Association who, thwarted in their desire to get control of the local fruit market so as to be able to run co-operative fruit auctions … decided to start negotiations with the Government … instead of a derelict brewery we have now a busy industry of a particularly wholesome and useful kind.

It was a spat that lasted until 1918 and caused a mayor to resign.

The Cheltenham Fruit and Vegetable Factory, as it was to be known, was housed in a block of buildings, formerly occupied by Stibb's Brewery, at the corner of Albion Street and Sherborne Place. For the fruit-pulping season, twenty workers and three male managers were employed. As the vegetable season got under way the workforce rocketed to eighty employees. The factory, which opened on Saturday,

11 August 1917, worked three shifts every twenty-four hours. Pulped fruit was useful because it kept longer than bottled fruit and would not use scarce, imported sugar. The large wood vats filled with fruit were cooked by applying steam until the fruit had been pulped and sterilised. It was then put into wine barrels and rum puncheons and sealed until needed for conversion into jam. Four hundredweight barrels of fruit could be pulped in five minutes with six vats pulping at a time. Barrels of fruit pulp – damsons, plums and apples – were stored on the Cheltenham Athletic Ground awaiting government instructions. The first season of pulping was a great success. There were so many barrels that they covered the athletic ground, piled two deep.

Cheltenham Athletic Ground with the result of a successful fruit-pulping season. The barrels are full of damsons, apples and plums ready to be taken to government jam factories. In 1919 the enterprise was taken over by the Cheltenham Market Gardeners' Association at larger premises in Dunalley Street. (*Cheltenham Chronicle and Gloucestershire Graphic*, 24 November 1917)

There was a secretive new industry in Cheltenham that came about as a result of the war – munitions. Cheltenham decorative craftsmen, H.H. Martyn & Co., had acted swiftly to compensate for work no longer coming in to the company such as the fitting out of luxury liners. The ill-fated *Titanic* had been worked on by H.H. Martyn & Co. The company had already started work on munitions in Cheltenham by 12 December 1914. A short report in the *Echo*, under the title 'War Office Contracts in Cheltenham', read:

> Workshops nearly as big as the Town Hall are alive with work … alongside a studio with plans for elaborate decorations for Buckingham Palace and Windsor Castle, The Town Hall at Johannesburg and the Parliament Buildings in British Columbia … H.H. Martyn has immediately started work for the War Office at present with something like £10,000 worth of ammunition cases in hand.

Four days later, 'A Cheltonian' felt the need to write to the newspaper to take issue with the report, which had stated 'contracts of this description are beneficial to Cheltenham'. The writer considered it a 'public disgrace' to have War Office Contracts which would reduce the workers' wages and suggested the company reduce their profits instead. The following day a reply from H.H. Martyn & Co. pointed out that, although there had been a downturn in their usual work, voluntary reductions in the staff and directors who were non-producers had been made at the beginning of the war. The remaining workers were paid at a higher rate than any other firm in Cheltenham.

Chancellor of the Exchequer David Lloyd George, on 9 March 1915, introduced a new bill in the House of Commons 'of the most sweeping character' – another addition to DORA. It enabled the government to take over control of any works or factories which were judged suitable for the making of munitions, e.g. motor and engineering works, and set them all to making shot, shell and 'war-like material'. In his speech on the new bill, Lloyd George brought in a new motto for the country: 'Not "Business as Usual" but "Victory as Usual"'. He explained that the bill would organise the industrial resources of the nation on a war footing, although it would lead to the 'subjection of business men to inconvenience … but the national need was overwhelming … at the critical moment.' This was just the beginning of a fast rolling need to step up production and consequently find a large labour force.

Foreseeing the growing need to find out how many women were available for work and exactly what their skills might be, the Board of Trade set up, in March 1915, a special Women's War Register inviting women of all classes to enrol. The *Echo* of 18 March considered this innovation to be of sufficient importance for a front-page report headed 'Women and the War – The Government's Call – Setting Men Free'.

The explanation was quite clear: women were needed to release men for the fighting line, as workers for the production of armaments and on the land to work on farms. As Sir John French, Commander in Chief of the Army in France said five days later, 'Munitions, more munitions, always more munitions … that is the governing condition of all progress.' The National Registration, carried out in August 1915, which then provided a record of all persons in the country aged 15 to 66 years of age and their skills consequently made the Women's War Register obsolete.

The people of Cheltenham would have been aware of the reason for the urgency of increased war production. Lloyd George, speaking in a debate in April 1915, said he would 'lift a curtain on some of the secrets of the war'. He did so by giving some salient and brutal facts, which were reported in the *Echo*: after eight months of war, there were six times as many men out there than the original six divisions of the British Expeditionary Force; every man who had fallen in battle had been replaced. In the two-week battle around Neuve Chapelle, almost as much ammunition was spent by our artillery as during the whole of the Boer War.

Bonar Law, in Parliament, added that workers weren't coming forward to work in factories to fulfil orders and production was not at the rate it should be. These facts had precipitated the shell crisis. Bonar Law urged: 'Let the country know of reverses as well as successes. Our people can stand the truth.' If only the truth could be read at all times in the newspapers. Censorship was severe in order not to demoralise people at home. When the soldiers came home on leave and the wounded arrived in the hospitals, only then was the reality and truth of the war brought home.

Lord Kitchener asked of the country's mayors that they hold a conference in their towns to consider how it would be possible to release men from work in the wholesale and retail trades and replace them with female labour. These men, it was hoped, would then be available for either munitions work or to enlist. Cheltenham's mayor, along with the town's MP Mr James Agg-Gardner, held this conference in the Town Hall on Monday, 17 May 1915. At the conference's conclusion it was agreed that, for Cheltenham, this '… readjustment of employment would be innocuous to trade interests and feasible. Government contracts … would give employment to Cheltenham's "industrial classes".'

LLOYD GEORGE MET OUR MAYOR

Three days into his new job as Minister for Munitions, Lloyd George visited Bristol and met with industrialists to form the West of England Munitions Committee. Present at this meeting were members of Cheltenham Chamber of Commerce and the town council. As a result, the mayor (William Nash Skillicorne), convened a meeting of local engineering firms at the (new) Municipal Offices in Cheltenham. Heads of twenty local firms formed the Cheltenham War Munitions Committee and acting as Secretary was Mr Edward Baring of Baring Brothers – local entrepreneur, impresario, husband and manager of Marie Hall, internationally famous violinist. A sub-committee for shell making was formed of the following local engineers: Samuel Such (of John Such & Sons Ltd, Caledonian Engineering Works, Swindon Road); W.J. Bache (borough electrical engineer); Harry Edward Steel (owner of a large garage on the former stable block of The Queen's Hotel); E. Green Jnr (probably Edwinson Green, son of a prize-winning Cheltenham gunsmith at No. 87 High Street); H.G. Norton (MD of H.G. Norton, ironmongers and garage owner at No. 416 High Street and Regent Street); John and Dale Marshall, sons of R.E. & C. Marshall. The shell-making sub-committee's first task was to ascertain what suitable machine tools were held by local engineering firms and what power was available to run equipment. It was ambitiously predicted that shell-making and the manufacture of fuses and other small articles would be started in Cheltenham within two weeks.

The *Echo*'s announcement on 17 June 1915 of a possible shell factory opened up a floodgate of letters from people unable to join the army but desperate to do something towards the war effort. One such read: 'Sir, I am over 55 and retired from India and am willing to give my services free if a shell factory is started in Cheltenham, for 4 or 5 hours daily.'

Four Committee members visited Woolwich Arsenal and Birmingham munitions factories the following week to consider what would be feasible for Cheltenham. A week later, an advertisement was placed in the *Echo* announcing that arrangements had been made for the opening in Cheltenham of a Munitions Bureau. This was in order to mobilise skilled engineering workmen for the munitions factory. They were to apply at the old Labour Bureau, No. 1 Portland Street. It is interesting to note that the times of opening included Sunday afternoons – most unusual in 1915.

A poster was put up around town inviting workers to 'Give your strength and skill to your country. Enrol for war work today. Each man will be given a certificate of enrolment.' In the case of men who were sent some distance from their home and requiring lodgings, they would receive a subsistence allowance of 2s 6d a day for seven days and for others there was a travel allowance. These were incentives the like of which the working man had never seen before.

The decision was made by 9 July 1915 to abandon the idea of a central shell factory in Cheltenham, but the town did have sufficient manufacturing capacity for four firms to make a start on shell making. At this point they were awaiting delivery of the steel and gauges to make 18-pounder shells for high explosives. Sadly, the services of the many volunteers would not be required. The material arrived in the form of highly tempered solid steel bars, the working of which required a skilled engineer. The assumption that many volunteers put forward, that they could be taught to do this in a matter of a few hours, was described as 'laughable, if the subject were a laughing matter'.

MUNITIONS WORK BUREAU.

THE ADDRESS OF THE NEAREST MUNITIONS BUREAU WHERE ALL

SKILLED WORKERS

IN THIS DISTRICT CAN ENROL, IS

1 PORTLAND STREET, CHELTENHAM.

HOURS:—

WEEKDAYS .... 6 p.m. to 9 p.m.
SATURDAYS .... 4 p.m. to 6 p.m.
SUNDAYS .... 3 p.m. to 6 p.m.

Where Full Particulars as to Rates of Pay, etc., can be given.

ENROL TO-DAY!

Cheltenham's own munitions industry advertised for staff.
(*Cheltenham Chronicle and Gloucestershire Graphic*, 28 June 1915)

Boys of Cheltenham College also contributed to munitions. They made shell bases
from rough cuttings of brass in their workshops, 100,000 steel punches for rifle
cartridges and 27,000 fuse plugs, working right up to the end of the war.

The West of England Munitions Committee placed a contract in July 1915 with
the Cheltenham War Munitions Committee for 10,000 high-explosive shells, which
were to be delivered at the rate of around 250 shells per week. A month later five
or six workshops were operating in Cheltenham and the Committee reported that
'it was possible Cheltenham may rise to something even larger'.

STRIKING MUNITIONS

All did not run smoothly at H.H. Martyn & Co.'s munitions work. In January 1916,
ninety employees of the Sunningend Works went on strike. An assistant manager
had been appointed to oversee the munitions work in the Joinery Department and
the men felt aggrieved and objected on the grounds that this cast aspersions on their
work. One can see why this was the case, as John Whitaker wrote: 'Men didn't last long
if their work was not up to the high standards demanded; even their peers would be
intolerant if the side might be let down.' However, it was forbidden under DORA for
those working on munitions to go on strike. Knowing this, the men had been cautious
and clever. All the strikers had tendered their resignations and worked out the required
amount of notice. Upon expiry of notice, the workers were given their insurance cards
and left, not turning up for work on the Monday, 31 January as they had no jobs to
turn up for. So, technically they were not striking and avoided prosecution.

On Tuesday, 1 February the newspaper reported that the workers were on strike but
the issue was not about wages. On Friday, an official from the Ministry of Munitions
intervened to resolve the dispute, heard both sides of the matter and found a way forward. It is not known how it was resolved, or if the assistant manager stayed, but the
men returned to their jobs on the following Monday and nothing more was reported.
H.H. Martyn & Co.'s contribution to the war effort was eventually to be much more
than just ammunition cases and involved a bold and brave leap into the unknown.

In September 1916 there were still three or four firms in Cheltenham engaged in
activities for the manufacture of munitions but after this date there appears to be no
mention of munitions work in Cheltenham. In January 1917, Cheltenham working
women were to be involved in an altogether much bigger munitions enterprise.

SPECIALLY CHEAP PURCHASE.

LADIES' DARK BLUE MUNITION OVERALLS

OF SERVICEABLE DRILL, WITH HOOD.

PRICE 5s. 11D. EACH.

These are made from hard-wearing untearable Bluette.

OVERALL COATS AND BREECHES FOR FARM WORK, FRUIT PICKING, Etc.

"The Famous."

PRACTICAL TAILORS & BREECHES MAKERS

350-351, HIGH STREET, CHELTENHAM.
PROPRIETOR · A · N · COLE ·

EVERY DESCRIPTION OF MOTOR, MUNITION, ENGINEER OVERALLS IN STOCK.

This advertisement has to be for Cheltenham's munition workers as Quedgeley Filling Factory provided the workers with uniforms and Cheltenham women were not working in Quedgeley until January 1917. (*Cheltenham Chronicle*, 1 July 1916)

CHAPTER 5

Cheltenham Hospitality

Cheltenham, whilst being a haven for retired Indian army officers, had never been a garrison town as such. That was to change within two months of war's outbreak. As pointed out in the *Echo*, 'The old terrace houses which many would have gladly seen dynamited are coming in useful.' Nationally 800,000 men were billeted in the winter of 1914/15. Cheltenham became part of that. The Cheltenham Chamber of Commerce, the Cheltenham Traders' Association and the borough council had all made efforts canvassing the War Office to acquire billeted solders. Their success would provide a lifeline for town businesses, provide employment and become the means by which Cheltenham could show its support for the troops and contribute to the war effort.

The 9th Battalion Gloucestershire Regiment in Lansdown in an assortment of uniforms, including 'Kitchener's Blue'. (By permission of the Soldiers of Gloucestershire Regiment Museum Ref 6083)

Kitchener was completely unprepared for the housing of large numbers of recruits in 1914 and the training camps were desperately unsuitable. On arrival at the camps, the reality for Kitchener's new army was the lack of uniforms, carrying brooms in place of weapons, having to wear old clothes and accommodation under canvas – and they had arrived in early winter. This new army had to be issued with any leftover uniforms available and one uniform, known as 'Kitchener's Blue', which was made of blue serge left over from Post Office stock.

With a change of clothes in a brown paper parcel tucked under their arms, the prospect of three square meals a day and an adventure, most Cheltenham recruits were sent to the Gloucestershire Regiment's base at Horfield Barracks in Bristol. The new 9th and 10th service battalions of the Gloucestershire Regiment contained 450 Cheltonians – hence, both of these battalions were unofficially referred to as 'The Cheltenham Battalion'. However, for many recruits they had to stay wearing the clothes they went to camp in. They were a motley selection, some wearing Sunday best suits and boaters, others rough, labourer's clothing. Unsuitable boots and clothes soon became tattered with the hard wear of soldiering and marching.

This letter from a Cheltenham lad from the 9th Battalion Gloucestershire Regiment at Codford appeared in the *Echo* on 17 October 1914:

> Very few of the regiments have got khaki uniforms. What they are served with are old red coats with vari-coloured collars and cuffs, some yellow some white some other colours. Some get the uniform of Kitchener's Second Army. These look very much like convicts from a distance on account of the blue cloth.

This desperate situation was alleviated somewhat by Kitchener, from 8 September 1915, giving an allowance of 8*s* 6*d* – raised two days later to 10*s* – to every recruit who provided himself with a serviceable suit, a pair of boots and an overcoat. The army paid for these to be posted from the recruit's home address.

From Horfield the 9th and 10th battalions were sent to their training camp at Codford St Mary in Wiltshire, described as 'an awfully out of the way place on Salisbury Plain', to face 'some of the roughest and wettest weather remembered'. They should have been in huts, but at Codford tents had been pitched on fields which flooded. It wasn't long before the ground was a quagmire of mud and the soldiers' feet were constantly wet. Worse still, the huts that *had* been built were not weatherproof, having been constructed with unseasoned timber by unskilled labourers. Galvanised sheeting was unobtainable as almost all of the zinc trade of the world was under German control. One group of soldiers had to pitch a tent *inside* their hut it was so wet!

Mass meetings were held at Codford in November 1914 as the soldiers, incensed by their worsening conditions, exacerbated by continuous rain, threatened to strike. Quoted by Nick Christian, Sergeant Ernest Chadband of the 10th Gloucesters explained: 'Codford was a terrible place to pitch a camp … we were 17 in a bell tent. Well, we rioted and went on strike as we couldn't sleep … so we protested … and in almost three days, the 9th and 10th were billeted in Cheltenham …' A soldier from Cheltenham writing home said: 'Everything was mud … in places it was possible to sink a good eight inches.'

Uniform production was stepped up as fast as machines could make them. The National Chamber of Trade had been asked by the War Office to investigate where manufacturing contracts for military clothing could be placed. To this end, the Cheltenham Traders' Association held two meetings with Cheltenham tailors, but it was apparent their machines were not suitable to make military clothing. Cheltenham tailors worked at a small scale so it was not economically feasible to accept the work for the rates the army offered. However, large War Office contracts were taken on by the Stroud clothing industry. Holloway Brothers Ltd advertised in Cheltenham in November 1914: 'Wanted Immediately Hands of All Kinds – Machinists, Basters, Fellers – Constant Employment.' In an end of year report on the Stroud clothing industry, the *Stroud News and Journal* of 18 December 1914 reported '… undiminished industrial activity in Stroud … working at high pressure in endeavouring to cope with the Government's urgent demand … chiefly in the manufacture of khaki … the greater output now is in respect of greatcoats for soldiers and the overtime is considerable.'

At the Eagle Factory of the ailing Tewkesbury Manufacturing Co., a War Office contract ensured the company was kept afloat for a while longer. An advertisement in Cheltenham papers on 27 November 1914 read: 'Wanted 200 Women to make Shirts and Collars. Weekly Wage – Good Bonus.' This was the final gasp for the factory, which couldn't keep going during the war, after the military contract had been fulfilled. The Eagle Factory was auctioned at The Bell in Tewkesbury in November 1915 and the company, employing over 300 people, was closed. For Cheltenham boot makers W.J. Melville Ltd of No. 408 High Street, the war provided a commercial boost in October 1914. Melville's secured the government contract to supply all the boots for the Cheltenham, Gloucester and Cirencester men of the National Reserve.

At Codford one Sunday, the 9th Battalion Gloucestershire Regiment were assembled for church parade. The sergeant tried to separate the men of different denominations – 'Roman Catholics?' evoked no response, 'Wesleyans?', no response, 'Any Presbyterians?', one recruit stepped forward. 'Any more Presbyterians? Hurry up!' A dozen men formed into a line. The sergeant eyed them up 'You're all Presbyterians?' he asked dubiously. 'Yes, we be all from Prestbury!' they replied.

'The Famous' in the High Street had an inspired copywriter whose advertisements reflected the need for military stock. One advertisement heading was 'On the War Path' and the goods advertised included 'Sleeping Helmets and Army Shirts for drilling and Khaki shirts'. Another was clearly aimed at the soldiers sartorially challenged in 'borrowed' uniforms: 'Welcome Glo'sters. Service Caps, Tunics, Breeches, Trousers, Braces, Underwear. Overcoats to order in three days.' Another advertisement was for the families of soldiers, encouraging them to buy clothes: 'Hurry Up With Your Army Orders – The Men are taking our Place. Let us see they do not starve.' What did that mean – that they should eat their own hats?

THE INVASION OF CHELTENHAM

On Saturday, 7 November 1914, the *Echo* reported:

> We hear from 2 or 3 sources, but cannot get it officially confirmed that the 9th battalion of the Gloucestershire Regiment, at present stationed at Codford, in Wiltshire will be billeted in the town … because their camp is a veritable quagmire … huts being built will take a couple of months.

National Reserves leaving the Drill Hall, North Street, on 4 November 1914. The Empress Tea Stores are now Primark. Melvilles Bootmakers of Cheltenham were awarded the contract to supply the National Reserves with footwear. (*Cheltenham Chronicle and Gloucestershire Graphic*, 7 November 1914)

No exaggeration there! Two days later, on Monday, 9 November, the imminent arrival of the 9th Battalion in Cheltenham prompted a report that 'Quite a rush by Cheltenham householders has been made to have troops billeted upon them.' But this was not to be. The army had plans for Cheltenham.

The next day the headline in the *Echo* must have scared the daylights out of many in Cheltenham. It read 'Invasion of Cheltenham' and was followed by the explanation that 2,700 infantry were 'awaited by the townspeople with pleasurable anticipation' and the length of stay was expected to be six weeks or longer. However, the mayor, when introducing a speaker at a lecture on 13 November, let slip that he had not, in his capacity as mayor, received notice from the War Office of the troops' arrival, hence the short warning he had given the citizens of Cheltenham!

Yet again, under the Defence of the Realm Act (DORA), the War Office had commandeered property – this time a large number of empty houses for billeting the troops, where the army could keep an eye on them. A few of the Cheltenham boys did go home but had to appear in the early morning at 6.30 for drill. Local building firms, A.C. Billings and Collins & Godfrey, worked day and night using every man available to prepare the empty houses, or 'voids' as they were called. To start with, twenty-one houses were taken: six in Lansdown Terrace, seven in Lansdown Crescent and a number of single houses – Eckington House, Rokeby, Douglas, Oakhurst, No. 1 Bayshill Lawn, Nos 5 and 6 Malvern Place and No. 2 Queens Parade. The Lansdown Terrace and Crescent houses had accommodation for around eighty men each and the single houses for 100–120 men.

A postcard of Cheltenham available to billeted soldiers. This one was sent to his wife by a soldier billeted in Parabola Road, Cheltenham. He asks, 'What has happened, I have not had a letter from you for a week!' (Author's collection)

ANOTHER INVASION? THE RUSSIANS HAVE LANDED – IN CHELTENHAM!

With only newspapers and word of mouth to broadcast news, to verify stories people had to rely on asking friends if they knew of someone who knew someone who knew! One widespread rumour regarding the Russian Army was heard by Colchester-Wemyss. He wrote on 8 September 1914, that it had been said:

... England sent ships to pick up 80,000 Russians from Archangel, landed them at Aberdeen, and entrained to Ostend and thence to France ... I asked a member of the House of Lords who had met a Cabinet Minister who had spoken to Lord Reading who denied it but, as he said 'You would expect someone in Government to deny it'.

Vera Brittain was told by her dentist that 100,000 Russians, with snow on their boots, had passed through Stoke-on-Trent and jammed the station vending machines with kopeck coins. The *London Evening News* a week later reported, 'A grey cloud of fierce, whiskered men went rolling down to Cheltenham, at Euston their passing closed the station for 36 hours ...' The rumour was firmly scotched in Parliament on 18 November 1914.

Mr C.H. Rainger, acting as Cheltenham's official War Department Contractor, liaised with Royal Engineers from Bristol to organise the fitting up of houses and field kitchens. Gas or electric light had to be fitted in every room of the houses, additional lavatories provided and rooms disinfected and scrubbed with carbolic. Soldiers slept on a straw mattress on the floor. At this time, Dicks & Sons Ltd, drapers in the Art and Economy Building in the High Street, were advertising hessian for soldiers' mattresses, as supplied to the Mayoress's Linen Committee. One wonders if the ladies of the Committee were asked to contribute some 2,700 mattresses for the 'Invasion of Cheltenham'!

By Wednesday, 11 November, it was confirmed that the 9th and 10th battalions were to arrive in Cheltenham on Friday, 13 and Monday, 16 November. Each battalion, now both 950 strong, with 30 tons of baggage apiece, was to arrive at St James' station in two special troop trains per day. Each train was met by the Dean Close School Officer Training Corps, which acted as a guard of honour, and the school's bugle band, which marched at the head of the soldiers. The parade marched via Ambrose Street, High Street, The Colonnade and the Promenade to meet up outside The Queen's Hotel from where they dispersed to their allocated billets.

The 9th Battalion occupied houses mainly in the Lansdown area. The officers of the 9th Battalion were billeted at The Queen's Hotel. No. 2 Queen's Parade, a few doors from the mayor's residence, was used as the headquarters of the commanding officer, billets and a mess for the battalion's fifty-six sergeants. A field kitchen was installed in a field adjoining Bayshill Court in Parabola Road. The soldiers were supplied from this with their cooked rations, using Aldershot ovens with gas stoves and brick trenches with wood fires, to provide practice for conditions at the front. On alternate days, half the battalion would eat roast meat and vegetables and the other half stewed meat and vegetables. Temporary sheds were used as pantries for storing bread and meat. Orderlies fetched the rations from the field.

The coffers of Cheltenham traders were boosted by roughly £1 per soldier with the billeting of the troops, particularly Morgan & Co. (see box on p.82), as all provisions were bought locally. One soldier of the 9th Battalion wrote to the *Echo* on 28 November: 'What a difference between Codford and Cheltenham! We have found carrots and other vegetables in our mid-day stew and greenstuff in the form of cabbage made its initial appearance … we have also had butter to help digest our jam with and for breakfast, liver and bacon.' The cuisine of the 10th Battalion may have improved as three groups of twelve cooks from the battalion had been sent each week to attend sessions at the School of Domestic Economy at Marlborough House, Winchcombe Street. Here they were taught to make chips, Cornish pasties and how to roast meat.

The 10th Battalion installed their field kitchen in a field at the back of Eckington House, cooking entirely by gas. Sheds were built to cover twenty gas cookers and the heating apparatus was by a series of Bunsen burners 12ft long. Security was not as tight as it should have been and the 10th Gloucester's cookhouse was robbed on 8 March 1915 of 14lb bread, 6lb sausages, 1lb of tongue, 1lb cheese, 19lb cooked beef and 15lb potatoes. Was it an inside job? A corporal of the battalion and two civilian 'dealers' were arrested after a police stakeout.

The presence of so much food acted as a 'honeypot' for another, altogether different, kind of group to be seen around the Lansdown area and provoked a spate of red-hot letters from angry residents. 'A Resident' voiced concerns thus:

> … since 'our soldiers' have been quartered in this neighbourhood, increasing numbers of urchins from the lower parts of the town, have made it a custom to collect scraps left over from the soldiers' meals … they come armed with cloth bags, wandering around, often in droves of twenty or more, causing great annoyance to the residents of Lansdown They are noisy and ill-behaved and are a menace to the traffic. In the daytime they are often in evidence during school hours, loafing about to their own educational and moral detriment … Can nothing be done to stop all this?

Another resident of Lansdown Terrace was equally outraged: '… the thing has become a perfect scandal. It is not only the children but there are crowds of noisy and very undesirable people about … unless something is done it will end by driving all decent people away from this part of town.' There was no further comment. Perhaps the army had its own way of dealing with the miscreants.

The 9th Battalion Gloucestershire Regiment cooking dinner in field kitchens in a field by Bayshill Court, Parabola Road, and taking cooked food to the billets.
(*Cheltenham Chronicle and Gloucestershire Graphic*, 21 November 1914)

For the culinary needs of 940 non-commissioned officers and men of the 9th Battalion, Morgan & Co. of No. 2 Queen's Circus was awarded the contract to supply, each day:

230lb Bacon	140lb Jam	Bread 1,165lb
940lb Meat	170lb Granulated sugar	Tea 37lb

'Don't frighten the horses' must have been a cry heard from many a Cheltenham carter. Apparently, on 28 November 1914, in Lansdown Road, three horses were frightened by the noise of the soldiers' boots on the tarmac road whilst the 9th Battalion made its way to early morning parade. The route to the temporary parade ground wasn't far from the Lansdown billets. Mrs Brewster of Hatherley Hall had placed at their disposal three of the fields on her model farm, amounting to around 15 acres, for purposes of drilling for the 9th Battalion. By December 1916, other areas had to be used for drilling. The borough surveyor asked Colonel Christie not to use Montpellier Gardens in future for troop training due to the damage done to the turf.

OUR NEW FRIENDS OF THE 9TH AND 10TH

The arrival of over 2,000 troops in Cheltenham provoked both interest and disinterest and a reaction against the lack of reaction. The *Echo* reported a large crowd had welcomed the troops, but one writer to the *Echo* on 14 November 1914 considered that the reception of the 9th Gloucesters by Cheltenham townspeople had been as damp as the weather: 'Scarcely a cheer – scarcely a wave of the hand. Really, I feel ashamed of this "military town" … Cheltenham may be fashionable but oh! so apathetic.'

Frederick Wright supplied tobacco to the soldiers at competitive prices and gave the use of their company's billiard room, which was next to the Soldiers' Welcome at The Rotunda. (*Cheltenham Chronicle and Gloucestershire Graphic*, 21 November 1914)

Once the troops settled in, there were moments of genuine warmth and generosity shown by Cheltenham townspeople. One lady, seeing a soldier buying cigarettes, at once paid for 200 packets to be distributed. An anonymous benefactor gave half a ton of coal to each house where soldiers were billeted. Whilst watching soldiers march down the Promenade, one lady wrote, 'It is very noticeable that many were suffering from bad colds as a result of the soakings … as there was much coughing!' This lady promptly visited a chemist and when the soldiers marched back she handed out packets of cough sweets. There were some Lansdown residents who invited groups of soldiers to dinner and another householder gave orders to her servants that baths were to be prepared at her house for four men each night.

A week after the soldiers arrived, the *Chronicle* commented:

> Although the man in the street did not enthuse over the 9th and 10th Gloucesters … I think Cheltonians as a rule are very pleased to have 2,000 plus men who responded to the call. Even the few people up Lansdown way who objected … must realise without them we may perish.

On the other hand, inevitably, there were complaints, like the medically unfit young man who '… whilst watching the soldiers pass in Lansdown Road, was greeted with jeers: "Join the ranks", "Show your pluck" and "There's another coward".'

There were reports covering every activity of the 9th Battalion: one hour's physical exercise before breakfast, company drill and bayonet practice from 9 to 12, and from 2 until 4 skirmishing and miniature battles and occasionally night operations from 6 till 8.30. During one such night operation, the 9th Battalion had 'taken' Hatherley Bridge, and Swindon Iron Bridge and either 'blown to atoms' or 'heroically defended' these local landmarks. Another regular route march consisted of travelling via the Promenade and Pittville out to the racecourse, through into Prestbury, along Cemetery Road into Hales Road and back to billets.

Whilst billeted in Cheltenham, the 9th Battalion were presented at a ceremony in Montpellier Gardens in February 1915 with complete new instruments to form a drum and fife band by Colonel Evan Jeune of Whaddon Manor, Cheltenham. Significant was the fact that the 9th Battalion was the only one of Lord Kitchener's new regiments that had started a regimental band for marching purposes. As Rudyard Kipling said: 'The New Armies were born in silence.' Now, it could be said, 'except for the 9th Battalion Gloucester Regiment'!

One January afternoon, whilst marching back to billets, having been thoroughly drenched in a terrible storm a half hour earlier, the 9th Battalion met a party of injured Belgian soldiers in the Promenade. One of the Gloucesters, still dripping wet, shouted, 'Are we downhearted?' and hundreds of soldiers replied loudly 'No!', which seemed to amuse the Belgians. Generally, after early morning drilling and breakfast, the battalion assembled at 9 a.m. and could be seen marching down the Promenade, headed by a band, on their way to high ground above Leckhampton, ascending the steep hill by the quarries, advancing in battle formation to the rifle butts at Seven Springs, having practised an attack en route. For a spot of trench-digging on the way, two companies carried pickaxes and shovels. All enjoyed al fresco luncheons on the hills of pork pies, bread, cheese and oranges, served up with mineral water or beer from barrels having been taken up by cart to the rifle range.

'DRINK-RIDDEN' CHELTENHAM?

Giving soldiers beer whilst on duty seems odd considering there were letters in the press from the mayor and others asking that soldiers not be 'treated' to beer in the pubs '… as it is really productive of much harm to discipline and good order. Treating is therefore unpatriotic.' One would have thought it was more dangerous to a soldier with a gun in his hand! Moreover, Lloyd George in February 1915 considered drink was doing more damage in the war than all the German submarines put together. Even the King signed the pledge and banned alcohol from the palace.

Under DORA, opening hours for licensed premises were severely reduced, especially in towns where soldiers were billeted. In the Petty Sessional Division of Cheltenham, a legally enforceable order came into effect on Saturday, 18 November 1916 forbidding the purchase of alcohol by soldiers to be taken out of licensed premises at all times, by military authority. More shocking for Cheltenham drinkers was that pubs in Cheltenham could sell alcohol only during the hours of 12 noon to 2 p.m. and 6 p.m. to 9 p.m. One pub landlord told the *Echo*: 'It seems very funny to see pubs turn out at 9 p.m. but even funnier after 9 p.m. to see men sat around drinking Oxo and lemonade!' Brewers were ordered, legally, to water down their beer.

A clergyman visiting the town in 1915 felt compelled to describe Cheltenham as 'drink-ridden'. Five letter writers agreed with him that there was a problem in the poorer areas of the town. Mr E.L. Daubeny wrote to the *Echo* of 'An unpleasant sight': 'Sir, Since the war, children are frequently seen loitering near public houses. If questioned the reply is usually "Waiting for mother".' This was a concern in Cheltenham with the working class in particular. Colchester-Wemyss agreed with Mr Daubeny and wrote in November 1915 '... the very poor are careless and improvident and just drink or waste their extra money.' Some wives received more in allowances from the army than the wages their husbands brought home during peace time, and munitions workers, of which there were close on 1,000 in Cheltenham, were earning higher wages than they would have done for peace time work. For some, this was a sore temptation leading to ruin, such as the case of one soldier's wife, of Little's Court, New Street, Cheltenham. This mother of six children, the youngest of whom was 2 months old, was charged with drunkenness and damage to police cells six times within one year. The magistrate declared: 'Sober, [she] is quite a good specimen of the working class woman of early middle age, drunk she is a tartar.' This time she went to prison and her children sent to the workhouse.

THE 'SUBMERGED 10TH'

The arrival of the 10th Battalion Gloucestershire Regiment, three days after the 9th Battalion, was met with 'a limited crowd present'. The *Echo* reporter particularly noticed their clothing '... not the khaki great coat but overcoats of miscellaneous cuts and patterns that had been served out to them ... and their caps were not all of the same style.' The commanding officer and his second in command were brothers – Lieutenant Colonel Henry Edward Pritchard and Major A. Pritchard. The 10th Battalion's headquarters was at No. 8 Lansdown Crescent.

Very little was reported of the activities of the 10th Battalion, a fact which did not go unnoticed by one *Echo* letter writer in February 1915, who referred to the 10th Battalion as being 'The Submerged 10th'. The writer asked if anyone knew the fate of the battalion: 'Are they by any chance swallowed up at the front or have they got lost on Cleeve Hill during a snowball fight?' The following day another reader replied to say:

> If the writer had finished his luncheon and had been out yesterday at 2 o/clock he would have seen 'The Submerged 10th' march by and if he was not in bed at 10.30 the same evening he would have seen the same 'Submerged 10th' return after a 20 mile march.

Two hundred soldiers at a time dug from 10 a.m. each day to build a 9in trunk main for improving water pressure at Leckhampton. The trench, 4ft × 2ft, stretched from Sandford Road to Leckhampton Road and took eight days to complete. (*Cheltenham Chronicle and Gloucestershire Graphic,* 26 December 1914)

The mystery was solved by a note from the editor of the *Echo* who commented that the newspaper team had done their best to get news concerning the 10th, but those in command preferred that 'as little should be said as possible'. Because the main activities of the 10th Battalion appeared to be soldiers charging up and down Leckhampton and Cleeve Hills, in preparation for what was to come, they were dubbed by the press 'The Fighting Tenth'.

The one significant piece of work carried out by the 10th Battalion, as a training exercise, was trench-digging for Cheltenham Corporation in December 1914. The council needed a 9in trunk main for improving water pressure at Leckhampton. A trench 4ft deep by 2ft wide for a distance of 1,600 yards was necessary, stretching from the corner of Sandford Road and College Road, through College Lawn, Thirlestaine Road, Naunton Lane to Leckhampton Road. Two hundred soldiers at a time dug from 10 a.m. each day for two hours and a night shift worked for part of the time. It took eight days to complete the trench. The Corporation was willing to pay for the work but the commanding officer, recognising the consideration

Roman snails, escaped from Chedworth perhaps, had been discovered around the walls and gardens of the buildings in Lansdown Crescent. Soldiers were sent to ferret out these large but tasty gastropods in order that they should grace the tables of the officers of the 10th Gloucesters.

extended to the soldiers by the townspeople, said he was '… not desirous of viewing the work as a business transaction'. In return, Cheltenham Corporation was to provide 'sundry things as required by the regiment'. The exercise saved the council 1s 9d per yard. A good arrangement all round but probably a cold, damp exercise as, by 28 December, snow was particularly heavy and then thawed overnight whilst they dug the trench.

SOLDIERS' WELCOMES

The spirit of voluntarism was alive and well in Cheltenham – the 'troops' willing and able to take up the mantle of voluntary work were aplenty in Cheltenham. As Braybon wrote, 'Wealthy women who wanted to do something for the war effort took up voluntary work … working class women, meanwhile, had no other jobs to turn to.' Elsewhere, the volunteers were described as 'leisure-class women'. There were large numbers of retired Indian Army officers' wives, used to 'taking charge', 'running the show' and organising – which many did through one organisation or another – and spinster daughters in abundance. Many of these ladies were able to find an outlet for their untapped potential.

With so many troops in town, the need for somewhere central for soldiers to meet and spend time relaxing was considered paramount. Within half a day of the news of the troops' arrivals, an ambitious and unique venture for the town rapidly materialised, under the auspices of the local churches – the taking over of The Rotunda as a Soldiers' Welcome. Mr Herbert Unwin of Arle Court generously footed the rent and Frederick Wright, the tobacconist, who was to profit handsomely from the troops, gave the use of his billiard room next to The Rotunda. This venture required the organisation of a small army of volunteers in its own right. It was run by thirteen departmental committees, with extra help provided by the YMCA and the Boy Scouts. It contained a writing room and post office, refreshment bar, billiard room and tobacco store, central reading lounge with games, sing-song room and a prayer room. The Churches Soldiers' Welcome opened for the first time on Friday, 13 November 1914. It was quite a novelty for the town as curiosity had got the better of some in Cheltenham. A note in the local paper read: 'Will all our friends resist the temptation to "have a look round" or to "show their friends" except before 10.30 a.m. After that we all help most by keeping out of the way. We have already learnt that a place flooded with ladies, clergy and laymen is not what soldiers want.'

In charge of refreshments was the ubiquitous Miss Mina Wethered with her mother. Letters appeared regularly asking townspeople for varied contributions. On 5 December 1914 it was for Christmas puddings to be delivered to the Town Hall for distribution amongst the restaurant bars of all the soldiers' clubs in

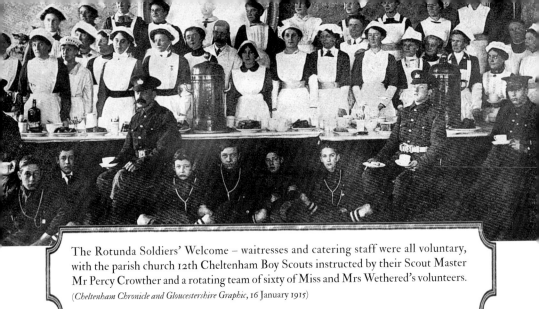

The Rotunda Soldiers' Welcome – waitresses and catering staff were all voluntary, with the parish church 12th Cheltenham Boy Scouts instructed by their Scout Master Mr Percy Crowther and a rotating team of sixty of Miss and Mrs Wethered's volunteers. (*Cheltenham Chronicle and Gloucestershire Graphic*, 16 January 1915)

town. Contributors were asked to 'Kindly put your name on the bowl so that we may return them after use. Or, you could send oranges or nuts … we require a huge stock.' Three days later Mrs Wethered appealed for cocoa, coffee, rice, sugar, ham, gammon, beef, mince pies, apples, bananas and custard powder.

Mrs Wethered, at this time, commented that the soldiers were 'Such well-behaved fellows; such gentlemen'. In return, the soldiers described her as 'second mother to them all'. A former Mayoress of Cheltenham, at the end of her husband's term of office, Mrs Wethered had presented to the borough a handsome gold and enamelled badge (with the design of the borough arms) to be worn by future mayoresses in office on ceremonial occasions.

The culinary delights purchased by the soldiers at The Rotunda, at cost price, included rice pudding one penny, tea and coffee a halfpenny, boiled beef sandwich a halfpenny and homemade cakes. For their supper the home-cooked fare consisted of sausage and mash one night, next night fish and chips and another night rabbit pie. Eventually nine to twenty different dishes a day were on offer. Cooking was done by seniors of the parish church 12th Cheltenham Scouts instructed by their Scout Master Mr Percy Crowther and a rotating team of sixty of Miss and Mrs Wethered's volunteers. Such was the success of the kitchen that they had gone from cooking 500 meals a day in November 1914 to 1,200 a day four weeks later. Every ten days twenty reams of notepaper, 5,000 envelopes and 2,000 postcards were being supplied free to soldiers.

Other clubs opened; Wesley Lecture Hall Soldiers Club, St George's Street, was managed by ladies from four local Wesleyan chapels. In the ten days it had been open from 15 November 1914, the club had already dealt with 700 ongoing parcels and letters and several hundreds of letters received. There was a room fitted up for hot baths and footbaths, safe custody of valuables, banking of money and a popular facility, the offer of darning and mending for the soldiers. In December 1914 a Soldiers' Waiting Room opened at St Mark's Wesleyan Sunday school, near Lansdown station, to provide 'rest and amusement … as a counter-attraction to the streets and other evils that exist whilst long waits between trains'. Within six weeks, 1,100 soldiers had visited.

'WRETCHED LITTLE FLAPPERS'

The influx of so many troops into the town caused the *Echo* to exclaim, 'Every girl found a soldier last night, if they wanted one!' Concerns about the moral welfare of young females in a town awash with young men, away from wives and sweethearts, were taken up by two parties – the Women Patrols and the Cheltenham Association for the Care of Friendless Girls. Canon Young, speaking at the Association's annual meeting at St Catherine's Shelter in Hewlett Road, pronounced: 'At present when there were so many soldiers in the town and the danger was very much intensified … It was the wretched little flappers between 13 and 16 years of age the workers should keep an eye on.' An anonymous writer to the *Echo* on 2 January 1915, warned '… mothers should see that their girls under 18 should be at home at night instead of running after the soldier boys. They will find there will be trouble by and by if they don't look after them.'

As for the Women Patrols, they were originated by the National Union of Women Workers (NUWW) to help keep order in the streets to combat 'khaki fever', as it was commonly called – others called it patriotic immorality. The members of the Women Patrols were predominantly middle class and middle aged. The girls fraternising with the soldiers, in the main, were young and working class – hence a class, age and culture clash.

The subject of women patrols was discussed at a meeting of the NUWW at Cheltenham Ladies' College in October 1914 where it was emphasised that the work was 'entirely preventative'. The idea was that there would be little chats with the girls to persuade them to join girls' clubs. Women patrols were in force in Cheltenham by the end of 1914 when the soldiers were billeted in the town. The leader in Cheltenham was Miss 'Nellie' Andrews, who taught German at Cheltenham Ladies' College. The patrol members wore a striped black and white armlet on their left arm and a black silk medallion on which the woman's number and letters NUWW were embroidered. Two patrols went out nightly for two hours and, as Miss Andrews wrote '… the mere presence of the Patrols had a restraining effect on the girls and there is no doubt the soldiers welcomed us, they used to salute when they met us on our beat.' These patrols could be considered to be the forerunners of the first two policewomen appointed in April 1918 in Cheltenham.

Soldiers wishing to understand the lyrics to *Mademoiselle from Armentières* could study French for Soldiers at the technical schools every evening for an hour, free of charge, in December 1914.

Whilst it was inevitable that some children would be born 'the wrong side of the blanket' during the war years in Cheltenham, it was an ill-founded belief that there would be a rise in illegitimate births. As was written, 'The war baby was a gigantic scare born of morbid hysteria of old ladies of both sexes!' Illegitimacy in Cheltenham was, in 1915 about normal: of the 772 registered births, 59 were born without sanction of fathers, eight more than in 1914. However, one can't help wondering about the circumstances behind a classified advertisement in the *Echo* of 6 July 1918: 'Would some kind person adopt a baby girl, 14 days old? £40 premium. Write 4587, Echo, Cheltenham' and another on 9 November 1918: 'Would any kind lady adopt a healthy baby girl for love only?'

A postman of the Army Service Corps delivering post to Woodleigh, The Park – a house which features later on in the war in a different role. (*Cheltenham Chronicle and Gloucestershire Graphic*, 27 February 1915)

By mid-December 1914 it was clear that more room was needed for the 9th and 10th battalions of the Gloucesters as the regiment, with new recruits, had expanded to full strength. Lansdown Court East and two houses in Royal Parade became new billets. Eventually, the tally of houses the 9th and 10th battalions used was extended to thirty-nine large residences and their stay extended from six weeks to six months. The 9th Battalion left on Monday, 26 April 1915 for Fovant, Salisbury Plain, and landed in France on 21 September 1915. The 10th Battalion departed on Thursday, 6 May 1915 to be moved to Sutton Veney, Salisbury Plain, before leaving for the front on 8 August 1915. Unlike the battalions' arrivals, there was no apathy on their departure. There were thousands of Cheltenham townspeople cheering the troops on their way, giving them an 'affectionate farewell'.

There was a rumour in Cheltenham that troops were being taken away because of a 'disease' affecting over 200 men. It was denied by the army, who said, '… the rumour is a gross libel on the soldiers'. Further troops identified to have been billeted in Cheltenham, after the 9th and 10th battalions of the Gloucesters left, up to October 1916 included the Army Service Corps, 5th Battalion Royal Warwickshire Regiment and the 3/4th, 3/5th and 3/6th battalions of the Gloucestershire Regiment, who left in January 1916.

This postcard from Frank Artus of Cheltenham, posted on 21 July 1915 to his mother, tells of the impending departure of the 10th Gloucesters to France. Frank sent it from Sutton Veney where the 10th Gloucesters were camped waiting to go to the front for the first time. (Author's collection)

THE 10TH GLOUCESTERS AFTER CHELTENHAM –
A SOLDIER WRITES TO HIS MOTHER

The postcard on page 91 from Frank Artus of Cheltenham, posted on 21 July 1915 to his mother, tells of the impending departure of the 10th Gloucesters to France. Frank sent it from Sutton Veney where the 10th Gloucesters were camped waiting to go to the front for the first time. He writes: '… according to the orders we had today they say we shall not be long now before we goes [sic] out to France, we are having all the rifles serve out today so there is something on the board that means the winter for us out there …' Seventeen days later the 10th Gloucesters left for Southampton and at 5 p.m. boarded a steamer for Le Havre. All the months of training, skirmishes and manoeuvres on Cleeve and Leckhampton hills were to be for real.

It was reported in the *Echo* on 6 October 1915 that:

> Mrs Artus of 3 Granville Street, Cheltenham has received a letter from her husband's nephew saying that her husband Sergt. E. Artus in the 10th Gloucesters was killed in action on September 25th in France … His brother, Corpl. F. Artus was wounded in the thigh in the same engagement.

Members of the 10th Gloucestershire Regiment in billets, posing behind Lansdown.
(By permission of Jimmy James and John Dowling)

Frank's brother Ernest, a plasterer with A.C. Billings, was one of thirty-six Cheltenham men out of 163 men of the 10th Battalion Gloucestershire Regiment who lost their lives at the Battle of Loos. Eight men from Cheltenham in the 8th Battalion also lost their lives at Loos that day. As Nick Christian writes, '... 163 of those who had proudly posed for photographers in Lansdown Crescent now lay with sightless eyes, cold and stiff on the field of battle'. Those were men who had been billeted in Cheltenham and over the next two months news would filter through to forty-four Cheltenham families that their son, brother, husband or sweetheart would not be returning.

Nick Christian described those eager young recruits in the aftermath of the Loos, thus: '... gone were those recent cocky Cheltenham smiles, now replaced with grim, careworn stares from eyes that had witnessed unspeakable suffering.'

Between 24–29 September 1915 there were 459 casualties of the 10th Battalion Gloucestershire Regiment, 'the Cheltenham Battalion', either killed, wounded or gassed at Loos. The battle also took the life of Clement Mitford, the eldest son and heir of Lord Redesdale of Batsford Park, Moreton-in-Marsh, and brother of the six Mitford sisters, and of Jack, the beloved son of Rudyard Kipling, who never got over the guilt of sending his son into war. This battle was the first time gas had been used by the British Army – 5,243 cylinders of chlorine gas were used on 25 September starting at 5.50 a.m. The wind turned and much of the gas blew back into the British trenches.

CHAPTER 6

What Did Cheltenham – and the Ladies – Do?

War changed the lives of women of all classes. They were to come out of their homes, mix together, participate in activities they could not have imagined would be necessary one year before and be given a level of freedom never previously envisaged. For women, pre-war life, as Kate Adie explains, '… was defined by what you couldn't do rather than what you could do … it remained very much a man's world.' At the beginning, many Cheltenham women initiated appeals on their own, mostly related to the particular military allegiance of a family member, causing overlap and duplication. Nonetheless, what was needed was coordination and channelling of effort and resources. In August 1914 the army's focus was using women as a means to encourage men to enlist. Neither military nor civilian authorities had given serious thought to how women's practical contributions to the war effort might best be utilised – so women organised for themselves.

In Cheltenham voluntary work was master (or mistress!) minded by a few simply remarkable women who should never be forgotten, the worth of whose contributions has been lost in the ensuing years. As 'The Chatterer' wrote in the *Chronicle* on 19 August 1916: 'The Garden Town has so many of the leisured classes, especially ladies, who back up the driving force of organisation … the leisured class in Cheltenham has always itself been strong in organising ability … something in our social structure favours the getting up of fêtes and the getting out of money.' The ladies of Cheltenham took no time at all to emerge from their drawing rooms and mobilise for the war effort.

THE MAYORESS AND HER LINEN COMMITTEE

Within a day of the outbreak of war, the mayoress (Miss Edith Skillicorne, sister of the mayor) set up a Linen Committee. A meeting on 10 August 1914 at the Town Hall called together 'ladies for linen parties to cut up linen for the treatment of our wounded soldiers and sailors' with Miss Skillicorne as President. Unprecedented though this activity was, it was the precursor of very much larger organisations in Cheltenham, which contributed significantly to the local and national war effort.

Two days after the meeting, the Mayoress's Linen Committee began holding working parties daily from 11 a.m to 1 p.m. and 3 p.m. to 5 p.m. at the Town Hall. Garments were cut to regulation patterns and work could be taken away to complete at home. Subscriptions to the fund for materials were opened, starting at 1s. One month later, September to October, the variety of the 3,521 goods despatched and the recipients included the following:

Soldiers' Club Isle of Wight:	36 glass cloths
Torpedo Flotilla:	40 scarves and caps
HMS *Maidstone* submarines:	83 scarves
5th Gloucesters:	768 garments
Indian Cavalry (Mrs Hearle Cole):	30 scarves
Refugees in Cheltenham:	186 bed linen

By November 1914, the Committee not only had a large band of ladies working away but twenty-four women and girls being paid out of the fund's subscriptions. The mayoress had made it clear she was 'anxious for it to be known in town that the organisation only gives out work to women who are really in want of employment'. The goods were stored in a room at the Town Hall, which began as a central depot for all war relief clothing, with Miss Mina Wethered as Honorary Secretary until she was called upon to use her expertise in a much larger exercise.

Clearly the Town Hall space had been outgrown as the Mayoress's Linen Committee needed to set up another War Supply Depot by March 1916. The venue for this was Marlborough House, Winchcombe Street, which was also home of the School of Domestic Science. Under the management of Mrs Forsyth Forrest and Mrs Richard Davies (wife of Alderman Dr Richard Davies), the depot held work meetings on Tuesday and Friday afternoons for the making of bandages and swabs which were sent to local hospitals, Cheltenham doctors at the front and Royal Naval hospitals. The volunteers were asked to wear white head coverings, sleeves and aprons, and tea could be had for thruppence (3d). A small weekly contribution was required to pay towards materials.

Eventually, by August 1918 there was also an Evening War Supply Depot. But no one in Cheltenham could fail to be impressed with the output of the Mayoress's Linen Committee. In the four years of the war, the output amounted to 90,938 garments and 'requisites'. The founder of the Committee, Miss Edith Skillicorne, died on 5 February 1918 'having been laid aside with a nervous breakdown', according to the *CLO* and the work was continued by the next mayoress, Mrs Rees Jones.

A much larger, countywide organisation was set up as the result of a meeting convened by the Lord Lieutenant of the County, Earl Beauchamp, and held in Shire Hall on 19 October 1915. He appointed a woman of remarkable organising ability and boundless energy, daughter of a former Mayor of Cheltenham – Miss Mina Ricketts Wethered – to Honorary Organising Secretary of the Committee to Co-ordinate Voluntary Work on 23 October 1915. In January 1916, Miss Wethered set up the Gloucester County Association for Voluntary Organisations depot at No. 8 Queen's Parade, in a house lent by the mayor, William Nash Skillicorne, and next to his and his sister's home. It seemed that the waste from overlapping supplies from the disparate working parties that had been set up willy-nilly throughout the county had become 'almost an embarrassment'.

Miss Mina Wethered, Honorary Organising Secretary of the Gloucester County Association for Voluntary Organisations, sat at her desk at the depot at No. 8 Queen's Parade. Just one of her wartime roles in Cheltenham for which she was awarded the OBE. (*Cheltenham Chronicle and Gloucestershire Graphic*, 20 October 1917)

A stockroom at Gloucester County Association for Voluntary Organisations at 8 Queen's Parade. (*Cheltenham Chronicle and Gloucestershire Graphic*, 20 October 1917)

The purpose of Miss Wethered's organisation was to coordinate, direct the output and despatch supplies from 140 voluntary working groups throughout the county. The depot was part of the supply chain to Red Cross hospitals in the county, with the exception of Cheltenham hospitals, which were supplied by the Mayoress's Linen Committee. Within three months of being set up the military hospitals, ambulance trains, casualty clearing stations as well as the local hospitals had been supplied with 3,200 garments and 40,000 bandages. There were always twenty to thirty bales of goods awaiting despatch in the hall of No. 8 Queen's Parade. When America declared war on Germany in April 1917, the American hospitals in the UK also asked for supplies of swabs and bandages. In addition to the workrooms at No. 8 Queen's Parade, Miss Wethered had to open a room in her parents' house at The Uplands for working groups to carry out additional work requested by the American Red Cross.

A report in the *CLO* of 7 July 1917 gives an indication of the scale and magnitude of the output from the depot:

> This year alone the record of work totals 30,276 garments and 111,000 bandages. 'Garments' covers an extraordinary collection of goods in 44 different collections including pneumonia jackets, sunshields, mosquito nets, walking sticks, splints, bandages, swabs. These have been sent to home hospitals and to others in Egypt, Salonika, Italy, Romania and France and to our troops there and to mine-sweepers. Women's work in the war is very apparent here and no 'Tommy' is likely to forget it.

By the end of the war, Miss Wethered and her voluntary staff had despatched a total of 7.5 million items. In recognition for this and her other voluntary war work in Cheltenham, in June 1918 Miss Wethered was awarded the newly founded OBE.

SCARVES FOR SAILORS AND
BINOCULARS FOR BATTALIONS

The war saw a plethora of appeals in Cheltenham, all competing for what seemed like bottomless pockets. Many appeals were made directly to the local newspaper either by the soldiers themselves or by families of local men appealing on behalf of specific regiments. In many cases the need was for articles to relieve boredom: magazines, local newspapers, musical instruments, games and boxing gloves. The appeals nearer to home included those for money, for help, for cars and drivers, horses, nuts and puddings. The lists became endless.

Private George Harker of No.14 Albert Street and with the Royal Marine Light Infantry missed his gramophone and requested one to be sent to him. Sister Pridmore at New Court Hospital asked for books in French as none of the wounded Belgians could read English but some could read French and she would like to start a library. Mrs Gwatkin Williams of No. 2 Lansdown Parade wrote saying she would be grateful for helmets, cardigans (with long sleeves), socks, scarves and mittens for the crews of submarines. In June 1915, a concertina was sent by Mr J.H. Olivant, printer of Bennington Street, replying to the 1/5th Battalion Gloucestershire Regiment's

Cheltenham Reservists, guarding a railway bridge at Winchester, appealing to passengers in passing trains for coal and newspapers from Cheltenham. (*Cheltenham Chronicle and Gloucestershire Graphic*, 27 February 1915)

Knitters provided sufficient scarves for every man and officer of HMS *Gloucester*. Here Mrs Richard Longland of Tate's Hotel in the Promenade, Honorary Secretary to the local branch of the Navy League, shows the collection. (*Cheltenham Chronicle and Gloucestershire Graphic*, 26 September 1915)

appeal – it was one 'of value' which belonged to his late father. He expressed the hope that '… the concertina band may march up Cheltenham's High Street playing "When Tommy comes marching home"'. Sergeant Earnest Thursfield, one of the original 'Fighting 30' from Cavendish House, wrote from Fovant Camp in May 1915 asking for any spare cricket gear to form a club within the 9th Battalion Gloucestershire Regiment.

Mrs Richard Longland of Tate's Hotel on the Promenade, the local secretary of the Navy League, asked for men volunteers to undertake patrol duty on the east and south coasts, saying motorcycles and motor cars would be most useful. By 15 August 1914 Mrs Longland had received over 100 offers of help and many ladies had said they were willing to receive wounded officers and men of the fleet in their homes. Mrs Longland appealed particularly for lady knitters to make navy blue scarves for the sailors. Eight ounces of wool costing 2s was sufficient for a scarf 54in in length. Four weeks later the knitters of Cheltenham had supplied sufficient scarves to give every officer and man aboard HMS *Gloucester* a scarf. Well done the lady knitters of Cheltenham!

An early appeal in the Cheltenham newspapers came from Field Marshal Lord Roberts, a man who was known in Cheltenham, having opened the Drill Hall in North Street in 1906, home of the 1/5th Gloucesters. He asked if sportsmen, unable to enlist, would send him their binoculars. These were for non-commissioned officers who were going to the front. By 31 October, nationally, 14,000 pairs had been sent in. Rear Admiral Grogan of Belmont in Malvern Road put a notice in the paper to say, on behalf of the Lord Roberts' National Service League, that anyone wishing to send field glasses, military prism-compasses, saddles and bridles, could have them forwarded by him. In addition, he pointed out, if these articles had the owner's name engraved upon them they would be returned at the end of the war. Wishful thinking! Strangely, Lord Roberts' letter to the *Echo* was later sold for £300 by a stationer in the Promenade, with funds donated to the war effort. Roberts died suddenly in France on 10 November 1914 whilst inspecting the Indian troops. The flag on the Municipal Offices in Cheltenham was flown at half-mast as a mark of respect.

MRS AGG HAS TWO GOOD IDEAS

Everyone in Cheltenham found ways to contribute, as can be seen by this announcement in the *Echo*: 'A fund is being started for providing socks for soldiers and sailors to be supported by domestic servants in Cheltenham who are asked to contribute one shilling each. Contributions should be sent to Miss Molly Green, Netherleigh, Lansdown Place.' One shilling was quite a considerable amount for a servant. Mrs Eleanor Agg of Foxcote House, Andoversford, thought she had hit on the perfect idea for raising funds, having read a letter in *The Times*. Mrs Agg wondered if it had ever occurred to the heads of households amongst the *Echo*'s readers to invite their indoor servants to contribute. The suggestion was for servants to donate one day's wages to the Queen's Work for Women Fund in aid of their less fortunate sisters. The staff of George's, caterers, let the newspaper know that practically all of their employees had agreed to a weekly levy on behalf of the National Relief Fund. Staff at A.C. Billings, builders, supported a family of Belgian refugees. Donating and raising money for the cause was now a culture across the classes, not confined to those who had plenty to give.

A rather different appeal came from Mrs Eleanor Agg, in her capacity as Chairman of the Women's War Club Committee of No. 5 Royal Well Terrace. In December 1914, the organisation had acquired premises at No. 25 Clarence Street for the purpose of providing free entry to rooms where wives and relatives of soldiers and sailors would find 'much to cheer and console them during the absence of husbands and sons'. Subscriptions from 2s 6d upwards were requested to be sent to the Honorable Mrs Jamieson at Thirlestaine Lodge and also the loan of tables, chairs and a piano. Four weeks later the mayoress opened 'The Tipperary Club'.

The War Office asked for volunteers to make much-needed nets for horse fodder, sending instructors to Cheltenham in June 1915. The instructors taught a group of local citizens who set up a workshop in Cheltenham College's gymnasium. The volunteers were told that it was important that the work must be continuous and not done spasmodically. Pupils from Dean Close School, Cheltenham Ladies' College and Pate's Grammar School for Girls also set to making the nets. It was hoped Cheltenham would be able to contribute 500 nets per week and, true to its word, the following week it was reported that Mr Tyler of Plant & Co., who had offered to pack and despatch nets, had sent 500 to the War Office Depot.

Making haynets for horses at the front in Cheltenham College gymnasium, one of a few venues for the War Office haynet workshops. (*Cheltenham Chronicle and Gloucestershire Graphic*, 24 July 1917)

PARCELS TO SOLDIERS – OR NOT!

A fund from 'Soldiers' Day' collections was set up to send parcels to Cheltenham soldiers at the front. On Wednesday, 15 July 1915, shop workers – described as 'those of the distributive trades' – helped to pack parcels. The ladies were allowed to carry articles to the men, who packed. The parcels included soap, sardines, chocolate, Oxo, condensed milk, sweets, cigarettes and tobacco. Packing had to be suspended when the supply of acid drops ran out. Then it was found that some of the parcels had to be unpacked, being over 3lb in weight, and 300 parcels were sent the following day.

The Church Lad's Brigade was ready and willing to help farmers as messengers, cyclists, patrollers or guards of railway and property. More interestingly, a company of lads was offered to farmers whose horses had been commandeered, to haul harvest wagons! Apply to Mr H.E.C. Townley, South View, Cheltenham.

This postcard was published by Cheltenham Traders' Association especially for Soldiers' Day, June 1915. The sale raised money to send parcels to Cheltenham men at the front. (Author's collection)

One grateful soldier wrote a letter of thanks, dated 25 September 1915, showing how far the parcels travelled. Trooper Herbert Hicks in the Dardanelles (Turkey) said that the parcels from Cheltenham were brought from the coast under the cover of darkness on pack mules.

However, it seems parcels didn't reach all Cheltenham soldiers. There was a plaintive appeal in a letter to the *Echo* from Lance Corporal Alfred Wixey of the 7th Battalion of the Gloucesters, with the British Expeditionary Force, somewhere in the Mediterranean in September 1915:

> One thing that strikes all of us Cheltenham boys is that Cheltenham seems to forget that the first Gloucestershire regiment to enlist in Lord Kitchener's Army was the 7th Gloucesters. I should like to tell the people of Cheltenham that they did so without a lot of recruiting meetings to beg them in … We haven't been mentioned a dozen times in the *Chronicle*. We don't want anything given us, but we would like to think we are not forgotten.

Also, Sergeant Kilminster of The Stores, Church Street, Charlton Kings, with the 7th Battalion, sent his own letter, writing of '… the good work the ladies of Cheltenham are doing for the boys of Cheltenham but I assure you we have

Soldiers' Day raised money to send parcels to Cheltenham soldiers at the front. Amongst those packing in this picture on 15 July was the Cheltenham entrepreneur and publisher Ed Burrows. (*Cheltenham Chronicle and Gloucestershire Graphic*, 15 July 1915)

not received any parcels whatever.' A sad state of affairs as the letters talk of the lives of 7th Battalion soldiers sacrificed in the battle on 8 August 1915 in the Dardanelles, mainly of Cheltenham men who enlisted early on in 1914. Fifty-one photographs of local men wounded or killed in the battle appeared in the *Chronicle and Graphic* relating to this battle. Included in those killed was the editor of the *Echo*, Captain Edwin Willoughby, and a 19-year-old *Echo* boy, George Parnell.

COMFORTS FROM THE INDIAN CONNECTION

Robin Brooks referred to Cheltenham during the first two decades of the twentieth century as 'Anglo-Indian Paradise'. This soubriquet becomes apparent when looking at the intended recipients of several appeals, giving an indication of the allegiance of one element of Cheltenham's population. Mrs Hearle Cole, later of the Cheltenham Prisoners of War Committee, asked for shirts, socks, mufflers, cigarettes or money for the men of the Indian Cavalry with the BEF. Her grandfather had been Inspector General of Hospitals in Madras, both her parents and she herself had been born in India and her father, Colonel Elphinstone Shaw, and uncle, General Macintyre, had both served with the Indian Army.

On 28 September 1914, the *Echo* carried the notice, 'Comforts for Indian Troops Serving in France'. It seems extraordinary that the Indian troops were not supplied with trousers. Cheltenham's Anglo-Indians responded immediately – the first six subscribers to the fund listed in the Cheltenham paper were retired colonels. In October an advertisement informed readers that the Government of India supplied the troops with thick jerseys, mitts and balaclavas but no pants. During the Afghan war and on the Frontier the Sepoys (Indian soldiers) constantly complained of feeling very cold from the knees up. The appeal continued:

> As we have so many Anglo-Indians and friends of India residing in Cheltenham it is suggested they show their appreciation of the Indian soldiers by supplying them with pants. Anyone who can spare an old pair or two of thick pants or drawers send to Plant and Co., Colonnade who have offered to pack and forward. The wholesale cost of a pair of pants is 3 shillings.

By 14 November, 2,160 pairs of pants had been sent to France for the Indian troops.

Miss Heath of Wellesley Court, Pittville, collected knitted comforts for the Lahore Battery of the Indian contingent now in France whom, she had heard, were also suffering from the cold. Whereas, Mrs Hunter Campbell of Eildon, Lansdown, received navy blue scarves etc. for HMS *Hindustan*.

Knitting, it would seem, was not just an urgent local activity, as Kate Adie writes: 'In the first few months of the conflict the upsurge in knitting attained heroic heights. Knitting became a kind of moral duty – no woman should be seen just sitting, she should be sitting knitting! Queen Mary knitted!' But, the knitting groups and Needlework Guilds the Queen had encouraged, and with which the Queen was much enamoured, caused consternation. Much as the work of the sewing and knitting ladies gratified the need to supply troops with warmth in one of the coldest winters on record in 1914, and the wounded with comforts and nightshirts, adversely they were depriving working women of a living.

Nationally, up to September 1916, 150,000 women had lost jobs in domestic service and workshops such as dressmaking. Many dressmakers could no longer find work in households. Ladies were economising by dispensing with the services of their servants and commissioning fewer dresses for 'the season'. On the other hand, pre-war, millions of pounds worth of readymade clothing had been imported from Germany and Austria into this country. With the inevitable shortage there ought to have been work but cutbacks and shortage of material were causing problems for the dressmakers.

The *CLO* of 29 August 1914 rallied the society ladies under the headline 'Women and War' with the words:

> Each woman can be of incalculable service if she will assist to keep things normal, particularly in the world of domestic commerce. In our trade war against Germany active cooperation is most necessary. They [women] should see to it that no articles of German or Austrian manufacture are allowed to enter the home.

Unbelievably, on the same page, in the adjacent column headed 'Austrian Velour Hats' the fashion correspondent wrote: 'Fortunately, the consignments of the popular Austrian velour hats for autumn and winter wear, had reached London before hostilities broke out. Therefore, they will be sold at the usual prices.'

In an unlikely alliance, the Queen, with Mary Macarthur of the Women's Trade Union League, launched the Queen's Work for Women Fund (QWWF), aimed at employing those women textile workers and seamstresses put out of work. This was done with the belief that '… prevention of distress is better than its relief, and that employment is better than charity'. The Queen had telegrammed the Chairman of Cheltenham Council on 9 September 1914 approving the formation of a sub-committee in the town for the QWWF. There had been a reluctance to form a QWWF as the Council Chairman felt that there was a danger of too many of these kind of committees.

By December 1914, a letter appeared in the *Echo* from one such unemployed dressmaker asking where she was to find work to support herself as, in this 'classic town of Cheltenham', dressmakers were not allowed to tout for work. She enquired if all the clothes had been made for Kitchener's million men. A reply the next day came from Mrs Gardiner of No. 6 Paragon Parade asking why the dressmaker had not seen the notices in the paper and outside the Municipal Offices. Apparently, the Mayor's Committee had considered opening a workroom but so few dressmakers filled in the forms it was considered a workroom was not needed.

By February 1915, under the auspices of the QWWF, a workroom was opened at No. 8 Queen's Parade, in the house lent by the mayor. Forty-four dressmakers and tailoresses were employed there and the number continued to grow weekly. No work was sold, as the purpose was not to compete with the trade of the shops. Wages were paid for out of a grant made by the Mayor's War Relief Committee, which also supplied some of the materials – purchased locally, of course. The workers made children's clothes out of worn garments and materials suitable for young servants' outfits, given away through the Mayoress's Linen Committee.

One novel way of raising funds was taken up by the ladies of Cheltenham Golf Club. *The Gentlewoman* magazine had devised a scheme whereby they would offer medals free to all ladies' golf clubs which arranged competitions with an entrance fee of not less than sixpence. The money was to go to the QWWF.

There must have been some speedy knitters in Cheltenham. The mayoress appealed on 18 December 1914 asking for knitted mittens so that a pair of mittens could be given to every soldier billeted in Cheltenham at the time – over 2,000 men – as a small gift from the residents of Cheltenham. Not much notice to knit a pair of mittens and organise Christmas! Many appeals were made to knitters of the town. But no worries as W.H. Gibbs, Wool Merchant of No. 3 Montpellier Walk, had 'Wools for Soldiers' on special offer the week of 13 March 1915. Surely the boys appreciated socks knitted in 'Extra soft khaki wool at thruppence ha'penny an ounce'!

The requirement for knitted goods didn't slacken throughout the war and still knitters' skills were being required in October 1918 when Miss Wethered asked for knitters urgently to make 200 mufflers. The request had come from the American Red Cross, which had also donated the wool. Further, Miss Wethered needed sleeveless sweaters to be knitted but no recipients were mentioned.

A colonel of a battalion of the Gloucesters at the front felt compelled to write to the *Echo* on 24 December 1914 to let knitters know – knitted belts are a mistake! Insects of all sorts get in and breed and the insect pests are perfectly terrible! Two or three yards of flannel seven inches wide would be better; fastened with two or three safety pins.

COBBLERS AND SLIPPERS

What a hive of activity No. 8 Queen's Parade must have been. In addition to the dressmakers and the Gloucester County Association for Voluntary Organisations, there was one room set apart for the cutting out and constructing of slippers for men at rest stations and in military hospitals, under the chief cutter, the Revd C.W. Birley, set up by Mrs Ernest Rogers. This group of voluntary workers – 'ladies and gentlemen banded together to make the slippers calling themselves the County Cobblers' – not only gave of their time but paid for the materials they made up. To start with, on average they were making 136 pairs of slippers a week. In addition they cut out slippers for the Belgravia Workrooms to make.

By May 1918 the demand for their slippers was so great that an appeal was launched through the columns of the *CLO* for both materials and money. In 1917 they had made 3,800 pairs of slippers and in the first four months of 1918 output had risen to 1,600 pairs, sent to France, Salonica and local hospitals. By now they had become 'the Slipper Department' which they did admit 'may first appear to be a somewhat insignificant or less luxurious piece of war work … but had plenty of willing hands.' There were by now eighty workers, a large number of them working at home. The slippers proved to be of therapeutic value to the wounded soldiers and the Red Cross used their patterns as examples for working parties throughout the country.

Belgravia Workroom making slippers for soldiers at No. 14 North Street. Most of these volunteers worked during the day. (*Cheltenham Chronicle and Gloucestershire Graphic*, 28 July 1915)

By the time of the appeal in 1918 the Slipper Department had outgrown the workroom at No. 8 Queen's Parade and moved to bigger premises. This was in a ten-bedroomed house in Bayshill Road called 'Edginswell', next door to Curtis's Private Hotel – later to become the Savoy Hotel. The Slipper Department's funds and resources were completely depleted. What's more, materials had become scarcer as the war progressed and subsequently their appeal was for materials. What they asked for were cuttings from linings, old hunting coats and riding habits, faded felt surrounds and cork lino – or money!

By August 1918 'Edginswell' was the home for yet another organisation which sprang up as a result of the war. It had the complex title of the Cheltenham branch of the Surgical Requisites Association Orthopaedic branch of the Queen Mary's Needlework Guild for Plastic Work. The organisation was to make special splints and surgical boots for wounded soldiers in Cheltenham hospitals and was asking for subscriptions for an initial outlay of £50 and £160–£200 annually.

BELGRAVIA WORKROOMS

The Belgravia Workrooms, working from No. 14 North Street, were started in July 1916 with the help of Cheltenham Chamber of Commerce and the Traders' Association. Within eleven weeks of opening they had 300 voluntary workers, making bandages, clothes and slippers, cut outs sent from the County Cobblers and, of course, a band of knitters. By the end of the first year, 15,000 articles, including 8,000 garments, had been sent out from the Cheltenham branch. Unlike most voluntary work, which was undertaken by women with time on their hands, the Belgravia Workrooms' production was, for the most part, carried out after working hours by women employed during the day in government offices, in the banks or in business. The Belgravia Workrooms was a national organisation, the Cheltenham branch having been set up in July 1916 by Miss Alice Crawley, a singing teacher from Cheltenham Ladies' College. As well as being the Workrooms' superintendent, Miss Crawley's musical expertise was put to good use arranging musical concerts to raise money for the Workrooms.

To celebrate their first year of work the Belgravia Workrooms held a bridge tournament at the Town Hall on 1 December 1917. In attendance was the Chairman of the Central Belgravia War Supply Depot in London, Romilly Fedden, who told the audience in no uncertain terms what their responsibilities were, as women: 'Desultory and individual work is not wanted … no woman has the right to work at home just because she wants to but ought to join some body … to best utilise every minute of her time, every yard of material and every penny spent to the best possible advantage.' By June 1918 this organisation had made 42,324 bandages and 9,995 garments and had been renamed as the Cheltenham Evening War Hospital Supply Department and, like the County Cobblers, had completely run out of funds.

ODD JOB CLASSES FOR WOMEN

'Odd Job Classes for Women' were advertised in October 1915 at the technical schools, reflecting a need for the ladies to learn new skills, including the use of tools. The classes were intended to '… help women to perform little "jobs" about the house, and in these times of crisis men can be more worthily employed than in stopping leaks in washers, repairing door-fastenings, cords and blinds or soldering kettles etc.'. It was quite clear which class you belonged to depending on whether you attended the Monday class at 2.30–4.30 p.m. at a fee of 10s for the course or 7.30–9.30 p.m. at 5s for the same course of demonstrations and practical work. The classes were a great success and were still running in February 1916 when the *Echo* watched a class in action and observed 'a lady with a little short-stocked plane make the shavings fly with a dainty elegance whilst smoothing a floor board, the exercise is as good for the arms and shoulders as tennis.'

APPEAL FOR CIGARETTES

An officer had written, 'When Tommy has a cigarette he doesn't mind the German "coal-boxes", the only thing the Hun doesn't like is Tommy's inscrutable smile and his cigarette! Feed the Smile the German Hates.' This patriotic sentiment drove the *Echo*'s appeal, started as a fund for the readers to subscribe to, which would provide cigarettes for the men of the Gloucestershire Regiment. Every packet carried a printed greeting stating it had been sent by a subscriber to that fund. Within two weeks of the commencement of the fund in October 1914, 15,200 packs had been sent to the front. By November 1914, 30,000 cigarettes had been sent from Cheltenham. Miss Porter and Miss Sweeney appealed for cigarettes for Tommies under the slogan 'When you offer your pal a cigarette, please spare one, or a copper (one penny) for Tommy at the Front'. Within a few weeks the ladies had sent 88,000 cigarettes, dozens of boxes of matches and patent lighters to the front. They added, 'Now that the cold weather has really set in, the need for smokes is greater than it was before. We want to send out at least 10,000 cigarettes a week.' They weren't the only ones to ask for cigarettes. The *CLO*'s appeal 'Tobacco for the Troops' on 17 October 1914 stated: 'Nothing gladdens the heart of our brave defenders in the firing line of France so much as the gift of a smoke … with a cigarette between their lips, they can face their discomforts cheerfully. The British soldier is an inveterate smoker.' The mayor, on sending the recruits out in the early days in Cheltenham, gave them all a box of cigarettes. Tobacco was considered to be a universal panacea, supposed to calm the nerves – an essential in time of war. However, to those who objected on health grounds, the *Echo* reiterated most people's opinion of the day '… happily, the anti-tobacco faddist is in a miserable minority.'

Mr J.S. Gibbons of Boddington Manor was appointed the Purchasing Officer for the Cheltenham area and bought over fifty horses in just two days, Thursday, 6 and Friday, 7 August 1914. Forty of these were for the use of the 9th Lancers, under the escort of Lieutenant Lennox Harvey, the well-known steeplechase rider. The appeals for horses in the Cheltenham papers was constant at the start of the war. The Master of the Cotswold Hunt opened the Hunt Stables to Mr Gibbons and told him to take what he liked and pay what he thought fair, most horses being bought for an average of £50. Six days later, due to the army mobilisation, Mr Gibbons was calling for more cavalry horses, light or heavy, also artillery horses (light vanners) and light draught horses. Then came the call for saddlers, blacksmiths, grooms, and rough riders for the Remount Service.

Whilst horses were leaving in their droves from the Cheltenham Horse Repository of Messrs Warner, Sheppard and Wade at Winchcombe Street, more were arriving. Canadian horses, 144 of them unbroken, arrived in Cheltenham. They were destined for an establishment in Prestbury, where they would be broken in before being sent to the front. Closer to home, Mrs Eva Daubeny of No. 10 Pittville Lawn, Honorary Secretary of the RSPCA, offered to defray the veterinary costs for the horses remaining in Cheltenham which had a heavier workload, if their owners couldn't afford to pay for their treatment. Mrs Daubeney also offered help in finding homes for solders' pets left behind.

WHAT HAPPENED TO THOSE LADIES IN THE SUFFRAGE MOVEMENT?

At war's start Maynard Colchester-Wemyss considered that:

> The Militant Suffragettes have for the time being buried the hatchet and are offering themselves as nurses and as workers for 'other capacities', for the common zeal. Very probably in this case, very many of them were not sorry for an excuse to cease practices which they could not but feel were abhorrent to a civilised society; and we may hope that the hatchet once buried will never again be un-earthed.

Perhaps this was wishful thinking. Cheltenham had long been a hotbed of the suffrage movement, as far back as 1871. Cheltenham worthies associated with the movement were people such as Miss Flora Kelley, Mrs Frances (Rosa) Swiney and Miss Theodora Flower Mills – the last two being President and Honorary Secretary of the Cheltenham Women's Suffrage Society. Rosa Swiney frequently, if not weekly, wrote letters to the local newspapers and especially contributed to the *Chronicle*'s 'Our Suffrage' column. Dr Alice Burns, the local Schools' Medical Inspector and Dr Alice Sanderson, one of the doctors who treated the Belgian refugees, were also Cheltenham suffragists.

Two daughters of John How, grocer of Cambray, became leading members of the suffrage movement in Cheltenham and in one case, renowned nationally. Florence Earengey, wife of local Cheltenham solicitor Dr William Earengey, later to be a High Court Judge, was the Secretary of the Women's Social and Political Union (WSPU), set up in 1903 by Emmeline Pankhurst. The Union's motto was 'Deeds not words'. Florence later defected to the Women's Freedom League of which her sister had been co-founder, both of the women not being in such full agreement with the extent of the militant tactics of Emmeline Pankhurst. On the 1911 census form Florence's husband had written 'The other members of the household were away as a protest against women having no parliamentary vote.'

Edith, Florence Earengey's sister, had married a son of H.H. Martyn, the local industrialist, and was known as Edith How Martyn, campaigning with a well-known suffragette Mrs Charlotte Despard. Mrs Despard was the sister of Sir John French, Commander-in-Chief of the British Forces in France. Edith How Martyn was sent to prison for two months in October 1906 for 'causing a disturbance within the sacred precincts of Parliament'. In the same year, the Cheltenham Ladies' College Vice-Principal and thirty-three members of staff signed the Women's Suffrage Declaration.

Miss Flora Kelley, as local Honorary Secretary of the Conservative and Unionist Women's Franchise Association, wrote in the *Echo* of 5 September 1914: '… we are putting suffrage work to one side and are devoting our whole energies to helping our country in the best way possible.'

Six days after war was declared, the government announced it was releasing all suffragettes from prison. In return, Emmeline Pankhurst's organisation, the WSPU, agreed to suspend militant activities and to pledge their workers for the war effort. True to their word, one of the organisers of the WSPU and a militant suffragette, the Honorable Mrs Evaline Haverfield, and a society singer and actress, Decima Moore, founded the Women's Emergency Corps. A meeting was held in the Drawing Room of Cheltenham's Town Hall on 12 November 1914, under the patronage of Miss Edith Skillicorne, the mayoress. Before 'a large gathering of ladies', Miss Pertwee of the Women's Emergency Corps spoke of how the organisation wished to register and control the vast body of women's voluntary services in the country and 'middle-class women will be trained and helped to win a living in this country'. Cards were handed out to the ladies but it is not known how many signed up.

In February 1915, the Women's Emergency Corps led to the Women's Volunteer Reserve (WVR). This organisation was composed of a mix of feminists and women who would not otherwise have mixed with such dangerous types! In their fascinating book *Working for Victory: Images of Women in the First World War*, Condell and Liddiard describe these types as 'the radical suffragette and the conservative aristocrat' and 'adopting a quasi-military uniform, a chain of command and rank structures, the clear implication being that they too were soldiers ready and willing to fight a common foe.' The WVR uniform was expensive at £2 10s and well beyond the means of working women. It consisted of a khaki wool jacket with large buttoned pockets, a skirt of 100in circumference around the hem which was to be 10in from the ground and a felt hat, shoes and puttees.

Three Women's Volunteer Reserve members, Captain Florence Earengey, Lieutenant Rogers and Sergeant Ruck in the tidy uniform competition. (*Cheltenham Chronicle and Gloucestershire Graphic*, 3 August 1918)

In February 1915 a letter in the *Echo* from the Honorary Secretary of the WVR invited prospective members for a possible WVR corps to be formed in Cheltenham. She (the lady is not named) stated that there were 800 WVR members in Worcester and asked, 'Now, why should not Cheltenham too recognise this need … Let our women now come forward'. The *Echo* of 19 February 1919 reported a meeting at Royston House where a movement was 'on foot to organise a Cheltenham corps of the WVR'. The initial objects of this organisation were, in the case of the invasion of England, which it was thought possible, taking over the duties of the men in the reserve line when the men were needed on the firing line. These women would be: 'cooking weary men's dinners, signalling duty, carrying despatches and orders, on either motors, horses or bicycles, putting up tents, arranging camps and putting fodder ready for horses – in fact everything a man would do but fight!'

A Mrs King, speaking at the WVR meeting, considered that girls needed drilling: '… for women to work well, they must work together. This is not a thing we have been well taught – discipline is a thing girls are not very good at, are they? Drill teaches prompt obedience, discipline and cohesion.' However, Mrs King pointed out that they were to be 'womanly women and not second-class men' and their motto was 'Efficiency and Strength'. Drill was to take place two to three times a week, signalling was compulsory but first aid, nursing, fencing, shooting, Swedish drill, cooking and handicrafts were voluntary. A small fee was charged for classes. After the meeting the participants were given tea by no less than Mrs Wilson, mother of the Antarctic explorer, who was the Cheltenham corps medical officer.

There must have been a recruitment meeting at some stage between 18 February and 5 March as the first advertisement to call the WVR members appeared on 5 March 1915. It announced that 'Drill and Signalling will commence on Saturday 6th inst at Montpellier Baths, Cheltenham at a quarter to five o'clock.'

NOT A WOMAN'S PLACE?

The grand Easter Recruitment Parade on 10 April 1915 was the first time the corps had appeared publically and the *Echo* reported it thus:

> The Cheltenham Women's Volunteer Reserve under Captain Despard totalled about 30 and were the only ladies in the procession. But they did honour to their sex or the bachelor members of our staff are no judges. Their khaki uniforms are neatness itself and the ladies marched in a manner which turned the Boy Scouts yellow [*sic*] with envy.

Queen Mary's Army Auxiliary Corps Grand Recruitment Rally, 18 July 1918. Speakers included Colonel Ingram and Mrs Florence Earengey of the WVR. (*Cheltenham Chronicle and Gloucestershire Graphic*, 27 July 1918)

The response of the *Echo* reporter was not shared by a 'Corporal in the British Expeditionary Force, somewhere on the Continent' whose reaction to a photograph of the WVR presence in the parade was extreme. He wrote this letter which appeared on 1 May 1915, in the *Chronicle*:

> Sir, – In your issue 17th April one picture of the recruiting procession struck me as being very ludicrous ... I fully recognise the patriotic sense of the Englishwomen but when it comes to parading the streets and making absolute fools of themselves, as will be seen by the photo (they are all giggling like a lot of small schoolgirls) I think it's about time something was done. I cannot imagine what the world is coming to when it comes to women (and Cheltenham too) who want to be soldiers. To tell you confidentially, it's enough to make a good soldier weep.
>
> I am sure, Mr Editor, you will agree that a woman's place is her hearth and home and not promenading for notoriety. Can you tell me of what earthly use they would be if the Germans really came? By taking the places of men who want to enlist a woman need not don a suit of khaki and parade the streets as our women of Cheltenham are doing.

In response, Honorary Colonel of the Cheltenham WVR, Lady Thiselton-Dyer, on 8 May 1915 wrote:

> … I think many people do not understand the aims and objects of the movement (which) … is to help in an emergency that may arise owing to the shortage of men … and, as I feel there will be an ever-increasing necessity for women to earn their livelihoods, I should like to make the training so thorough that its effect may be a permanent one.

GARDENING GIRLS – OR TENNIS?

Lady Thiselton-Dyer, the Honorary Colonel, wrote a letter the same week in the *CLO* asking if anyone in Cheltenham could lend the WVR an empty house, with a fair-sized kitchen garden that the corps could cultivate with the help of 'a practical gardener'. She was well qualified, being the wife and daughter of former Directors of the Royal Botanical Gardens at Kew and a well-respected botanical illustrator in her own right. It was an ambitious project but the corps was loaned close on 2 acres of land that had formerly been Heath's Nursery (where A&E at the General Hospital is now). The intention was to grow vegetables for sick and wounded soldiers.

At a meeting held at Cheltenham Ladies' College on 28 May 1915, the Honorary Colonel reported that the corps in Cheltenham was flourishing with a membership of some sixty women in only three months of recruiting. Included on the new committee was the Vice-Principal of Cheltenham Ladies' College, Miss Guinness, and the Honorary Treasurer was Miss Wayre-Taylor of Segrave, The Park, where the Honorary Colonel had an office. Drill classes were under Miss Despard and flag signalling under Mrs Florence Earengey. Motors were assigned to Miss Wayre-Taylor, cooking to Mrs Stanley Wilde and sewing sandbags and sheets to Mrs Wilson. Collecting money and sheets for Red Cross hospitals in the Cheltenham area was under the control of Mrs Barrington Piers.

The committee also decided to arrange classes as diverse as book-keeping and massage. Agriculture classes would be taken including milking, butter and cheese making and the cookery class was to teach corps members to prepare soups, puddings and invalid dishes for wounded soldiers. Mechanical construction of all kinds of motors was to be taught so that the ladies could 'execute repairs when called upon'. Lady Thiselton-Dyer also pointed out that there was a great need in some shops in Cheltenham for messengers to carry parcels, run errands etc. which she thought the corps might well do! Voluntary work and WVR activities replaced leisure.

The demise of the garden project at Heath's Nursery was reported on 29 May 1915:

Sadly, Lady Thisleton-Dyer announced that she was … grieved and disappointed at hearing that some of the corps had given their names for the gardening but had since withdrawn on the plea that they could now play lawn tennis. Surely this was thoughtlessness. How can we think of playing games while our country is passing through this most appalling crisis.

By December 1915 it was reported that the officers of the WVR felt that they were not numerically strong enough to undertake the gardening work. However, by June 1916 the WVR was 'cooperating in the movement of women's war work on the land'. No reports mention what exactly they were doing.

But all was not sweetness and light amongst the voluntary linen suppliers of Cheltenham – toes were stepped on and noses put out of joint! Lady Thiselton-Dyer had written a letter, which appeared in the *Echo* on 17 June 1915, thanking people for the outcome of a WVR appeal for sheets for a local Red Cross hospital. There was a great need of a fresh supply of sheets owing to wear and tear from constant use. Donations from her appeal comprised 196 sheets, 54 pillowcases, 3 blankets, 6 breakfast napkins, 2 pillows and a collection of £18 10s 6d. The next day, Miss Edith Skillicorne, the mayoress, wrote on behalf of her Linen Committee stating that 'We cannot help regretting very much that a separate appeal had been made for gifts for one of the hospitals without any reference to this depot. We hear some of our generous supporters have been naturally annoyed at being asked again.' Oh dear! Without further ado Mrs Helen Stanley Wilde on behalf of the WVS replied: 'I cannot help expressing my regret that Lady Thiselton-Dyer's kind response … should be misconstrued and caused the Mayoress uneasiness … If so many people have been annoyed, how is it our girl-collectors have met with utmost generosity?' There was no further comment!

By November 1915 Florence Earengey had been appointed captain to replace Miss Despard and the WVR had taken offices at 17 the Promenade. In October 1916 the WVR opened a soldiers' club in their Promenade offices, in addition to work as messengers for the Red Cross office, which took them to practically every VAD hospital every morning. They held whist drives for wounded soldiers, then took the soldiers to the Picture Palace and afterwards gave them tea and sold flags in aid of the Lifeboat Institution. When the third Communal Food Kitchen was established in Cheltenham in February 1918, the WVR supplied the staff on Mondays and Fridays.

In April 1918 street operations for the Spring Flower Day for Voluntary Organisations were under the directions of Mrs Earengey of the WVR 'who had many helpers' and at another event raised £20 18s 6d by selling lemonade. Two weeks later, at the Sailors' Day concert at the Town Hall, Mrs Earengey was '… a wonderful Golly' and the WVR assisted with the seating and programmes.

In February 1918 a new organisation was formed, the Cheltenham Women's Council (CWC), which was made up of 'societies engaged in community work in Cheltenham'. The vice-chairman was Miss Clara Winterbotham. The next month, the CWC held a joint lecture with the Cheltenham branch of the NUWW, the subject of which was the 'Citizenship of Women: responsibility of the enfranchised womanhood of the country'. The speaker at the CWC May meeting was Mrs How Martyn, nationally known suffragette and social reformer and sister of Florence Earengey, captain in charge of the WVR.

By June 1918, a special meeting was held at the WVR headquarters of the CWC and the speaker at the meeting was a Mrs Ralph Durand, recruiting controller of Queen Mary's Army Auxiliary Corps (QMAAC), introduced to the meeting by Florence Earengey, now President of the CWC. At the request of the mayor, the CWC had been asked to help with recruitment as '… the reason for the special demand for women in the QMAAC (is) to take the places of men in the army who could be transferred to the fighting line.' Florence Earengey stood side by side with members of the QMAAC in their grand recruitment drive in Cheltenham.

It would seem that the life of the politico-social movements – and the pre-war suffrage movement – in Cheltenham had come full circle. Women of a certain age and status had been given the vote in February 1918, the aims of the QMAAC were the same as the original WVR aims, the use of women power was now formally recognised as a branch of the army and the work was on a paid basis.

CHAPTER 7

'We Are But Warriors for the Working Day': Women, Work and Warnings

For the men, war in the trenches blurred class divisions quite considerably. At a recruitment meeting in Cheltenham, Captain Baldwin of the 11th Battalion Gloucestershire Regiment so succinctly summed this up: 'In a little ditch called a trench in France, there is only one class – the class that answers to its country's call. In future there will only be two classes among men, the class who went and the class that stayed at home.' For both officers and men from the ranks, this would be the first time they had met and mixed in such close proximity and realised they weren't so different after all. Women didn't have quite the same opportunity. War was a great separator of the sexes.

WHERE DID ALL THE SERVANTS GO?

There was a large domestic servant class in Cheltenham, who would never have mixed with their employers on anything other than servant/mistress level. Opportunities for betterment or travel for servants were few and far between. As Brooks writes, in Cheltenham '… if your name didn't appear in the "resident gentry" pages, employment opportunities meant going into domestic service – and not much else.' The home front for domestics was just as it said; in situ, in the town, at home. There was no choice – until the war.

In the course of the war in Cheltenham there was a decrease in domestic positions as economic cutbacks hit and the size of household staff was reduced. Colchester-Wemyss pointed out: 'Those with a fixed income … are suffering, some of them terribly, their income reduced, the war claim upon it terrible, income tax is at 25% now and it will increase.' The effect of the war worked both ways. The *CLO* of 25 March 1916 stated that it was the patriotic duty of the 'woman of the house' not

Servants of the future? Girls learning how to lay afternoon tea in a model sitting room, taught by Miss Wright at the School of Domestic Science, Marlborough House, Winchcombe Street. (*Cheltenham Chronicle and Gloucestershire Graphic*, 26 February 1916)

to be disloyal and selfish in employing superfluous servants and a crime against the community to retain women servants who could be dispensed with, due to the urgent demand for women workers in the munitions factories. However, the writer realised the hardship this would cause: 'How to get through the complicated work of a large household with less help will be a serious question for numbers of housewives.'

Maynard Colchester-Wemyss recognised this trend for the working class:

> The effect of the war on those whom we call the working class is that there is a wonderful betterment in their position ... it is getting almost impossible to obtain domestic servants, all the girls are off shell-making ... the merest duffer can earn 15 shillings a week ... and if she becomes expert, and some of them do rapidly, they can earn £3, £4, £5.

This quote from a munitions worker gives a good indication of how domestic servants were treated '... the indignities of never being thanked or addressed or acknowledged at all ... and the mistresses who prefer food to be thrown away rather than let their servants have it ... working in the munitions factory was like "being let out of a cage".'

This letter from the *Echo* of 10 March 1916 paints a clear picture of what one servant in a Cheltenham house predicted the domestic situation would be post-war:

> Does anyone think the girls who are doing men's work in shops, also motor drivers, bus conductors etc. who work a certain number of hours a day will go back to 'servitude'? That is what it amounts to when she has to work from 6.30 a.m. to 10.30 p.m. ... with one evening a week and every other Sunday afternoon and evening off ... and has to ask permission to go out to post a letter. Once she has tasted freedom she will not give it up and go back to a life in slavery. Some mistresses think servants are machines ... and can work all day on a very little food ...

It was the munitions shortage that precipitated the expansion of women's employment which, in turn, would provide work for close on 1,000 women in Cheltenham from 1917–1918.

THE SHELL CRISIS

In June 1915, munitions committees were formed in areas chosen for impending munitions factories. Gloucester's industrialists were headed by the managing director of the Gloucester Railway Carriage and Wagon Co., John Julius Steinitz. The same month, Lloyd George, now Minister of Munitions, made an informal visit to Gloucester. After the visit, Colchester-Weymyss wrote: 'I think England has at last woken up and become alive with the necessity of pouring out munitions of war in a steady unbroken stream. The whole country is being organized as England has certainly never been organized before.'

The Shell Crisis of May 1915 also presented itself as an unlikely opportunity for the assertion of women's rights within industry and trade unions. Lloyd George had an inspired move up his sleeve. He did the unexpected and persuaded Emmeline Pankhurst, one of the foremost suffragettes and certainly an antagonist of Lloyd George, to front a propaganda campaign to convince both women and employers of the need for female labour. Lloyd George provided £3,000 worth of funding from the Ministry for Mrs Pankhurst to organise a mammoth parade through London on Saturday, 17 July 1915 – 'The Women's Right To Serve March'. Forty thousand women with ninety bands playing martial music marched to the Ministry of Munitions on the Thames Embankment. By 6 p.m. there were 60,000 women outside the Ministry. Lloyd George came out of his office to speak to the crowd and in his speech said: 'The women of this country can help us enormously through to victory ... Without them victory will tarry.' A woman in the crowd demanded, 'What about the vote?' and Lloyd George replied jokingly, 'We will get her into the shell factory first!' And they certainly did.

'WE ARE BUT WARRIORS FOR THE WORKING DAY'

Manor Farm, Quedgeley, whilst still being a working farm had also been a convalescent depot for shell-shocked horses. Under the Defence of the Realm Act, the government was able to requisition 257 (of the 298 acres) acres of good-quality arable and pasture land. In September 1915 Lieutenant Colonel J. Curtis-Hayward, owner of Manor Farm, had no choice – the land was needed urgently for the new munitions factory. Work commenced at the site on 20 October 1915.

Output began at Quedgeley in early March 1916 at the National Filling Factory No. 5 and by June there were 2,113 women and 307 men working in the factory. By July 1916, 156 wooden buildings had been constructed – eventually there would be around 250 wooden buildings – twenty workshops, shifting houses, locomotive sheds, canteens, rest rooms, laundry, cobblers, stores, magazines etc. The power house, cartridge box store and gunpowder magazines were the only buildings constructed of concrete. The Midland Railway track had been extended into the factory compound in December 1915 and the passenger train service was ready for passengers in May 1916. In total there was eventually almost 4 miles of standard-gauge railway. There was 9 miles of narrow-gauge rails throughout the site, on which hand-hauled trolleys were used to shift shell casings and ammunition around the factory site, to and from the workshops.

National Filling Factory No. 5, Quedgeley in 1918, where many Cheltenham women worked from January 1917. The high-explosive sheds have blinds over the windows to prevent the sun's rays igniting any inflammable material. (Loaned by the late Jerry Jenkinson of Gloucester Local History Society)

'Never before has a General Commanding Armies in the field addressed the civilian population, at home, in terms as if it were the fighting force,' said the *CLO* on 22 July 1916. Haig had sent a telegram asking the munitions workers to postpone the two days' holiday promised to them in August to replace the Whitsun holidays they had worked through. 'I fully appreciate how tired you must be but two days cessation of work would have the most serious effect on our operations ... to make enough ammunition for the greatest battle the British Army has ever fought.'

As the demand for shells increased so the workforce grew, peaking at 6,364 workers. In early 1917 the Quedgeley factory started night working to keep up with the demand. The *Gloucester Citizen* and the *Gloucestershire Echo* newspapers carried advertisements on 23 and 27 January 1917 for more women workers. These advertisements were placed in the same day's newspapers as a letter signed by the mayors of Cheltenham and Gloucester and Bishop George Frodsham, Chairman of the Advisory Committee for Women's War Employment. In the letter the three made 'an urgent appeal to women to volunteer for munition work'. The three were keen to point out that they were anxious to avoid any further depletion of local industries connected with the supply of food or fabrics to the army and in agriculture or with the Red Cross. The advertise-ment asked for 'Women of All Classes' with the added proviso 'who are not already engaged in work of national importance', to register at the Labour Exchange for the work. The women had to be over 18 years and under 35 years of age and of unblem-ished character. This left a diminished pool of people qualifying on all counts and consequently those applying were mostly those in domestic service and shop workers. Ironically, a news item on the same page as the advertisement reported the 'Munitions disaster in the East of London, 69 killed 328 injured.' Kate Adie referred to munitions work as '... a production line of death which ended on the Western Front.'

From February 1917, in order to bring the new workers directly from Cheltenham, one of the Gloucester to Quedgeley trains was altered to start from Cheltenham, Lansdown station, stopping at Gloucester and directly into the factory compound at Quedgeley. One of the Cheltenham evening trains brought day shift workers back at 6.10 p.m. and returned taking the nightshift to the factory. Munitions worker Mrs Lena Merrett of No. 1 Victoria Parade, Gloucester Road, wrote to the *Echo* on 23 July 1918, concerned at the lack of safety with close on 500 women rushing out of the Lansdown station, asking for another exit from the station. Mrs Merrett told the readers: 'As you may know, it is one continual rush when once we leave our workshops until we are outside the station. A very frequent occurrence when once outside is that someone faints, owing to the dreadful crush trying to get up the steps or out of the door.'

On entry at the factory gates the workers went past a 'Recogniser' who asked 'Are you free of prohibited articles?' Items not allowed into the factory were tobacco, any smoking equipment, especially matches. Strict punishment followed infringements of this rule, with 150 men and 3 women prosecuted. William Hooper of No. 2 The Retreat, Cheltenham, was found with a pipe and tobacco when challenged by a 'Searcher' and fined £5 – a lucky man as others were jailed for the same offence. It is ironic that the Chairman of the Petty Sessions where these court cases were heard was none other than Lieutenant Colonel Curtis-Hayward, 'owner' of the land at Manor Farm where the Quedgeley factory was built.

Marjorie Pendry from Prestbury, a munitionette or 'Tommy's Sister'.
(Courtesy of Bob Wilson)

For their safety, workers wore wooden clogs or felt slippers, depending on what work they did, to reduce the likelihood of sparks. The women wore special protective clothing – flannel overalls or tunics, caps and trousers, coloured to indicate their work area – blue, khaki, grey, brown, black or white. White overalls showed the wearer carried out work with the most dangerous materials. The overalls were supposed to have been fireproofed but to save costs, this was not done. Uniform trousers had no turn-ups or pockets where explosive dust could lurk. The wearing of trousers by women was considered inappropriate and unladylike but it was safe and practical for munitions work. Most of the women would

OUTPUT AT QUEDGELEY BETWEEN 13 MARCH 1916 AND 21 NOVEMBER 1918

Complete assembly and filling was as follows:

18-pounder shells	10,279,557
Filled cartridges	7,005,746
TNT exploder bags and cartons filled	8,489,084
Fuses assembled and filled	3,078,162
Primers filled	11,501,459

Louise Bosworth, so described, was an overseer at the munitions factory at Quedgeley and became famous locally for her untrained but sweet singing voice. Her first appearance at a music hall was at The Hippodrome in Cheltenham on Easter Monday 1917. Louise was so successful she was booked for the rest of the week and for music halls at Gloucester and Stroud during the next two weeks. The review in the *Chronicle* read: 'The measure of her popularity is accentuated as she is a munitions worker at a factory which is taking a substantial share of pulversing the Huns on the Western Front. She is gifted with a soprano voice which, if not over-endowed with power, is singularly sweet.'

never have worn trousers before. When the munitions workers were in the procession at the peace service in Cheltenham the Sunday after the Armistice, some members of the crowd jeered at the women. The hostile criticism was that they were a disgrace to their sex for debasing themselves by wearing trousers and unmaidenly to be so enthusiastic at the cessation of mass slaughter that they themselves had contributed to.

For some, the TNT dust caused their hair, hands and faces to turn yellow – giving them the nickname 'Canaries', but to neutralise the effects of the poisonous explosives they were using they were given a free pint of milk twice a day. The munitions girls other nicknames were 'Munitionettes' and the lesser-known 'Tommy's Sisters'.

Six days before the signing of the Armistice on 11 November 1918, the factory management were ordered to take on no more staff and reduce output at Quedgeley. On Armistice Day all workers were given three days' paid holiday and, when they returned, it was to clear up and close down the factory. One week later 75 per cent of the workers no longer had a job.

WOMEN'S WORK – TAKING ON MEN'S WORK

Cheltenham's new female workforce mirrored the national picture. In the main, they were either producing war supplies, as in the case of the Quedgeley women from Cheltenham, or working in non-industrial jobs where they wouldn't have been considered for the work, such as taking on men's work. Cheltenham was no exception to the national work scene as can be seen by a letter to the *Echo* in September 1915, although the writer appeared to be concerned that the women were not up to the job:

> I notice the Tramway Company have followed the example of other towns in appointing Women Conductors … but when watching the girls dragging the trolley arm, enforcing order amongst a lot of silly youths out for a lark, or upon the half-drunken members of society who wish to argue a point, I am not so satisfied it is ideal girl's work.

WOMEN CAN FIGHT!

Ladies should release men for War Service by Qualifying for Positions in Offices, Shops, and Factories. Boys can help by Training for Engineering.

Particulars and Advice Free (call or write)— Mr. W. M. WHELEN, Business Organiser, 9 Pittville-street, Cheltenham.

Stirring words. It demonstrated the Pankhurst plea that women had 'The Right to Serve'. Nationally, women in paid employment increased by almost 2 million from July 1914 to July 1918. (*Cheltenham Chronicle and Gloucestershire Graphic*, 6 November 1915)

However, one lady tram conductor reached the rank of inspectress (as they called it) but she still had to give up her work when the men came back in 1919.

The local newspaper's pictorial edition, the *Cheltenham Chronicle and Graphic*, was less generous in its attitude towards working women. Its editor chose to show very few pictures of women in men's roles and when it did, the captions were somewhat patronising. Gertrude Healey had the writer flummoxed as to how to refer to her and so he settled on 'Cheltenham Woman "Boatman"'! He continues by explaining, 'During the absence of Boatman H. Healey from Pittville Park on active service, his wife has taken on his work and can now be seen sculling a party round and letting out boats with a professional adroitness.'

This letter writer to the *Echo* in September 1915 seems not to object to women working in shops:

> I was better pleased in visiting a big establishment in the Promenade that the shop is manned by a large number of young ladies … their work wasn't strenuous but they went about their duties in a bright and businesslike manner and when my pen nib breaks I know where I will be shopping!

Pictured in 1916, two girl gardeners, we were told, '… were successfully taking the places of men in the tomato and cucumber houses at Kingsville.' The 'Lady Billposters' from May 1917 caption reads, 'Two quite prepossessing young ladies in very serviceable male attire …' Are they referring to the breeches the girls are wearing?

The caption on a lady porter's picture of June 1917 was less patronising and rather vaguely informs us that 'The Midland Railway Company are now employing a large number of women on their staff and at Cheltenham station quite a lot are at work.' Women at this time were employed on the railways in only a few roles, such as the filthy job of cleaning the engines and lamps and, obviously, portering. Some railway companies used women as signallers and ticket collectors – but nowhere were they allowed to drive the trains.

Forty auxiliary postmen had been employed at the Post Office. It is not known if any of the 'postmen' were actually 'postwomen'. However, what was reported was that '… several women who have been instructed in the art of sorting during the last three weeks … won the loud praises of the Postmaster for the splendid zeal with which they helped to lighten the task of their male colleagues.' In 'The Red Cross in Gloucestershire Report of 1916', Captain Frank Colchester-Wemyss, son of the Chairman of Gloucestershire County Council, wrote: 'The Post Office, some months ago, without any warning, put its Postwomen – thousands of them – into hats and ribbons exactly the same as those worn by our Commandants.' One could assume, as the captain was reporting on events in Gloucestershire, that there might just have been some 'Postwomen' in Cheltenham!

Lady billposters in the Promenade. The caption in the newspaper read, 'Two quite prepossessing young ladies in very serviceable male attire …' (*Cheltenham Chronicle and Gloucestershire Graphic*, 26 May 1917)

Mr Webb, of the Cheltenham Window Cleaning Co., was a lucky man to have a business to come back to in 1919. His wife, daughter and four of his employees' wives carried on the business when their husbands and Mr Webb were away fighting. Likewise, Mr Samuel Field, lessee of the Winter Gardens, who, when he signed up under the Derbyite scheme, went off to war in May 1916 leaving his wife in charge of arranging concerts and films, which was a significant and considerable undertaking.

CHELTENHAM AS SEEN BY MAYNARD COLCHESTER-WEMYSS, 22 JUNE 1916

Go into the town you see nothing but boys, old men and women in the streets. The Bus Conductor on the tram, perhaps also the driver, will be a woman; go into the shops and you will be served entirely by women, even in the grocers' shops – the last of the tradesmen to introduce women assistants. Go into the church practically the whole congregation women; go to a cinema – nothing but women, children and a few khaki men on leave … few motor cars on the roads and of those, at least half will be driven by women. Walk along the streets you will meet parties of 2 and 3 men dressed in loose blue uniform, some hobbling on crutches, some in bath chairs … go into offices, banks … girls fresh from Board Schools but many others daughters of rich men, of Clergymen, of officers.

In the summer of 1914, the manufacture of aircraft was very much a fledgling industry. The British had fewer than 113 aircraft in naval and military service and their use was held in low regard by military authorities. Sir John French, the British Expeditionary Force (BEF) Commander, considered cavalry more useful for reconnaissance work than unreliable aeroplanes. However, some sixty aircraft of four squadrons of the Royal Flying Corps flew to France with the BEF.

The Cheltenham firm of H.H. Martyn & Co., better known pre-war for fitting out ocean liners and ornamental artwork, kept afloat financially, during the war, by taking on contract work building aircraft frames as well as making munitions. In 1914 Hugh Burroughes of the Aircraft Manufacturing Co. (Airco) of Hendon, approached the company looking for a manufacturer to whom he could trust to subcontract the woodworking construction of wings and fuselages for de Havilland and Farman planes. Pitching against two other heavyweights in the business, one of whom was Maples, the furniture maker, Martyn's won the contract. Burroughes had appreciated the particular skill and dedication of the workforce and their willingness to adapt those skills.

At the end of 1916, after eighteen months of contract work, Alfred Martyn, son of the founder H.H. Martyn, realised the need for the company to design and build aircraft rather than fulfilling contract work for another company. As a result, H.H. Martyn & Co. formed a partnership with Hugh Burroughes and Airco and the Gloucestershire Aircraft Co. came into being. Registered on 5 June 1917, the new company was formed to acquire the aircraft manufacturing business of H.H. Martyn & Co. The significance of this new venture to Cheltenham is reflected in the minutes of the Electricity and Lights Committee of Cheltenham Borough Council. It reported on 6 January 1917 that:

> … the Gloucestershire Aircraft Company had now decided to take a supply of energy for their premises … for three years … cost of the cable extension being about £750 … this is one of the largest developments in the history of the town … the increased output heralding a brighter outlook for the prosperity of the town … hoped it would be crowned with the success such a courageous venture deserved.

The company name was later changed to the Gloster Aircraft Co. because, it is said, foreigners couldn't pronounce the company's name! As well as wings and fuselages the company also built complete Bristol F2B and Nieuport Nighthawk fighters. The new aircraft company leased space at Martyn's 5-acre Sunningend works in Lansdown, utilising the skilled workforce. In addition, the new company was able to take over a proportion of existing Airco contracts. Eventually, the value of air reconnaissance work at the front being carried out by the Royal Flying Corps became widely recognised and thus led to increased demand for planes. Constructing aircraft frames needed large spaces and, as a consequence, the company moved the making and assembly of DH6 and Bristol Fighter fuselages into part of the Winter Gardens (behind the Town Hall), where they stayed until after the war, sharing their building with the concerts, roller skating and cinema.

Here, teams of women cut out, stitched, treated and fitted fabric to the air frames. The treatment required the application of 'dope' to the stretched fabric. This work was unpleasant and unpopular – fumes from the 'dope' causing sickness. To offset the harmful effects, workers were given one pint of milk a day and underwent a medical examination every two weeks to ensure there were no long-lasting effects on the women's health. The women were paid a farthing (a quarter of a penny) extra per hour for this work.

The women earned £2 9s for days and £2 12s for night shifts, which were day and night 6.30 to 6.30. The company also made observation balloons which required four rows of heavy stitching on each seam or joint to make it gas proof. By June 1918 H.H. Martyn & Co., with the Gloster Aircraft Co., employed in total 780 people in Cheltenham and at Sunnningend produced forty-five aircraft a week. By Armistice Day £1.5 million worth of government orders had been carried out by the company. When fighting ceased in November 1918, the Royal Air Force was operating 22,000 aircraft.

Aircraft workers at H.H. Martyn's works at the Winter Gardens. The girls at the back are sewing canvas onto aircraft wings with large needles. (By permission of John Whitaker from his book *The Best*)

THE DANGER FROM THE AIR – CHELTENHAM PREPARES

Since December 1914 when German warships shelled three of England's east coast towns, a certain vulnerability and insecurity pervaded the country. That fear was felt in Cheltenham. For the first time women and children were the victims of war in their own homes in England and British blood had been spilt on British soil. In all, there were fifty-one Zeppelin raids and fifty-seven aeroplane raids, which resulted in 1,413 deaths and 3,407 injuries as a result of bombing during the First World War. As Kate Adie points out, 'This changed women's status in war: They had no say in going to war, yet they were dying in it.'

The Cheltenham Original Brewery took advantage of the raids by placing an advertisement inviting those from the east coast to 'Come to Cheltenham for the waters' and the mayor wrote to the mayors of the towns affected offering them safety in Cheltenham. What's more, Cheltenham Borough Council debated as to whether it should pay £300 extra insurance for council buildings to be protected against air raids. It was decided not to at that point.

Zeppelins were aluminium-framed airships named after Count Ferdinand von Zeppelin, who pioneered their development. They were a frightening sight, being the size of two football fields and described as looking like 'silver dragonflies'. They needed the cover of darkness to be effective and were slow and ponderous. Once children had been killed by the bombs dropped from Zeppelins the airships' new nickname became 'baby killers'. Eyewitnesses said they could actually see the faces of the men pushing the bombs over the side of the Zeppelins.

The events on the night of Monday, 31 January 1916 shocked Cheltenham's inhabitants. Seven airships dropped more than 300 bombs over seven counties as far afield as Derbyshire and Staffordshire, killing fifty-nine civilians and injuring 109 people. Cheltenham felt vulnerable. It was now within range of airships. The report of the raid, almost filling the front page of the *Echo* of 3 February, contained harrowing and graphic accounts of injuries, whilst playing down the severity of the bomb damage, as would be expected of a War Office-censored report. The next day, reporting on 'Odd Job' classes for ladies, the *Echo* reporter's opinion was that, 'With the threat of Zeppelin raids, it is well that our ladies should be prepared to put in a pane of glass!' Being Gloucestershire's Honorary Acting Chief Constable at the time, Colchester-Wemyss wrote:

> I was rung up about 11 o/clock last night from the County Head Police Station at Cheltenham to tell me that telegrams had just come in from Birmingham and Wolverhampton that a fleet of Zeppelins were dropping bombs. Notice was immediately given to Gloucester, Cheltenham and Stroud and other centres of population in the county to put out all lights in the towns, after sounding the 'hooter' which is the prearranged signal for an air-ship raid.

The Cheltenham Chamber of Commerce at their meeting on 8 February 1916 passed a resolution to impress upon the town council the absolute necessity of timely warnings to be given of the approach of Zeppelins. The warning that Colchester-Wemyss had written about had been delayed until 11 p.m., whilst police rushed around town urging people with bright lights shining from their buildings to extinguish them. Mr Dicks of Adderley, Leckhampton Road, wrote to the *Echo* to ask why trams were running fully lit in Leckhampton Road during this raid warning.

From spring 1917 the Germans began using long-range Gotha bombers which could attack during daylight and travel further inland. For Cheltenham that meant the town was within range and consequently in danger of air raids. Over the course of the war there were to be raids by both Zeppelins and aeroplanes as far inland as Wednesbury, Staffordshire. It was mistaken for Manchester!

LET THERE NOT BE LIGHT

It didn't take long for the Home Secretary to issue a Lighting Restriction Order on 9 February 1916 to be observed in Gloucestershire every night from one and a half hours after sunset until half an hour before sunrise, to begin 16 February 1916. The Zeppelins were dropping bombs on areas of concentrated light. All external lights had to be shaded, inside shop lighting reduced or obscured and blinds lowered on railway trains. Houses were to have dark blinds, thick curtains or shutters closed at night. Street and public lights were extinguished at 10 p.m., unless safety was endangered. For motorists, life became perilous at night-time. Cavendish House and Dicks & Sons also lost no time in offering blackout material for blinds.

Another order followed that disallowed the use of headlights of any description within the boundaries of Cheltenham. However, drivers were unaware that on reaching Holy Apostles they were outside the boundary and could put their lights back on. The inside lamps of tramcars and omnibuses were to be lit only enough to enable fares to be collected and eventually the outside of the tramcars were painted a dull grey colour when they required repainting to further tone them down.

TRAM DRIVERS: WHAT TO DO IN AN AIR RAID

The Cheltenham Council Minutes of 9 January 1916 agreed instructions to tramway employees in the event of there being a raid by hostile aircraft:

A. On hearing the hooter all cars to be stopped.

B. All passengers to be removed and lights put out.

C. The driver and conductor to stand by the car until the all clear is given.

What were the driver and conductor supposed to do if the bombs were falling?

ZEPPELIN RAIDS.

A Large Stock of INEXPENSIVE MATERIALS SUITABLE FOR DARKENING WINDOWS, SKY-LIGHTS, &c., at

CAVENDISH HOUSE,
CHELTENHAM.

Advertisement for blackout material from Cavendish House. (*Gloucestershire Echo*, 11 February 1916)

Lighting restrictions posed problems for cyclists. If a bicycle was not lit up at night it could not be wheeled in the road. Wheeling a bike on the footpath was forbidden at all times; but you could carry your bike as far as you liked – or were able!

Arrangements were made to fix a hooter in the centre of town in addition to the steam whistle (siren) at the Electric Works. This hooter, costing £9, was sited on the roof of the Cheltenham Original Brewery, which was owned by the local MP. At a council meeting of 14 February 1916 it was further resolved that the hooter and siren should not be sounded unless aircraft were reported within the radius shown on a map held at the police station. One letter writer to the *Echo* expressed the opinion on the issue of the siren that:

> There appears to be a general feeling that the sounding of the Electric Works Siren is not the least alarming method; in fact many people believe that the siren, which is anything but musical, has an effect of disturbing the more nervous of the inhabitants far more than is necessary.

Now Cheltenham Borough Council reversed a previous decision and decided to pay £300 extra insurance for council buildings to be protected against air raids. Advertisements appeared in the local newspapers urging people to insure against Zeppelin raids and air raids: '… it is a mistake to suppose that any part of the country is immune from attack', the advertisement read. The insurance companies were quick to point out that the government would not accept any responsibility for damage caused by air raids and householders were not covered by their fire insurance policy.

Not everyone in town felt the measures were necessary, whilst others thought they hadn't gone far enough. Ed Burrows, who had expended such effort on enticing visitors to Cheltenham, was furious. London was being bombed but had no lighting restrictions. He considered Cheltenham was '... beset with panic ... the recently adopted panic measures ... were fatal to the prosperity of Cheltenham as a spa ... plunging the town into Stygian darkness.' Others thought that there were too many flagrant breaches of the lighting restrictions and the fines weren't heavy enough: 'It's worse than useless if nine-tenths of the townspeople comply and one tenth ignores with impunity!' Many wrote letters of complaint about the dangers of walking in the dark. But there was much time taken up in the Cheltenham Police Court fining people from all walks of life for incursions of the lighting order.

By 7 March 1916 the editor of the *Echo* felt it necessary to write: 'Rumour in Cheltenham was very busy and unusually wild, picturing Zeppelins as thick as locusts in the Midland shires.' Major C. Russell of Harrogate, who knew Cheltenham well, wrote to the *Echo* complimenting the town for '... taking the Zeppelin menace seriously' but making a suggestion by asking '... could the town not go one better and provide itself with a battery of anti-aircraft guns ... any of the hills around would be an excellent site ... there are long odds on hitting a Zeppelin but it would make

BOROUGH OF CHELTENHAM.

ÊNEMY AIRCRAFT.

NOTICE.

The following INSTRUCTIONS are issued as a precautionary measure in case of a Raid being made :—

The General Public are advised to remain Indoors during a Raid in order to avoid danger from bombs or defensive measures.

On news being received of the approach of Aircraft, warning will be given by sounding a Steam Whistle at the Borough Electricity Works.

On an alarm being given occupiers must Extinguish all Lights on their Premises visible from outside. It is of the utmost importance that this should be promptly and effectively done, so that no light may be visible.

Arrangements have been made for Extinguishing the Public Lighting.

REES JONES, Mayor.

Municipal Offices, Cheltenham,
February, 1916.

What to do in the case of seeing enemy aircraft. Advice from Cheltenham Town Council. (*Cheltenham Looker On*, 5 February 1916)

them fly higher!' Even the *CLO* agreed, proclaiming: 'It is high time anti-aircraft guns were placed in suitable positions.' Perhaps someone should have taken note of the talented inventor and brilliant art metal worker John Chandler. He designed and made the top section of Pittville Gates and designed splints for disabled soldiers. Chandler had invented a method of defence against Zeppelins but the government wasn't interested as it wasn't thought there was a need for it. Plus ça change.

It wasn't long before the government brought in an innovative plan, put forward by William Willett of Chislehurst, designed to maximise daylight hours. On 8 May 1916 Daylight Saving was adopted. One hour more of daylight was accessed by putting clocks forward, on Sunday, 21 May by one hour at 2 a.m. and then put back an hour at 3 a.m. on 1 October 1916. At the time it was estimated to save £2.5 million in gas and electric light bills. It's a plan that hasn't been altered in 100 years.

CHAPTER 8

Khaki Everywhere Again: Pilots, the PO and POWs

KHAKI EVERYWHERE – AGAIN

Maynard Colchester-Wemyss was often in Cheltenham. Having taken on the role of Honorary Acting Chief Constable, he worked from the Gloucestershire police headquarters at No. 1 Crescent Terrace. In a letter in 1915 he noted: 'Khaki everywhere … you cannot walk 20 paces … without seeing khaki.' The billeting of troops in Cheltenham was such a success that the War Office sent more.

In October 1916, the *Echo* announced the largest influx of troops yet to arrive and the newspaper reacted with a special news column entitled 'Pars for Soldiers', with short news pieces about soldiers in and from Cheltenham. At the same time, all Cheltenham VAD hospitals were full of soldiers, mostly wounded in fighting at the Somme. Cheltenham was to expect 5,250 troops, arriving within two weeks. The troops were from the Worcestershire Regiment, the Warwickshire Regiment, the Oxfordshire and Buckinghamshire Light Infantry, the South Midland Cyclist Corps, the Royal Army Medical Corps and the Buckinghamshire Regiment. It is no wonder that in January 1917 the 'Pars for Soldiers' column commented:

> Sociable burgesses and lady workers who have held converse with our soldiers quartered in Cheltenham must have noticed that there is a striking difference in the speech and idiomatic expressions used by the men – Middlesex, Yorkshire, Welsh, West of England and the high-pitched, jarring enunciation which betrays Staffordshire or Lancashire.

Most troops were billeted in empty houses in Lansdown, Christ Church, Bath Road, The Park, Painswick Road, Clarence Square, Pittville Circus and Charlton Kings.

This time some troops were billeted in private houses. In all, 116 Cheltenham houses were requisitioned and adapted during the war and the military authorities had to put the houses back into shape after the war.

MORE WELCOMES FOR SOLDIERS IN 1916

With the major arrival of troops in 1916 a plethora of clubs for soldiers was started, mainly run by religious organisations in Cheltenham. Amongst these were Rodney Hall Soldiers' Club run by Highbury, Royal Well, St Andrews and Cambray churches and chapels. A variety of institutes offered free admission to the soldiers, such as St John's, Albion Street; Baker Street Institute, Lower High Street; St Peter's Institute, Tewkesbury Road; St Stephen's Institute, Tivoli; Emmanuel Institute, Exmouth Street; St Philips Institute near the Norwood Arms; the Conservative Club, Albion Street and Cheltenham YMCA, Cambray.

Inside the Soldiers' Welcome at The Rotunda, underneath the dome. (*Cheltenham Chronicle and Gloucestershire Graphic*, 9 January 1915)

A Cheltenham landlady, who had six soldiers billeted with her in October 1916, was surprised to see all her tea things disappear as if by magic after she had given the soldiers their supper. She feared perhaps the men had stolen her best china. But no, in her absence, the men had simply carried the crockery into the back kitchen and washed up and put it away – obviously in the wrong place!

Red Cross Hospital Club for wounded soldiers in Clarence Street. (*Cheltenham Chronicle and Gloucestershire Graphic*, 23 March 1918)

Salem Soldiers' Club, Crescent Parade, was funded by fifty to sixty friends of the chapel giving between 3*d* and 1*s* a week each. Of their forty to fifty lady volunteers working the rota, each one, when on duty, brought along a pudding or homemade cake. So popular were the soldiers' teas on Sundays that a system of selling by coloured tickets for different times had to be brought in. One Sunday a few weeks later 400 soldiers wanted tea in a room set for 120 people.

In 1916, with double the previous number of billeted troops, the organisers of The Rotunda Soldiers' Welcome took up the challenge anew, reopened and expanded by taking on an adjoining shop. Again Mrs and Miss Wethered, past mistresses in the art of buffet organisation, took up the challenge. Space was always going to be a problem with over 5,000 troops in town and it was clear that an additional central venue was necessary. Consequently, on 23 October 1916, another soldiers' club was opened at what had been the recruiting station at the Imperial Rooms (behind Neptune's Fountain). This venue was run by the parish church, with eighty to ninety workers on the rota.

The Warwickshire Regiment was the only regiment to open their own club and the only club to have a boxing ring in Cheltenham. For this they took over All Saints' Institute and the club was referred to as 'Very much a men's club … there not being a skirt even behind the canteen counter!' The billeted soldiers were not the only ones to enjoy new clubs in Cheltenham. A Wounded Soldiers' Club was opened in Clarence Street on Tuesday, 20 March 1917 in premises previously occupied by the Military Police.

THOSE LADIES OF THE WVR AGAIN!

The Women's Volunteer Reserve decided to run a soldiers' club in October 1916. The WVR took over the whole of the building in the Promenade, where previously they had used one floor as their headquarters. To free up volunteers' time to run the club, the WVR had to reduce their drill time to half an hour a week and undertook to scrub and keep clean the whole of the building. Their club, open 4–9 p.m., was open fewer hours than other soldiers' clubs and had distinct disadvantages over the church-run clubs – less money and fewer members to run the club. Nevertheless, in the second week the club's participants had used 2,000 sheets of paper for the writing of letters. As the *Echo* proclaimed, '… the corps of the Amazon Army … has pluckily undertaken the running of a soldiers' club … this club is an Adamless Eden …' One wonders what the ladies thought of that description.

YMCA

Many of the soldiers' clubs were supported in one way or another by the local YMCA, not least by the thousands of sheets of notepaper supplied weekly and free to the clubs and the billet mess rooms. During the course of the war the YMCA evolved from a parochial institution to one of considerable usefulness; identifying needs and then finding ways of meeting them. During 'Hut Week' in Cheltenham, the enormous sum of £6,200 was raised by and for the YMCA, including £900 from Cheltenham College and £500 from Dean Close School. This financed a wooden hut to be built

New YMCA Soldiers' Rest Hut at Lansdown station built with the £6,000 raised from 'Hut Week'. (*Cheltenham Chronicle and Gloucestershire Graphic*, 9 June 1917)

at the Lansdown Midland Railway station in order that troops could be served refreshments at all times of the day and night. And who supervised the catering? The ubiquitous Miss Wethered, of course!

At the outset of the war, one well-known Cheltenham tradesman, Mr A.C. Cole, managing director of 'The Famous', was serving with the YMCA in Sling Plantation Camp, Salisbury Plain, looking after Canadian soldiers. His reports give an indication of the vast numbers of troops in just one camp, the volume of mail the postal service had to distribute and the scale of the work the YMCA undertook: 'We deal with thousands of men per day. Our mail bag is around 5,000 daily and we sell £20 worth of stamps every day.'

Mrs Ringer, organiser and 'controller' of the 'Prisoners' Day' parade in 1916, which raised money to send parcels to Cheltenham Prisoners of War. Here she is leading the parade dressed as St George, in chain mail. (*Cheltenham Chronicle and Gloucestershire Graphic*, 19 August 1916)

Another Cheltenham YMCA volunteer, the tireless organiser Mrs Ringer, staged entertainment for the billeted troops, which included teaching French to soldiers two evenings a week and musical evenings at the Racecourse Hospital. To raise money on another occasion Mrs Ringer 'hawked' fish for a day around Cheltenham, pushing a handcart, dressed as a fishwife and 'crying' 'Caller Herrin'', raising £10 in one day. For the Prisoners' Day fund-raising event in 1916, this formidable lady organised an extensive procession for which she personally collected sufficient money for prizes, designed decorated cars with the wounded soldiers from local hospitals and to top it all, led the procession riding astride a horse dressed as St George, in a coat of chainmail. It is said that Mrs Ringer learnt the skills of a properly decorated procession from her time at school in Hanover, Germany!

The man who had been Commander of the British Expeditionary Force at the start of the war was now Field Marshal Viscount John French, the first Earl of Ypres, and in this capacity he visited Cheltenham on 6 December 1916. He opened a bazaar at the Town Hall in aid of St Dunstan's and viewed a march past of troops who were training in Cheltenham in the fog and rain. In 1920, St Dunstan's opened a holiday home for blinded sailors and soldiers at Suffolk Hall, Lypiatt Road, once a VAD hospital during the war and now the Victory Club.

CYCLISTS APPEAR OVER THE HORIZON!

Any Cheltonian early riser on Thursday, 31 August 1916 may have noticed with surprise and some confusion a great number of lights appearing over the hills by the Seven Springs. As the lights came closer, the gradually increasing sound of singing could be heard – the cheerful chorus of soldiers. The sound was from 1,200 army cyclists verging on Cheltenham after a night 'march' of 42 miles from their camp in Wiltshire. By 5.30 a.m. the cyclists had settled down on Cheltenham College sports ground, rolled up in their blankets. By 7 a.m., a small crowd had gathered at the ground, equally surprised to see seven rows of dull green cycles stretched across the college field stacked in pairs.

The soldier cyclists, towels in hand, wended their way to Montpellier Baths but, alas, to their great disappointment as well as to that of the baths management, it was Ladies Day at the baths! By 10 a.m. the men had collected their bivouacs from where they had caught a quick snooze. Two hours later 1,200 men set off from Cheltenham on their cycles to travel 42 miles back to their camp. Riding in file on the open road the column stretched back 2 miles. Cheltenham was soon to see more cyclists when the Army Cyclist Corps of the South Midland Division, many of them Cheltenham men, were billeted in the town in November 1916. In December 1916 the council agreed to an extra payment of 5s per week to Mrs Shetton, caretaker at the baths, to allow washing baths to be open until 9 p.m. for the troops stationed in the town and Alstone Baths was taken over exclusively for the use of soldiers. The week after the troops left it was reported in the council minutes that the soldiers had taken a total of 30,604 baths during their stay.

Cheltenham's Territorial Cyclists. The South Midland Cyclist's Company recruited many from Cheltenham. The recruitment poster read, 'Are you fond of cycling? Why not cycle for the King? Bad Teeth No Bar'. (*Cheltenham Looker On*, 15 August 1914)

THOSE DARING YOUNG MEN
IN THEIR FLYING MACHINES!

The last billeting in Cheltenham must have set hearts a flutter amongst the ladies and small boys would have gazed in awe at the cadets of the No. 8 School of Aeronautics. Six hundred-plus cadets of the Royal Air Force were billeted in Cheltenham from August until November 1918. In May 1918 the RAF was recruiting in Cheltenham for 200 more trainee pilots. The council's Town Improvement and Spa Committee Minutes of 16 August 1918 stated that the Town Clerk had received an order, under the Defence of the Realm Act, taking over the Town Hall, with the exception of the main entrance, the spa and the portion of the building on the east side of the main hall. The War Office requisition was for the Town Hall's main hall, pillar room and supper room. A local riding school and thirty-three private houses were also taken over for accommodation. Meals were provided at the Town Hall and 140 girls and women volunteers were enlisted for the work – ninety as cooks and waitresses and the remainder as clerks, typists, draughtsmen, motor drivers etc. As the *Echo* explained, 'Girls and women of all classes are required who wish to help the boys in keeping the Empire's "end up" overseas … now is your chance … the pay is good and the uniform quite nice.' The No. 8 School of Aeronautics gave basic instruction to their cadet pilots at Marlborough House in Winchcombe Street, which must have been a fairly crowded place with domestic science classes, war supply workrooms and odd-job classes.

By September 1918 Cheltenham had become home to members of the Women's Royal Air Force who were billeted in Cheltenham. The YWCA had been asked by the military authorities to provide a rest house and tearoom immediately for the girls of the WRAF. After quick negotiations, the YWCA were offered No. 10 the Promenade and swiftly put out an appeal for furniture, pianos, sofas and carpets etc. After the Farewell Ball on 9 January 1919 the local members of the WRAF were demobilised.

The Parks and Recreation Committee also received a request on 23 October 1918, asking that the use of the town's recreation grounds be granted to the cadets for football and other games. Initially, the plan had been to take over the East Gloucestershire Cricket Ground for recreation and a small ground for practising taxi-ing planes. A Royal Flying Corps airfield had been established at Rendcombe from early 1916. John Lance & Co., the Cheltenham drapers, advertised itself as outfitters for the Royal Air Force. The pilots could keep themselves cosy with camel hair fleece helmets and Jaeger three-layered camel hair sleeping bags. After their brief sojourn in Cheltenham, the cadet pilots moved on to Shorncliffe in November 1918 and their place was taken over by No. 9 Observers School of Aeronautics.

The Post Office in Cheltenham encouraged its staff to sign up – all having received a letter to that effect. Of the 253 permanent male staff employed in Cheltenham, 125 went to war. Nine of them died, including two messenger boys. They represented all parts of the military and navy as well as the Post Office Rifles. The staff left at home were encouraged to subscribe to the Post Office Relief Fund and to support local charities. For example, in 1917 eighty-four members of the indoor staff of the Cheltenham Post Office paid for a spinal chair for wounded soldiers in St John Hospital, Gloucester Road.

John Woodington Morgan, pictured here with his family, was a telegraphist clerk at the general post office in the Promenade in Cheltenham. He lived at No. 7 Jersey Place, Cheltenham, with his wife Charlotte and daughters Janet aged 12 years and Irene, 8 years old. He enlisted on 25 April 1915 as a result of the massive Easter recruitment rally. Aged 42, John was too old for fighting

John Woodington Morgan, with wife Charlotte and daughters Janet and Irene, one of the 125 Cheltenham Post Office staff who went to war. He enlisted in the Royal Engineers Postal Section in a non-combatant role, being 42 years old. (By permission of Julia Manning)

Cheltenham Post Office's volume of business on Wednesday, 22 December 1915 made records. Despatched from Cheltenham over two nights were 171 postal cases containing parcels and overseas post to the army. Christmas morning's postal delivery was the heaviest ever known. It was reported 'With a greatly depleted staff ... thanks to the enthusiasm of the postal workers not a single parcel or packet sent overnight was undelivered.'

and was therefore in a non-combatant role in the military. Along with thirteen members of the Cheltenham Post Office staff, John joined the Royal Engineer's Postal Section, responsible for delivering mail to the military during the war. John Morgan would probably have been at one of the army sorting offices in Boulogne, Le Havre or Calais. All mail for the Western Front was sorted at the Post Office's London Home Depot, housed in the biggest wooden structure in the world at the time, covering 5 acres of Regents Park and employing more than 2,500 people. From here the Army Postal Service took over sending post overseas to the soldiers. In 1917 the Army Postal Service carried 19,000 mailbags across the Channel each day,

Cyril Caudle, formerly a well-known Cheltenham postman, was described as a clever and low amateur comedian, impersonator and vocal humorist when he signed up in June 1915. Having been badly gassed whilst serving with the 14th Battalion Gloucestershire Regiment (Bantams), Cyril spent some months in hospital but was back on base duty at Horfield Barracks in September 1916. Subsequent reports in the paper told of Sergeant Caudle's new duties when he often came to Cheltenham to escort absentee soldiers and conscientious objectors from the courts to wherever they had been sent.

A Roll of Honour of all the staff of the Post Office who had served in the war was unveiled by MP Sir James Agg-Gardner at a ceremony on 22 October 1918. It was to hang below the clock in the main Post Office in the Promenade and is now on a stairwell at the Sorting Office, not on public view. At the unveiling the Cheltenham Postmaster paid particular note of two of the postal staff who had received awards for bravery – Mr Reginald Evans, who had been awarded the Military Medal, and Mr F. Miller, who recieved the DCM and Croix de Guerre. Reg Evans, a postman, enlisted in Cheltenham in June 1916 and was called up in January 1917. He was awarded the Military Medal for his part in action on 30 November 1917 at the Battle of Cambrai. Nellie Wright, a sergeant in the Women's Land Army Timber Section, worked in the timber yard at Moreton-in-Marsh and at Shab Hill, outside Cheltenham. Nellie was billeted at No. 110 Fairview Road with Reg's family. The two married in December 1920 and, post-war, Reg continued work as a postman, retiring after forty-six years' service.

LETTERS FROM OUR TROOPS –
ONE LECKHAMPTON STALWART

The *Echo* regularly printed news about Cheltenham's soldiers and these snippets about Walter Ballinger are of particular interest. Ballinger was one of the rioters known as the 'Leckhampton Stalwarts', jailed for their actions nine years previously for defending rights of way over Leckhampton Hill. Henry Dale of Leckhampton Quarries and Dale, Forty Pianos in the Promenade, had fenced off the paths on the hill. The case went to court but the stalwarts lost their case. Known as 'Pooser' and dubbed 'King of the Common', Ballinger was a platelayer with the Railway Company and lived with his mother at 1 Karoo Cottages, Church Lane, Leckhampton. In his army record he claims not to have been in prison and to be 38 years 11 months. He was, in fact, a few weeks off his forty-sixth birthday – not only the young lied about their age to enlist! Ballinger joined the 1st Gloucestershire Royal Engineer Volunteers and was in the 113th (Railway Company) of the Royal Engineers. Like John Morgan, these were older men skilled in certain trades, enlisting for working not for fighting. Described as being 'powerfully built', as a sapper Ballinger was sent to France to build new railways close up to the trenches, repair damaged bridges and rail lines. As he left Cheltenham for training at Longmore, on 6 January 1915, along with thirteen others from Cheltenham, he told the *Echo* reporter: 'I'm off to fight for what I'm not allowed to walk over.'

A letter from Ballinger, written whilst serving in France in July 1915, was in thanks for having received a parcel from Cheltenham, from those sent out from the Drill Hall by the Cheltenham Traders' Association:

> … I am often reminded of my native town by surroundings, especially when I see the hills in the distance. I remember when I was but a youth and roamed the Leckhampton Hill at my leisure and when every part of the same was free to the public. But alas! When I see the barbed-wire entanglements here, I am reminded of the narrow paths with a wire fence either side to keep to the footpath on Leckhampton Hill! The fight we had for the people's rights; but we were defeated. Today we are fighting a different foe, and we will never quit the field until we have conquered this foe. Walter Ballinger, Corpl R.E. In the Field 22nd July 1915.

One letter from a Cheltenham soldier at the front tells of his chance encounter with another Cheltonian: 'The first Cheltonian I came across was Victor Barnett, despatch rider, tearing through our lines with a "and-there-ain't-no-copper-at-the-top-of-Lansdown-Road-to-stop-this-outfit" sort of manner!'

The Royal Engineer's Railway Brigade outside the Cheltenham recruitment office on 6 January 1915. The Leckhampton Hill riots 'stalwart' Walter Ballinger, a railway plate layer, is on the back row in a bowler hat. He told the reporter 'I'm off to fight for what I can't walk over.' (*Cheltenham Chronicle and Gloucestershire Graphic*, 23 January 1915)

Walter Ballinger is further mentioned when the *Echo* reported: 'Corporal Ballinger, who, big fellow that he is, writes with the smallest hand of the 451 soldiers whose notes we have read, has carried very poignant recollections of his beloved hill with him to the front.' Walter Ballinger survived the war and returned to live back in sight of his beloved Leckhampton Hill, being present at the ceremony when the council purchased the hill and declared it officially open to the public in September 1929. Walter died in 1939.

Sad letters from wives appeared in the paper such as that from the wife of a soldier. She asks, 'Have you seen my husband? Letters to him are returned "Wounded", "Hospital", "Unable to Trace"'.

CHELTENHAM'S PRISONERS OF WAR
AND TWO REMARKABLE LADIES

The large basement at Dumfries House in Bayshill (now Butler's Fuels) became the source of a lifeline to 197 prisoners of war (POWs) from Cheltenham. The house was the home of Mrs Elphinstone Shaw, wife of an Indian Army colonel and daughter and sister-in-law of Indian Army generals. Having been married in India, Mrs Shaw returned to Cheltenham in 1895 to join her sister and family. Since October 1914 Mrs Shaw had been sending parcels of her own accord to prisoners of war from Cheltenham. The Prisoners of War Fund Committee, part of the Cheltenham Traders' Association, was formed in July 1915, as a result of 'Soldiers' Day' held in the town in June. Mrs Shaw and her daughter, Mrs Hearle Cole, were asked to serve on the Committee and to take on, officially, the organisation and despatch of parcels to captured Cheltenham soldiers. At the time it was considered that 'their onerous duties will extend over some weeks, maybe months'!

The first batch of thirteen parcels, sent out in July 1915, contained sugar, Nestlé milk, café au lait, golden syrup, herrings, bacon, camp pies, towels and soap, pencils, tobacco, bread, cake and pipes. Local traders had to submit a tender to supply the organisation. A letter appeared in the *Echo* from Mrs Hearle Cole on 17 July 1915, advising people to note that the German authorities had requested that if they were to send their own parcels to POWs, the parcels must be sewn up in canvas, linen or sacking with the address to be written on linen and sewn on to the parcel, as brown paper parcels were falling apart.

Letters of thanks came flowing in to Dumfries House from POWs and their families and, as a result, in September 1915 Mrs Shaw was asking for warm vests and worn boots for the POWs, as they had requested. Three months later the *Echo* had started a fund to supplement money coming from the Traders' Association's efforts, so great was the need, and this fund continued throughout the war. Some townspeople 'adopted' a POW and gave money regularly to pay for his parcels. By December 1915 Mrs Shaw and her team of volunteers were sending eighty parcels a month at a cost of 5s each, weighing 11lb and including a cardigan jacket, muffler, cake, sweets, roast beef, raisins, tobacco and cigarettes, apple mould, milk, tea, cocoa, Vaseline and a handkerchief. Mrs Shaw was able to pass on, through the pages of the newspapers, useful snippets of advice to POWs' families. One returning soldier wrote, 'I shall always remember Mrs Shaw who gave me food when I was hungry and consoled me when I was sad.'

By September 1917, demand had risen to seventy parcels per week, packed by several lady assistants, and the *Echo* fund had raised £1,166 15s 7d. The work, by this time, was considered to be of sufficient importance to be taken under government 'control' but was still not given any government subsidies or grants. In effect, Cheltenham POWs were supported by their own people. When food rationing was brought in, the 'government control' was evident in that the only food allowed out of the country was to be specifically for POWs but not for internees. On 9 December 1917 Mrs Shaw died suddenly. She was held in such high regard that her obituary spoke of her thus: 'She was a grand old lady, one of those staunch, sterling, fine characters who sticks to a job however arduous.' Mrs Shaw was typical of Cheltenham's Anglo-Indian ex-military ladies, used to rallying support to look after 'the troops'. As one would expect, her daughter, Mrs Hearle Cole, took on the running of the organisation, with help from her own daughter, Mrs Austin Miller.

Eventually, ten lady volunteers, the domestic staff of Dumfries House plus the gardener, Mr Matty, were sending out an average of 1,020 parcels monthly, weighing 10lb. There were 'bonded' goods – tea, coffee, sugar, syrup, chocolate, tobacco and cigarettes, stores of which had to be checked weekly by Customs and Excise officers. Mrs Hearle Cole was answerable to the Central POW Committee in London and to forty-two regimental care committees. Letters from the men's relatives and hundreds of cards from the men had to be answered regularly and personally by Mrs Elphinstone Shaw and by the end of the war Mrs Hearle Cole had to take on a secretary to cope with the volume. One letter of thanks, written on behalf of the Cheltenham POWs in a German camp, told the ladies that their work was vital to the men but that sometimes parcels needed better wrapping, such as the one received where the soap had become mixed with the jam! Another from a Bishop's Cleeve man told of having been moved around POW camps and eventually receiving thirty-six parcels at once.

The financial situation in May 1918 was precarious; there was only enough money for one month's parcels – the cost of parcels had almost doubled to 8s each. In a newspaper appeal it was reported that 'Due to recent great drives by the Germans hundreds of prisoners were taken including some from Cheltenham … so it is only fair to warn that the demands of funds are now exceedingly heavy … and operations may have to be suspended.' In response, another, even larger 'Prisoners' Day' was held on August Bank Holiday Monday, with a total of forty-seven stalls and a procession of sixty-four entrants in fancy dress, organised and controlled by Mrs Ringer. The event raised a staggering £3,300 from the people of Cheltenham.

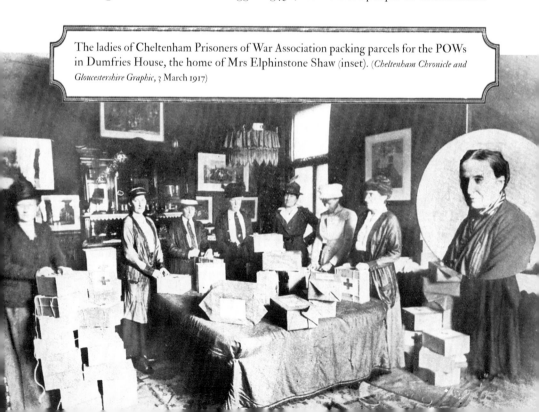

The ladies of Cheltenham Prisoners of War Association packing parcels for the POWs in Dumfries House, the home of Mrs Elphinstone Shaw (inset). (*Cheltenham Chronicle and Gloucestershire Graphic*, 3 March 1917)

BROTHERS IN GERMAN POW CAMP

The two sons of Mrs Marshall of Vine Cottage, Alstone Lane, Harry and Frank, had been missing since 21 and 25 April 1918. Imagine their mother's delight when she received postcards from both of them on the same day in 1919. Harry, serving with the Gloucestershire Regiment and Frank the Devon Regiment, had met at the same camp a few days after being taken prisoner.

Cheltenham POWs who presented themselves at Dumfries House when freed, received 15lb of food, a shirt, muffler and socks from Miss Wethered's County Voluntary Association, £2 on arrival and £1 per week for eight weeks from funds. At the POW Thanksgiving Dinner in December 1918, Mrs Hearle Cole received '… a tornado of applause such as she is unlikely to forget' and a rose bowl engraved with the Borough Arms of Cheltenham and an inscription with the names of 197 men who were POWs. The four maids were presented with gold brooches and the gardener, Mr Matty, with a case of pipes. Five days later eighty of the men made a pilgrimage to Cheltenham Cemetery and placed a wreath, crown and cross on Mrs Elphinstone Shaw's grave.

CHAPTER 9

Meeting Trains, Meeting Needs and Municipal Matters

'It really is too awful to think of the slaughter that is going on; our own losses are more than serious. Even in England we are getting wounded everywhere and they are all dressed in a blue uniform to distinguish them.'

Maynard Colchester-Wemyss

THE RED CROSS

Meeting Trains and Meeting Needs

Early on in the war, whilst the new recruits eagerly marched to Lansdown station for journeys to the army depots, their embarkation onto the trains often had to be delayed. It was not deemed good for the morale of the recruits to see the hospital trains full of injured soldiers. Cheltenham's Lansdown station was on the route from Southampton (one of the entry and exit points from the front in France) to the North of England where the wounded were heading to the big military hospitals. The town became the first stopping point for the hospital trains, for the recruits from the north travelling to training camps in the south and the trained soldiers going to the docks for embarkation to the battlefields.

The Cheltenham branch of the British Red Cross Society made a considerable contribution to the war effort in the town. Initially, the society took premises at No. 8 Spa Buildings, Montpellier Spa Road. In charge was Mrs Lord of Lilleybrook, ably assisted by Miss Alice Yonge, who, in this role, was described as 'a round peg in a round hole'. The Red Cross detachments throughout the town mobilised swiftly and efficiently to take orders for whatever was needed of them and the St John Ambulance mobilised their men. First-aid lectures and nursing courses for women were immediately put on at the technical schools and an advanced course was likewise

In October 1914, in one fully equipped Red Cross train on the way north, the *Echo* reporter felt it necessary to give this report: 'People on the platform thought they had discovered a Ghurka judging by the dark complexion and the figure of one of the wounded men, but inquiry elicited that the gentleman of colour was in the Manchester regiment, he being in everything but his skin, a "Britisher".'

commenced at the Town Hall for members of the Voluntary Aid Detachments, who would become so important to Cheltenham's eight VAD hospitals.

One such example of Red Cross activity happened on 9 September 1914. Nine ladies from the Leckhampton detachment were at the Midland station all night to cheer on seven troop trains loaded with 3,000 recruits. These ladies supplied fruit and water for every one of the recruits throughout the night and then received a wire asking for breakfast to be supplied for another 500 men – with less than two hours' notice. On time, they prepared over 1,000 sandwiches, providing coffee and cigarettes for all. One trainload of injured soldiers must have wondered where they were when, on 3 October 1914, they were treated to an 'abundance of splendid sandwiches and tea and an adequate supply of little luxuries such as petit fours and fresh flowers'. In time, the supplies became more functional.

Occasionally, there were local people amongst the wounded on trains stopping briefly at Cheltenham but, in spite of hospitals in the town, these local wounded were sent out of the area. One such was Private G. Drury of the Northants Regiment, whose home was at No. 8 Old Millbrook Terrace and who had worked at H.H. Martyn's machine shop: 'The poor fellow had received a pretty severe wound but was very cheerful and hopeful … his wife had no idea he was on the train and had only just received a card to say he was wounded.' Luckily the *Echo* reporter was able to tell his wife of his whereabouts.

Hospitals Open at Short Notice

Cheltenham was a town with plenty of large houses of a size suitable for conversion to use as hospitals and with owners willing to offer them up to the Red Cross for the purpose. Secondly, the town's geographical location, on the train route from Southampton, made Cheltenham the ideal location for transportation from the front to the eight war hospitals eventually sited in the town. Thirdly, amongst the town's population were ample numbers of willing, able and available volunteers, especially young ladies with time on their hands, to staff the hospitals.

Cheltenham's Red Cross Voluntary Aid Detachment hospitals began receiving wounded soldiers from October 1914, when the first patients – Belgian soldiers – were sent to New Court Hospital in Lansdown Road. It opened on Wednesday, 21 October with just twelve hours' notice of the arrival of the wounded. Fifty-five wounded Belgian soldiers arrived at the GWR station at Cheltenham by special train from Oxford at 1.45 p.m. The general public was not admitted to the station, except for a small group of male Belgian refugees on the platform. The wounded soldiers were put into motor cars and cheered en route to the hospital.

One week later, the Racecourse Hospital, equipped for over 100 patients, received twelve Belgians and two British soldiers. The first three wards were opened in rooms usually occupied by the Cheltenham Steeplechase Club. In use was the clubhouse – the principal lunching room having the added advantage of a verandah for fresh air for gas cases – the second dining room and the club's upstairs drawing room. Moorend Park Hospital followed on 5 November 1914, which then moved to The Abbotts, All Saints Road.

The Abbotts proved to be too small with only fifty beds and closed in October 1916. Patients then transferred to The Priory, London Road, which had provision for 100 beds. Most of the beds had been borrowed from St Mary's Teachers' Training College for lady teachers, who had moved out of their hostel dormitories at The Priory to make way for the hospital. By the end of 1915, the decision had been made to close the men's department of St Paul's Teacher Training College for at least one year. The intake had dwindled and the remaining male students were transferred to Saltley and Chester Training College. The St Paul's building was then taken over by 140 new female trainee teachers. The Priory was the only Cheltenham hospital with a small ward for officers. The hospital had a 'Cheltenham Ward' paid for by the townspeople who had contributed so much to equip the hospital.

Ambulance Train ward car (continental) which took injured soldiers from the front to ships for transportation home to hospitals such as those in Cheltenham. (Author's collection)

NEW COURT RED CROSS HOSPITAL, CHELTENHAM.

MARTYN BROS., CHELTENHAM.

Postcard of New Court Hospital showing the ward in the elegant main reception room of the houses, and opened on 21 October 1914 with just twelve hours notice of the arrival of fifty-five wounded Belgian soldiers. (By permission of Cheltenham Local and Family History Centre)

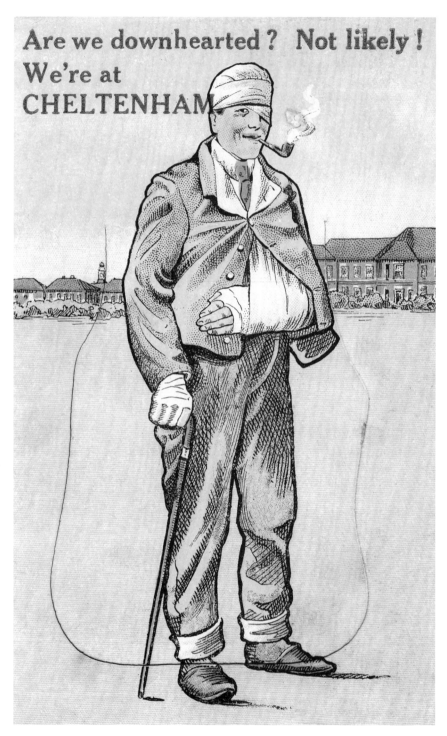

Are we downhearted ? Not likely ! We're at CHELTENHAM

This postcard was made to be sent by wounded soldiers in Cheltenham hospitals. The front has a flap for the soldier to write a message. (Author's collection)

Suffolk Hall, in Lypiatt Road, previously a school, opened in December 1914 and, post-war, became a St Dunstan's holiday home for blinded soldiers and sailors. It is now the Victory Club. Leckhampton Court was opened in February 1915, lent by Colonel and Mrs Elwes, the grandparents of Sir Henry Elwes, author of the foreword of this book. It is now a Sue Ryder hospice.

In May 1915 demand increased for Class A hospitals. Cheltenham saw the opening of three hospitals in schools – Naunton Park on 12 June, St Martins on 23 June and St John on 30 June. By now the military authorities had decided that whole trainloads of cases of any degree of severity – unselected in any way – were to be sent direct from the port of disembarkation to Cheltenham. Trains conveyed from 100 to 300 wounded cases at a time in specially adapted trains.

The arrival of casualties direct from the front into these hospitals meant that the allocation of the wounded to hospital beds would now be organised by Cheltenham's Emergency Committee of the Red Cross. For this new operation, Ticehurst Solicitors gave office space to the Committee at No. 1 Ormond Place. Telegrams were sent from Southampton where the wounded soldiers arrived from the front, to 'Nightingale, Cheltenham', giving the numbers and time of arrival of hospital trains – usually with only a few hours notice. Dr McAldowie, the senior medical officer at Leckhampton Court, as quoted by Eric Miller, recalled the arrival of '… mud-caked, blood-stained warriors straight from the battlefields, the first field dressings still round their limbs.' 'Walking wounded' were issued with a distinctive uniform of a blue suit with white lapels, white shirt and a red tie.

Schools as Hospitals

At Naunton Park Hospital the new commandant, Miss Ethel Geddes, later to be Cheltenham's first elected woman councillor, controlled fifty to sixty voluntary staff. The cookery housekeeping was in the capable hands of Miss Mina Wethered, who had masterminded the catering at the Soldiers' Welcome at The Rotunda with her mother and in 1916 became the organiser of the County Association of Voluntary Organisations. The Mayoress's Linen Committee provided 300 beds for the hospital – given or lent – including some children's cots! Dicks & Sons, the department store, had a good arrangement whereby those wishing to donate goods could buy direct from their Cheltenham store to be sent to the hospital.

One of the Naunton Park classrooms was used as a bedroom for four nurses until they were lent a house and housekeeper at No. 1 Fairfield Villas by Dr Beresford Jones, who was serving at the front. Number 10 Ward, containing eight beds, had been specially reserved for soldiers suffering from shell shock (called neurasthenia at the time) in accordance with the scheme of Dr Prosser, adopted in several London hospitals. The walls, bedsteads etc. were coloured primrose and the roof Cerulean blue, which was considered to be very restful and soothing in nerve cases. Naunton

Dicks' advertisement publicised Naunton Park Hospital's needs so that donors could buy from their store and Dicks would deliver to the hospital for them. (*Cheltenham Chronicle and Gloucestershire Graphic*, 29 May 1915)

Park Hospital also specialised in pathological and bacteriological work, including the Carrel Dakin treatment for wounds by the use of a specially produced antiseptic solution, developed in the field hospitals in France. Naunton Park Hospital admitted, up to 29 December 1918, 2,751 patients with only seventeen deaths.

The Grounds Committee of Cheltenham Council granted exclusive use of Naunton Park Recreation Ground to the soldiers of the hospital during certain hours of the day. Two members of the Committee were indignant that the War Office thought it necessary to rail off the wounded soldiers from the public. Councillor Haddock said it was done to protect the soldiers from the public, who were not to be trusted.

Gloucester Road School was the only Cheltenham hospital to be staffed entirely by members of the St John Nursing Division working with the Gloucestershire branch of the British Red Cross, with around seventy-five voluntary staff, hence the hospital was named St John.

Whilst a patient at Naunton Park Hospital, George Dyas (24 years) of Barton-on-Humber, married Edith Barrett (21 years) of No. 63 St James' Street, Cheltenham, at St Paul's church on 21 December 1917. Barrett was sentenced to two months' imprisonment in November 1919 for bigamy. She had married William Henry Barrett at the same church on 11 June 1916 whilst he was on sick leave. She said her husband had treated her badly and Dyas was very persuasive. It wasn't the only case of bigamy in Cheltenham during the war.

Medical New Ground – and then the Flu

For the medical staff, treating these wounded soldiers would have been a steep learning curve. They were treating wounds and diseases they could not have prepared for – trench foot, frost bite, gangrene, gas poisoning, shrapnel wounds, amputations, massive trauma and disfigurement and then the tropical diseases of malaria, enteric and yellow fever.

Added to this were the many cases resulting from the influenza pandemic in 1918, which killed not only soldiers, but nurses and civilians in Cheltenham. Anna 'Lina' Shaw, daughter of the Revd John and Mrs Shaw of No. 17 Lypiatt Terrace, was a Red Cross nurse at New Court Hospital. She died of influenza on 2 March 1917 aged 33 years and was given a full military funeral at Cheltenham cemetery. Elizabeth Roberts of No. 1 Hanover Street, was working for the Women's Royal Air Force 9th School of Aeronautics in Cheltenham and died on 28 October 1918 aged 20 years old. In October 1918 Naunton Park School pupils, scattered in other venues due to the use of their school as a VAD hospital, were not to attend school for three weeks, due to the influenza pandemic, when a third of the children were absent and many teachers. During a twelve-day period in October 1918, of ninety-six deaths registered in Cheltenham, sixty-nine of them were as a result of influenza, most of the victims being aged from 5 years to 30 years of age.

During the war, in total, 15,582 soldiers were treated in the eight Voluntary Aid Detachment hospitals in Cheltenham and yet there were only ninety-nine deaths. During the week of 26 October 1916, it had been calculated that there were 1,320 wounded soldiers in Cheltenham. Demobilisation of the hospitals started in November 1918 and was completed within four and a half months. However, on the streets, as De Groot writes, 'the ubiquitous presence of severely disabled ex-soldiers provided a constant reminder of war's cruelty.'

WHAT TO DO WITH THE CHILDREN?

That was the question asked at a special meeting of the Cheltenham Council Education Committee on Monday, 24 May 1915 regarding 1,700 Cheltenham schoolchildren. A request had been received from the Southern Command of the Red Cross on Saturday, 22 May asking for provision of 500 more beds in Gloucestershire for wounded soldiers, in response to the massive number of casualties from the front. In an emergency meeting, the council agreed to the use of two Cheltenham Borough Council schools – Naunton Park and Gloucester Road – which were approved on the Sunday as suitable by the Red Cross doctors, providing space for at least 300 of the beds. By noon Monday, 24 May the Education Committee had unanimously approved the idea and Monday evening the Board of Education had sanctioned the use of the schools as hospitals. But what were they to do with the children to be displaced – 954 pupils attending Naunton Park School and 750 attending Gloucester Road?

Cheltenham Education Committee met on Tuesday, 25 May 1915 to discuss where to put the children from Naunton Park School. One interesting option, favoured by the teachers, was to use two wings of the council-owned Winter Gardens, behind the Town Hall. But the £500 per year to compensate the existing lessee of the Winter Gardens, Mr Field, who staged films and concerts, was considered too prohibitive. The playground would have had to have been the bowling green in the grounds and that really would have caused uproar, not least amongst council members who used the green. Disused schools such as Wesleyan School in Great Norwood Street, St Philip's School and St Lukes' Emmanuel School were considered insanitary by the Borough Medical Officer, Dr Garrett. A double-shift system, like that in Reading, was thought possible, whereby the children would work alternate shifts from 9 a.m. to 12.30 and 1.30 to 5 p.m. Those taking the morning shift one week would take the afternoon shift the next week. The decision to take up this suggestion was made by the Education Committee's Chairman (Alderman Bendall), he being also the Chairman of Naunton Park School Governors. When school commenced on 31 May 1915, two classes went to Leckhampton School, two to St James' School and two classes worked the double-shift system at St Luke's School. The double-shift system ended on 1 October 1917 and the two classes at St Luke's moved to two large private houses with good gardens – North Devon Lodge and Northwick Villa.

As for the pupils of Gloucester Road School, they all continued their education by means of a double-shift system at the Parish Boys' Schools in Devonshire Street and Knapp Road. This avoided both expense on extra buildings and the splitting up of groups of pupils. By August 1917 it was found that by using Baker Street School and St Paul's Mission Hall for teaching the Gloucester Road School pupils, the double-shift system could be abolished.

The double-shift system caused problems, reducing the school day from five to three and a half hours. It set free, either in the morning or the afternoon, nearly half the population of school-age children in the town. To prevent the spare time now enjoyed by these children from being 'wasted in the streets', Councillor Merrett suggested to the Education Committee in June 1915 that teachers who were free at the same time as the children should organise games, or better still, take them on rambles and give them lessons in nature study!

A First for Cheltenham's Children

Cheltenham was one of the first places in the provinces to open an Evening School Play Centre in March 1918 at Holy Trinity Infants School, in order to '... provide a counter attraction to the life and loafing on the streets'. The advertisement for a superintendent required that he should be a good disciplinarian and would work for eighteen hours a week for £50 per annum. The Play Centre combined recreation with profitable handicraft employment such as boot making. The leading spirit behind this was Mrs Humphrey Ward, a well-known writer and Cheltenham resident, who pointed out that 'thousands of homes in Cheltenham have been left fatherless and there is an alarming spread of juvenile offences'.

WHAT THE 'LADIES' OF CHELTENHAM LADIES' COLLEGE DID

The contribution of the Cheltenham Ladies' College to the war effort was considerable, due to the foresight and energy of the principal, Miss Lilian Faithfull. As far back as 1910, two Red Cross Voluntary Aid Detachments (Nos 66 and 68) were formed at the college and students were entered for first aid and nursing examinations. As Lilian Faithfull explained, the reason for this was '… to act as a pioneer in training English girls to take their share in the work of national defence'. Little did she realise how soon or how valuable this would be. By 1914 some 400 members of the college had gained certificates.

Miss Lilian Faithfull, Principal of Cheltenham Ladies' College, in her car with nurses at St Martin's Hospital, Parabola Road. The hospital was funded and staffed by former and current teachers and pupils of the college. (By permission of Cheltenham Ladies' College Archives)

In March 1915, VAD Gloucestershire No. 68 was given notice of mobilisation and the college offer of a hospital in an empty house was accepted and sanctioned for forty to fifty patients. The house, 'Eversleigh', in Parabola Road, leased not owned by the college, was converted and furnished with funding supplied by the College Council. The house was renamed St Martin's – after the patron saint of soldiers – and each ward was named after a college boarding house. Girls from the relevant boarding houses looked after the simple non-medical needs of the patients in their ward. The hospital was staffed for the whole war period by former pupils and past and present teachers. With thirty-six hours' notice given of the first patients arriving, cooks, nurses and staff were summoned from all over the country. On 28 June 1915 thirty able-bodied convalescents arrived, tired of the restraint of a hospital and longing for home, determined to have nothing to do with a girls' school. They even threatened to make good their escape by nightfall! It didn't take long for them to change their tune. College was like being at home in a regiment – men wore the house ribbon of their ward and many attended college morning prayers.

By spring 1916, the wounded were coming straight from France or the Dardanelles (Turkey). In July 1918, the owner of the house wanted 'Eversleigh' returned to

Dr Grace Billings, part-time medical superintendent of St Martin's Hospital with nurses from the hospital. It is possible the cross-legged boy is Grace's son, Fred, who became a rear-admiral. (By permission of the Billings family)

private use. The hospital was transferred to Lisle House in Clarence Square, lent by Mrs James Winterbotham, after two months refurbishment. St Martin's ceased to exist as a college hospital on 8 February 1919. During the hospital's last four months, practically the whole staff went down with influenza during the epidemic. St Martin's had, up to March 1919, 690 admissions and only one death. The Ministry of Pensions had asked the Red Cross to provide a post-war hospital of twenty beds for paraplegic ex-soldiers. When St Martin's closed, the Red Cross took over Lisle House to provide this post-war hospital and equipped it with what was left over from St Martin's Hospital. Miss Alice Yonge, the Red Cross's 'round peg in a round hole', became commandant of the hospital.

CHELTENHAM'S FIRST WOMAN GP AND AN INNOVATIVE INVENTOR JOIN COMPANY

Dr Grace Billings was the part-time medical superintendent for St Martin's and also Cheltenham's first female GP, having set up a general practice in Cheltenham in 1899, probably the first woman to do so in Gloucestershire. During the war, Dr Grace, as she was known, was one of the first officers of the Cheltenham Infant Welfare Association and held a clinic from 1917 until her retirement. During this time she was the mother of two small children, Frederick and Brenda. Dr Grace was one of ten doctors giving their services free of charge to keep the Belgian refugees healthy.

Born Grace Harwood Stewart, the second daughter of Councillor (later Alderman) James Stewart, Grace married Frederick Billings, the son of A.C. Billings the local builder. One family story is that she may have been the first woman in Cheltenham to own a motor car. After Dr Grace had completed her medical rounds in the morning she would lend her car for wounded soldiers to be taken out for drives. Another story was that she smoked heavily during the flu epidemic and advised her patients to do likewise, as she believed it warded off the disease.

She encouraged John Chandler to set up the Gloucestershire Surgical Appliance Co. Chandler was an art metal worker with a forge, opposite Pittville gates, the top section of which, it is said, he made himself. Later on he was employed by H.H. Martyn & Co. Chandler was a prolific and innovative inventor, having developed devices during the First World War for improved accuracy for firearms, a lightweight lifebelt used by the navy and a defence against Zeppelins.

Alfred Martyn, who set up the Gloster Aircraft Co., recommended the aircraft company financially support John Chandler's Gloucestershire Surgical Applicance Co. of No. 1 Belle Vue Lawn, Cheltenham. The company came into being in 1915, developing metal splints far superior to the crude devices then in use. It was Dr Grace Billings who encouraged Chandler to specialise in this field.

MAKING – DOING – COLLECTING

Cheltenham Ladies' College staff and the 500 pupils' contributions were wide-ranging and innovative. At first, the girls sent out comfort boxes, gifts of pipes, electric torches, chocolate and musical instruments, accompanied by a letter, to unknown soldiers at the front. The college ran a war workshop where sunshields, sandbags and periscopes were made – the latter after a design by one of the staff. The college's total wartime output from its own hospital supply depot and workshops was over 55,000 articles.

In 1915 the Royal Society War Committee, working under the National Health Insurance Commission, asked forty university and college laboratories for help in producing certain stages in the preparation of Novocain. During July and August 1915, members of the science staff of the college and of other schools in Cheltenham, as well as qualified past college pupils, worked on the preparation of glycol-chlorohydrin. Until early 1916, the college and seventeen other laboratories collaborated in the manufacture of acetal towards another local anaesthetic called beta-eucaine. Another 'war industry' of the college laboratory was the making of iodine ampoules and the younger college girls were able to give some help in this work for the greater part of the war.

Pre-war, the principal source of medicinal herbs was Germany. The National Herb Growing Association was formed in January 1916 to act as an intermediate agency between small growers and the wholesale firms, who would only buy in large quantities. On summer mornings in 1916, some 200 pupils, six tram loads of girls, set out on herb-gathering expeditions to the country to collect some six or seven specified plants. When sold, the proceeds went to pay for a drum for sterilising wound dressings at St Martin's. The pupils also raised money to provide a mobile X-ray vehicle for use at the front.

DIGGING – CLERKING – RECYCLING

A patch of the Cheltenham Ladies' College playing field was dug up for growing potatoes, and vegetables were cultivated in the garden of an empty house. Mr E. Turner, at Shipton Oliffe Manor, had need of help with the farm. The 15 acres of potatoes he was growing for the Red Cross hospitals was in danger of being lost due to overgrown weeds until the college supplied parties of volunteers. A total of 125 girls worked on the land. The same year, Lilian Faithfull personally organised a party of old and present college girls to go fruit picking at Westbury-on-Severn. They rented a large old-fashioned house and worked between eight and eleven hours a day.

MASKELYNE'S UNUSUAL CONTRIBUTION

John Maskelyne, famous magician and the son of a Cheltenham saddler, had an unusual contribution to make to the war effort. At the outbreak of the war he was approached by the Admiralty. Battleship crews operating massive 16in guns were having to work in fifteen-minute relays as they were burned by the flashback after each shell was fired. Maskelyne was asked to supply the formula for the cream he used to protect his skin when handling live coals and red-hot pokers in his act – which he did. Being a pioneer of high-speed photography, Maskelyne was again aiding the War Office by photographing shells in flight on artillery test ranges to help in the development of new weapons.

Cheltenham Ladies' College girls on stretcher drill at their playing fields opposite Christ Church. (Courtesy of Cheltenham Ladies' College Archives LF 310 22a)

From one of the letters Maynard Colchester-Wemyss wrote in 1916 can be gleaned further college work. As Chairman of the Gloucestershire County Council, he asked Miss Faithfull to provide clerical help as so many of the male council clerical staff were serving with the forces. The Ladies' College pupils addressed 400 envelopes to farmers and also collected the results from the farmers' replies.

In 1918, the College Council lent two houses for the purpose of collecting waste material from the college boarding houses, which was collected weekly by the college gardeners and sorted at the houses. When a ton of paper was collected it was despatched to Avonmouth for munition making. Bones were sorted and made into glycerine, also for munitions. Biscuit tins and bottles were packed back to their original firms, jam jars and bottles sold to the local jam factory. Empty tins were collected in the yard and allowed to get rusty and when a ton was collected – a target which they didn't quite reach – they were to be crushed by a steam roller and sent to France for road-building. Even the soot which came down from the unswept chimneys in the empty houses was sold. The honey from a swarm of bees which had taken up their abode between the window frame and the wainscot of a college house was collected and sold. Nothing, but nothing went to waste!

THE TOLL OF CHELTENHAM'S OLD BOYS

Cheltenham College took a heavy toll of past pupils in the war. Fifteen masters were at the front. So many senior pupils left before the autumn term that one boarding house had to be closed. By the end of hostilities, 675 old Cheltonians (former pupils) had been killed, 726 wounded and six were awarded VCs. Canon Reginald Waterfield, Principal of Cheltenham College, wrote to the families of all former pupils who had died, offering condolences and asking them to send a photo for a memorial album he was compiling. By the end of the war he had thirteen volumes of 612 photos. It is said that he never recovered from the heartbreaking task of losing so many former pupils and writing to the bereaved families.

Of more than 400 Cheltenham Grammar School old boys who served, seventy-three died. Awards to ex-grammarians included four DSOs, twelve Military Crosses, two Distinguished Flying Crosses, four Military Medals and thirteen Mentioned in Despatches. From Dean Close School, 103 old boys died out of 681 who fought.

NEW MUNICIPAL OFFICES

It was apparent to Cheltenham Corporation as far back as 1899 that there was a need for bigger and better municipal offices. At this time the council advertised for land or buildings suitable for conversion. Thirteen sites had been proposed and there was also a suggestion that a new building might be erected in Imperial Square. The building being leased in the High Street was expensive but there were other disadvantages. Council Minutes report: 'It was really a disgrace that it should be necessary for the Town Clerk to go out into the passage to see anyone who came to speak to him on any confidential matter.' Council meetings were held in the Art Gallery and after 1903 in the Town Hall. Two sites discussed in 1902 were for a building on a disused graveyard in St George's Square or the Lloyd's Bank building in the High Street. A proposal in 1903 was to convert Montpellier Baths and in 1910 that the Imperial Rooms and building be used. By 1906 the proposals had included the Winter Gardens, the Post Office in North Street and the Liberal Club and, finally, the five houses in the Promenade all owned by different people, sited behind the bandstand where the present war memorial stands.

It wasn't until 1912 that local architects were asked to submit designs for a building, to be chosen by public opinion, for a site set aside within Imperial Gardens. A prize of £100 was offered for the winning design but the eight designs submitted were for a building costing more than the £10,000 allocated and were thus rejected. Unhappy at how the Corporation had treated them, the architects protested and the two best designs by Healing & Overbury and Chatters & Smithson were awarded £20. The remaining six were awarded £5 each.

In the opinion of the editor of the *CLO* in February 1913, the scheme to convert the houses in the Promenade was 'cheap and nasty … and would make Cheltenham an object of ridicule – there is already too much of the "has-been" about Cheltenham.' Using a loan from the Local Government Board, the Corporation finally bought the central private houses (Nos 21–26) in Promenade Terrace in 1913, having prevaricated about purchasing them in 1906. The original houses, part of a large 'palace fronted' terrace designed by the architect G.A. Underwood and originally known as Harward Buildings, were described by David Verey as 'the great terrace, equal to any in Europe'. The building cost around £14,000 to buy and renovate, with adaptations by A.C. Billings.

First to move in was the Rates Department, followed by The School Clinic. This was built in the basement of No. 22 and had moved from the 'insect slaughter house' (fumigation unit) in Bennington Street after stiff opposition. One room contained the 'vermin destroyer' (like a camp stove), a bathroom, two medical treatment rooms and a lecture room for mothers. All rooms had white glazed tiles, bordered with light green tiles. The entrance to the clinic was from Royal Well, possibly to ensure infested patients didn't contaminate those entitled to use the grand front entrance.

In the basement of Nos 23 and 24 were strongrooms that housed civic documents, town seals and mayoral chains of office. The first floor of No. 26 housed the council chamber, 36ft × 24ft, with windows both sides and carpeting, costing £53 – quite a luxury at the time. The Mayor's Parlour was at the rear of the building and the lavatories contained a neatly fitted lavatory especially for His Worship. All doors and woodwork were 'mahogany-grained'. Originally it had been hoped to put a big clock in the middle of the central pediment at the front of the building. The Corporation moved in 1915 and the council sat for the first time in the new chamber on Monday, 7 June 1915, having decided that because of the war it was not the time to hold any celebrations for the new offices.

THE SAD DEATHS OF TWO GOOD MEN

William Nash Skillicorne, Mayor of Cheltenham from the outset of war, descendant of the town's originator, four times Mayor of Cheltenham, son of the first Mayor of Cheltenham, twenty-seven years on the town council, died on 23 October 1915. The mayor, who was 54 years old, died of a heart attack some days after a car accident. Being driven back from Eastbourne to Cheltenham, a tyre burst on his car and overturned. Skillicorne, his two sisters and his chauffeur were thrown out of the car but he was pinned by his arm under the car. Sir James Agg-Gardner, local MP, described him as '… a man of unruffled temper and genial disposition. A familiar and beloved figure had been removed from our midst.' His sister, Miss Edith Skillicorne, founder of the Lady Mayoress's Linen Fund, died on 5 February 1918.

Whilst one newspaper prematurely declared the new mayor to be Mr George Dimmer, his name was withdrawn at the last moment. Although the controversy was not really explained it must have been of a serious nature as the selection committee stated emphatically that it would never sit again! Councillor Rees Jones became the new mayor.

June 1916 saw another death under tragic circumstances, that of Lord Kitchener. On his way to a secret meeting in Russia to co-ordinate strategy on the Western and Eastern fronts, Kitchener boarded the HMS *Hampshire* on the afternoon of 5 June 1916. It struck a mine and within fifteen minutes sank off Orkney. Colchester-Wemyss wrote of Kitchener: 'I certainly think he was the most remarkable man England or the Empire has produced in the last half century.'

Mr William Nash Skillicorne, Mayor of Cheltenham until his death on 23 October 1915, and his sister Edith, who acted as the mayoress and died on 5 February 1918 'having been laid aside by a nervous breakdown after her brother's untimely death'. (*Cheltenham Chronicle and Gloucestershire Graphic*, 16 February 1918)

Submarine Week. Each day this arrow on the front of the Municipal Offices was moved to show the amount of money raised towards the target. Cheltenham exceeded the target, raising £186,958 in one week. (*Cheltenham Chronicle and Gloucestershire Graphic*, 16 March 1918)

Throughout the war there were a multitude of calls on people's pockets to dig deep for one worthy cause or another – flag days, Soldiers' Days, concerts in aid of Belgian refugees, POW Days, Hospital Day, funds for Tobacco for the Troops. So much so that 'The Chatterer' in the *Chronicle* was to exclaim on 19 August 1916 that, 'No other town of the size of Cheltenham has been afflicted with so many Special Days. Where does all the money come from? That is a conundrum to which there is only one answer "Don't Know; Give Up!"'

Cheltenham's gargantuan challenge in the week of 4–9 March 1918 was to raise £100,000 to buy a submarine. Not for the first time was Cheltenham asked to loan money to the government. Residents of the Borough of Cheltenham invested £2¼ million in bonds and war savings certificates for the war loan and in 1919 the town was presented with a tank in recognition, which resided at Westal Green. In 1918 towns and cities were urged to raise enough money for an item of war; the amount was based on the town's population. For the cities it was a Super Dreadnought, some a light cruiser, for others a tank or an aeroplane. It was calculated that if each of Cheltenham's 50,000 population bought a bond costing £2, the target could be reached. The money was raised by buying War Bonds and therefore lent to the government at 5 per cent interest.

The task was in the capable hands of Mr W.J. Bache, the borough electrical engineer and Honorary Secretary of the War Savings Committee, who afterwards was praised as having 'commanded success, organised with imagination and carried through with spirit.' The council set up a fifty-rung target ladder against the front of the Municipal Offices, each rung representing £2,000. A council workman was sent up the ladder each day to move the pointer upwards. Submarine Banks outside the Municipal Offices were open from 10 a.m. to 8 p.m. and war bonds were sold in officially sanctioned shops and banks. Each day was designated for a section of the town's population. The *Chronicle* wrote 'the naming of the days suggested to each class that the other classes were "playing the game". And play the game they all have!' Alfred Martyn (of H.H. Martyn & Co. at Sunningend Works and the aircraft factory) offered every person who bought a bond or certificate at the Submarine Bank a ticket of admission to a temporary workshop set up in the Town Hall, where several aircraft were shown in various stages of manufacture. Shirer and Haddon, one of the official sellers, offered a draw with prizes of war bonds to the value of £5 for the first prize and six prizes of 15s 6d.

Amongst the large subscribers were:

Cheltenham Original Brewery	£10,000
Cheltenham Corporation	£5,000
Cheltenham Building Society	£5,000
Cheltenham Newspaper Company	£2,000
Sunningend Works	£1,000
Monday Professional classes and the private residents	£20,575
Tuesday Ladies' Day	£14,046
Wednesday Traders' Day	£28,746
Thursday Market Day – Land Day	£42,268
Friday Children's Day	£45,637
Saturday Workers' Day	£35,686

Such was the response that the total was reached and passed before the end of Thursday. 'A result,' the *CLO* wrote, '… that probably exceeded the most sanguine of expectations. The present effort somewhat discredits the "pretty, poor and proud" distinction some label the Garden Town. "Pretty", of course – "Proud", yes. But "Poor"?! Well, if we are not all millionaires, there must be some of us who are "warm" in the financial sense.'

The final total raised was a staggering £186,958.

NEW MUNICIPAL MATTERS –
WOMEN ON THE COUNCIL AND WOMEN VOTERS

> For the first time in history, women became fully integrated into the public and economic life of the industrial countries … worlds of men and women were two separate spheres – one that included politics and public life belonged to men the other covering life in the kitchen, the nursery and the boudoir belonged to women.

So wrote author Sean Lang. Under the Representation of the People Act 1918, women over the age of 30 years who owned property or were married to men with voting rights, were entitled to vote for the first time.

This women's enfranchisement caused much consternation in Cheltenham. The *Echo* editorial leader of 12 January 1918 claimed: 'It must be recognised that a woman's political intelligence is likely to develop somewhat more slowly than that of a man who devotes more time to the reading of newspapers … and discussion on imperial and local affairs.'

Cheltenham Town Council clearly disagreed. The first lady town councillor was elected by the council members on 1 July 1918 and co-opted as a member of the Corporation for East Ward – Miss Clara Winterbotham, firstly a staff nurse and from 1918 hospital quartermaster of St John Hospital, Cheltenham. Miss Winterbotham's brother 'Percy' had been elected as councillor for East Ward and had been allowed to keep his seat whilst he was serving with the 1/5th Battalion Gloucestershire Regiment. Over time, this was not practical and Winterbotham resigned. His place had been taken by Mr W.H. Horsley, estate agent, who had been co-opted by the council, until Mr Horsley was elevated to an aldermancy. Clara Winterbotham went on to become Cheltenham's first lady mayor in 1921.

Eligible female voters of Cheltenham, by exercising their franchise for the first time, may have been instrumental in voting in the first female councillor in a contested local election in November 1918. Representing Cheltenham's North Ward was Miss Ethel Geddes of No. 4 Suffolk Square, formerly commandant of Naunton Park Red Cross Hospital. The *CLO* commented during canvassing: 'I hear that hundreds of women in the North ward are unaware they are entitled to vote … when told she can vote her astonishment is only equalled by her incredulity!' The newspaper commentators clearly didn't trust Cheltenham women to know what to do. It was also said that, with so many women voting for the first time in Cheltenham, there would be endless spoilt voting papers. North Ward saw only ten spoilt papers out of 1,385 votes cast and there was no reason to believe these were spoilt by women – some men over 21 years of age were also voting for the first time! Clearly the *CLO* changed its tune once Miss Geddes had been elected in a three-way contest. The report speaks volumes about the content of Cheltenham Town Council: 'Miss Geddes and Miss Winterbotham, being the genuine article of the right brand, will be a welcome set-off to several musty imitations of the sex, camouflaged in trousers, who have too long sat around the council board.'

CHAPTER 10

Pigs and Protests: Trench Warfare on the Home Front

Messages to consumers in the early years of the war were: business as usual, buy locally and don't hoard. By 1916 shortages of commodities, in particular food, led to further exhortations to householders. Petrol rationing curbed motoring for pleasure. By now the message was a serious 'Save or Starve' – food economy or food rationing. Like army conscription, food rationing was considered anathema and 'unBritish'. There were those who considered that giving in to rationing would send the message to the Kaiser that he had won. But food queues caused endless aggravation to the British housewife and affected civilian morale more than price rises.

It was an issue whose effect separated the classes. Cheltenham ladies could send out for their supplies to be delivered, or bought 'under the counter', whereas the working-class housewife with little extra cash had to spend hours queuing for staple items – bread, margarine, sugar, tea and eventually meat. The middle classes complained vociferously; they were not used to being denied items they could still afford. The working classes clamoured for food rationing which would bring equality and fairness.

THE FOOD CONTROLLER

The new Ministry of Food was established in December 1916 with the object of 'promoting economy and maintaining the food supply of the country, increase production and reduce waste.' Lord Devonport, the founder of the International Stores, a national chain of 200 grocery stores, was appointed the first Food Controller. Colchester-Wemyss described him as 'One of the clearest headed of our great business men,' although Doyle referred to Devonport's contribution as '… egregious incompetence'.

In December 1916, restaurant lunches were limited to two courses. Dinners, of a maximum of three courses, had to be served between 6 p.m. and 9.30 p.m. By January 1917, as certain foods were becoming dangerously short, the first measures were put in place to effect food economy. Wheat for bread-making was substituted with anything from potato flour to chalk to bulk up the mix until, as Doyle writes, '… the universally detested loaf was dark in colour, rough in texture and unpleasant in flavour.' In 1914, 80 per cent of wheat consumed in Great Britain had been imported. Britain's sugar supply had been mainly in the form of sugar beet from Germany and Austria, a source no longer available, and sugar prices had risen 163 per cent during the first two years of the war. Sugar shortage meant production of milk chocolate was halted and sugar content was reduced in confectionary.

On 3 February 1917, Lord Devonport issued an appeal asking everybody, 'on their honour', to adopt a fixed standard of food, making it clear that unless this happened, rationing would be the only outcome. Some people, it was known, were laying in big stores of flour, sugar and tinned meats in case rationing became compulsory. People were asked to restrict themselves to 4lb of bread, 2½lb of meat and ¾lb of sugar per week. For the working classes it was a ridiculous suggestion as they couldn't possibly afford to buy that quantity of meat per week and sugar was almost unobtainable.

By early March 1917, bread had to be sold by weight in multiples of a pound. Joseph Robinson, a baker of Prestbury, was summoned for selling bread under weight and was fined 10s by Cheltenham Magistrates. All loaves had to be one of three designated shapes. In March it was announced that there was only enough stocks of potatoes in the country to last a month. Queues formed whenever rumours told of a certain shop which had a delivery.

Again, DORA was used to commandeer unused land, this time for allotments, as a measure to step up food production by all means. Cheltenham Corporation began to acquire unused land in the town, for war allotments, under the Cultivation of Lands Order 1917. Growing food on allotments was described in the *Chronicle* as '… a form of trench warfare in which we can all have a share.' It made people at home feel they were joining in the fight. In February 1917, the Allotments Committee had 140 applicants for portions of Agg-Gardner and Naunton Park recreation grounds, which were let for food production, but sixty-two people still needed land. During 1917, 42 acres of new allotments were acquired by the Corporation to add to the 20 acres already let, including 5 acres in Folly Lane, 6 acres in Albert Road, 4 acres in Hales Road, 4 acres at Orrisdale Terrace, 7 acres in Hall Road with 33 acres let privately by owners to amateur gardeners. Two acres at Heath's Nurseries in College Road, where the present-day A&E department of the hospital is, were rented to the council.

GERMAN POWS IN CHELTENHAM

Colchester-Wemyss in February 1917 noted that to increase arable food production, 'prisoners of war were sent to Gloucestershire to work on farms, but they don't send Germans but Austrians and Hungarians.' However, Toddington Orchards received

German POWs in London Road, Cheltenham, being marched to where they were billeted at Charlton House (Spirax-Sarco). (*Cheltenham Chronicle and Gloucestershire Graphic*, 15 June 1918)

seventy-five captured Germans on 16 March 1917. They were kept in a wired compound and guarded by Military Police from Cheltenham. The War Office sent a representative to Cheltenham with a view to opening a proposed camp for German POWs needed for agricultural work. On Monday, 10 June 1918, forty-two POWs were to be seen in Cheltenham, marching to Charlton House (now Spirax-Sarco), Cirencester Road, where they were housed. Two of them were seen, in August 1918, weeding Royal Crescent with just a young boy accompanying them. Any contact with German POWs, considered to be helping them, was illegal. One Cheltenham woman was heavily fined £7 1s in July 1918 for giving a German POW 1s.

A variety of pictures appeared in the *Cheltenham and Gloucestershire Graphic* showing Cheltenham's growing answer to food economy. In March 1917, Cavendish House employees were pictured making allotments on waste space in Sandy Lane. A well-known Cheltenham solicitor, a Lloyds Bank cashier and a local curate were shown, all digging, with the caption, 'Every able man and un-able man is digging with fervour to raise crops to neutralise the submarine menace.' Staff, both male and female, from Dale, Forty, the piano company in the Promenade, took over the whole garden at Woodleigh, a large house in The Park, previously an army billet. Staff members spent evenings and half-day holidays each cultivating a patch of

Dale, Forty staff growing fruit and vegetables on their own plots in 'Woodleigh', The Park, one of the houses used to billet the Army Service Corps in 1915. (*Cheltenham Chronicle and Gloucestershire Graphic*, 18 May 1918)

'A mischievous rumour has been in circulation during the past week to the effect that surplus allotment crops are to be commandeered by the government. There is no foundation for this rumour which has probably been started by enemy agents.' So wrote Mr F. Longworth of the Cheltenham and District War Agricultural Committee, February 1918.

their own growing fruit and vegetables. The servants of Mr Unwin of Arle Court in June 1917 rose especially early each morning during the growing season to garden before they started their household duties! However, 'The Chatterer' in the *Chronicle* asked: 'How many unused corners in Cheltenham have been turned over by the rich to the poor … we have seen one dear lady who refused to give a piece of land as the idea of cabbage and broad beans close to her window conflicts with her aesthetic tastes.'

THE ALLOTMENT MOVEMENT

The allotment movement became large enough in September 1917 for the Cheltenham Allotment Association Ltd to be formed, under the Chairmanship of Ed Burrows, entrepreneur and publisher. The organisation, working along cooperative lines, was able to buy in tools, seeds and fertiliser to supply their 600 members. At the end of the war the Association represented the allotment holders to campaign for a right of tenure on their plots. Within six months the Association had acquired a further 50 acres of allotments in Cheltenham, set up a depot in Bennington Street, formed a bee section and made a profit of £71. By May 1918 there were 161 acres of municipal and private allotments and 1,516 allotment holders in Cheltenham.

GERMAN THREAT TO STARVE BRITAIN INTO GIVING IN

When the war had not been won by 1917, the German Kaiser was determined to bring the British people to their knees. He threatened to starve the British people '… until they, who have refused peace, will kneel and plead for it'. The German navy was sinking 300,000 tons of shipping per month. In the month of April 1917 alone, the loss had escalated to 550,000 tons of supplies. One grain ship sunk at the beginning of May, with the loss of 5,000 tons of wheat, would have fed the combined population of Cheltenham, Tewkesbury and Gloucester for six months. The country had become so short of supplies there was only enough wheat to make bread for six weeks.

Under DORA, the Cakes and Pastry Order of 23 April forbade the manufacture and sale of crumpets, muffins and light pastries. Bread was not to be sold until twelve hours old. Strangely, no customer served between 3–6 p.m. could be sold more than 2oz of bread, cake, buns, scones or biscuits in teashops and scones were not to contain sugar. Restaurants were ordered to have one meatless day and five potato-less days each week. The poor potato harvest meant there would be fewer seed potatoes for planting the next year's crop. This prompted Lord Devonport to issue 15,000 tons of seed potatoes, mostly to allotment holders around the country, to try to ensure a crop for the coming season. Counties were asked by the Food Controller to set up, through county War Savings Associations, 'a vigorous food economy campaign'. At a meeting held on 11 April 1917, Cheltenham decided to form its own Food Control Campaign Committee to deal with food, food economy exhibitions and campaigns and to set up communal kitchens in Cheltenham. As the *Chronicle*'s 'Chatterer' exclaimed, 'Another committee … the food question is with us with a vengeance!'

The King issued a proclamation on 2 May 1917, read out in churches all over the country four Sundays running, asking people to reduce their intake of bread by at least a quarter and to abstain from using flour in pastry. On hearing this, one woman was overheard to say, 'In my household we hardly eat any bread at all. We practically live on toast.' Government propaganda suggested, 'Eat slowly, you will need less food.' Bread prices rose even higher, taking it almost out of the price bracket of the working-class housewife who spent one fifth of total food expenditure on bread and flour and relied on it to fill up a hungry family. In time the government had to subsidise the humble loaf, fixing the price at 9*d*. Under DORA the wheat crisis prohibited the sale of products such as wallpaper paste and starch for stiffening linen. Game shooting was forbidden, to preserve lead and grain, as was throwing rice at weddings, feeding wild birds or stray dogs and making sugar icing. Cheltenham Town Council Minutes of 5 May reported the arrival of an extra 8 tons of seed potatoes from the County War Agricultural Committee and a week later 17 tons more were distributed amongst allotment holders.

Lord Devonport asked the nation on 29 May 1917 to respond to the King's message by wearing a purple ribbon which read 'I Eat Less Bread'. The next day Devonport resigned his post as Food Controller for health reasons, to be replaced on 15 June 1917 by Lord Rhonnda, the Welsh 'Coal King'.

Food economy messages targeted all social classes in Cheltenham, and were even shown to cinema audiences between screenings. The Mayor of Cheltenham, in a speech at the Town Hall on Saturday 5 May, told the audience, 'It is up to the well-to-do classes to leave the cheap bread – the wheaten loaf – for the poorer people as bread is their staple food and manual labourers require 7lb of wheaten bread a week. Meat – leave the cheaper cuts for the poor.' The same day, the Food Campaign Committee organised a procession from the Municipal Offices, led by a bugle band and a troop of Boy Scouts holding banners which read, 'Spare Bread and Win the War', 'Gluttony is the only enemy you need fear' and 'There should be no food hoarding, which is a crime, and no waste, which is a sin'. Giving speeches along the route, at the Gordon Lamp and the Midland station, standing in a decorated motor car, were Mr Bache (the borough electrical engineer), Councillor Alfred Mann (a coal merchant) and the rector of the parish church, the Revd H.A. Wilson. The rector had also spoken on the stage of The Hippodrome in between 'turns'. However, 'The Chatterer' in the *Chronicle* felt that 'Giving over the Long Garden outside the Municipal Offices to vegetables not tulips would have been more effective than the Rector's excellent three minute speeches at the picture houses.'

A meeting on 'Food Economy for Housekeepers, Cooks and Domestics', chaired by Miss Lilian Faithfull, Principal of the Cheltenham Ladies' College, was advertised for 14 May 1917 at 3.30 p.m. requesting: 'It is hoped Ladies will arrange to allow their cooks to attend.' Miss Faithfull firmly believed in the need for rationing. In the Christ Church Boys' School log it is recorded that on Empire Day 24 May 1917, 'The older scholars attended a parade of elementary schoolchildren ending at the Municipal Offices, where the Mayor addressed the assembled youngsters urging

Food Saving Campaign. The Scouts' bugle band heads the procession with Mr Bache, Councillor Alfred Mann and the Revd H.A. Wilson on 5 May giving advice on food economy.
(*Cheltenham Chronicle and Gloucestershire Graphic*, 12 May 1917)

them not to eat more than they needed.' The children would have been less happy that the Food Controller had written to all churches and chapels in May, asking that activities involving food, such as Sunday school treats, be ceased. Others may have taken offence when the *Chronicle*'s editor stated that '… these publicity campaigns are absolutely necessary to reach the denser sections of our community', but did emphasise the seriousness of the situation on 19 May: 'Unless the heedless thousands who, through careless ignorance or wilful disobedience … can be made to see the ghastly consequence of their criminal disregard … then food rations will be fixed.'

CHELTENHAM'S FOOD ECONOMY EXHIBITION

Cheltenham's War Savings Committee organised a grand eight-day War Economy Exhibition, held in the Town Hall between 16 and 23 June 1917, from 2.30 p.m. – 9 p.m. There were thirty stands from local contributors and 300 volunteers. The purpose was 'to illustrate economy in the production and preparation of food and clothing'. The *Chronicle* described the exhibition in advance as '… a veritable paradise for our housewives, assuming they are still getting sufficient nourishment to give them the strength to go there!'

Stalls included information on Food Reform (meatless and vegetarian food), wartime economy recipes, useful wild plants to eat, goat management, rabbit rearing, home contrivances, the Glove Waistcoat Society – which showed how to make wind-proof waistcoats out of discarded gloves – clothes made from cast-off clothing, objects made from empty tins, toys crafted from waste made by the Cheltenham Toy Industry (a workshop for young girls at St John's church), child welfare and the Corporation Electrical Department showing the domestic uses of electricity. There were over thirty competitions, with cash prizes, for innovative ideas such as articles made of worn out stockings and meals made without meat, potatoes or flour at a cost less than 10*d*. The staff of Cheltenham Ladies' College and the School of Domestic Science gave cookery demonstrations. There were lectures on domestic repairs and renovations and one on how the war affects the temperance question. Cheltenham's voluntary war workers showed their skills and the County Cobblers gave lessons in slipper making. Sugarless war teas were served by the Cheltenham Canteen Corps for 6*d* and demonstration food was sold each day to avoid wastage. Mr Bache, the principal organiser of the Cheltenham Food Economy Campaign, had certainly done all he could for the food economy message to hit home.

It was never going to be enough. The food problem was overwhelming. One letter writer to the *Echo* in July 1917 claimed he heard a rumour that Cheltenham Borough Council had a store of hundreds of bushels of wheat and asked when it was going to be released. At the same time Colchester-Wemyss wrote '… no one really knows how serious the shortage really is and millions don't want to believe there is any shortage and act accordingly.' Newspapers had given conflicting reports, partly due to censorship, in order not to demoralise people. In April, the *Echo* reported the Food Economy campaign had been successful in reducing bread consumption by 15–20 per cent in the town. However, this was contradicted four months later when the *Echo* reported that bread consumption had gone up during 1917.

Food rationing became a reality as Lord Rhondda announced on 6 August 1917 that sugar cards were to be issued to all householders in October and the sugar rationing scheme would become effective on 30 December. The Food Controller outlined possible schemes to deal with bread and meat at a later date and that a scale of prices would be fixed for all important foodstuffs. The three main principles to the policy were that supplies must be conserved, shared equally by rich and poor and prices must be kept down. Councils were asked to appoint Food Committees that would control prices and register grocers and retailers, and issue cards to householders.

On 22 August 1917 Cheltenham Town Council held a special meeting to form a new Food Control Committee, as instructed, to replace the War Savings Committee. The new Committee would have, as the *CLO* stated, '… drastic powers of control over the retailer and whose first duty was to safeguard the interests of the consumer.' In effect, it would be responsible for setting up and policing food rationing in Cheltenham. Chaired by Alderman Waghorne, the Town Clerk and Mr A.E. Hudson, Chief Sanitary Inspector (and Inspector of Nuisances) were appointed as joint executive officers. On the Committee was the ubiquitous Mr W.J. Bache (borough electrical engineer), Councillor E. Silk representing grocers of the town, Mr W.H. Hudson of George's the caterers for the bakers and millers and Mr Leigh James for the Butchers' Association. It was made up of no more than twelve local people to include at least one woman (Miss Alice Andrews, a teacher at Cheltenham Ladies' College) and one representative of labour. The Committee was to control the distribution and prices of essential foodstuffs and to set up Central Kitchens, which became known as Communal War Kitchens and then National Kitchens.

Captain Frank Colchester-Wemyss, County Director of the Red Cross, and son of Maynard Colchester-Wemyss, wrote in the Gloucestershire Red Cross report:

In August 1917, I was warned by Mr Morton of Cheltenham, who has an estate in India, that there might be a shortage of tea … I was able to buy 8 tons at 2s 3d per lb, directly from India and very much to my surprise, the Tea Controller let us have it. It was excellent tea and lasted us for a year!

Colchester-Wemyss also purchased tons of potatoes which Gloucestershire farmers grew for the Red Cross hospitals.

'Not a charity or philanthropic agency but a state socialistic institution based on the principle of cooperation, the main object is to save food by eliminating the waste of labour, fuel and material involved in the system of separate household kitchens': this was how Lord Rhondda's Communal War Kitchens were described by Alderman Margrett. The motto was 'Not free meals but thrift meals' and the intention was that it was to be patronized by all classes. Cheltenham's War Savings Committee, for an initial cost of £25, opened the first Communal Kitchen, as an experiment, on Wednesday, 20 June 1917 at Holy Trinity Mission Hall, Sherborne Street, to coincide with the War Economy Exhibition. The opening day's menu, which sold out, was oxtail soup (1*d*), salmon cutlets (3*d*), stuffed pork (3*d*), greens (1*s*) and flaked rice pudding and treacle (3*d*). In the initial two weeks, Holy Trinity Kitchen sold 2,350 meal portions. It could be described as Cheltenham's first takeaway restaurant. The scheme was that people brought their own jugs and plates to be filled to take home. The kitchen was open every weekday from 12 noon – 1.30 p.m. The kitchen's regular customers were soldiers' wives and children, elderly persons and those living on their own. So popular was the venture that in December 1917 the decision was made to open kitchens in North and South Wards of Cheltenham.

There was a subtle name change between setting up of the first Communal War Kitchen and the second Cheltenham National Kitchen at 27 Upper Bath Road in South Ward on 22 January 1918. Many 'National' kitchens started out as 'Communal' kitchens but the name changed, as Arnold Bennett, novelist and temporary member of the Ministry of Information, explained: 'The popular antagonism to the word "communal" should be noted as Britons are too individualistic

St Paul's National Kitchen and some of its customers. (*Cheltenham Chronicle and Gloucestershire Graphic*, 23 February 1918)

CHELTENHAM

NATIONAL KITCHENS

EAST WARD.	SOUTH WARD.	NORTH WARD.
Sherborne Street, Berkeley Avenue.	27 Upper Bath Road.	Borough Laundry, Swindon Road.

OUR MOTTO: ECONOMY NOT CHARITY.

MENU.

MON. 18 : Soup 2d. Meat Patties 2d. Potatoes 1d. Date Pudding 2d. Milk Pudding 1d.

TUES. 19 : Soup 2d. Irish Stew 3d. Cabbage 1d. Potatoes 1d. English Pudding 2d. Milk Pudding 1d.

WED. 20 : Broth & Dumplings 2d. Fish Pie 3d. Vegetable Hot Pot 2d. Potatoes 1d. Treacle Roly 2d. Milk Pudding 1d.

THURS. 21 : Soup 2d. Boiled Beef 3d. Cabbage 1d. Potatoes 1d. Apple Turnover 2d. Milk Pudding 1d.

FRI. 22 : Soup 2d. Fish Cakes 3d. Stewed Beans with Savoury Dumplings 3d. Potatoes 1d. Chocolate Pudding 2d. Milk Pudding 1d.

SAT. 23 : Soup 2d. Roast Beef 4d. Cabbage 1d. Potatoes 1d. Treacle Tarts 2d. Milk Pudding 1d.

(This Menu is subject to alteration)

OPEN EVERY WEEK DAY from 12 to 1-30.

☞ *BRING your own Jugs and Dishes.*

THOMAS HAILING LTD. PRINTERS 150 HIGH STREET AND OXFORD PASSAGE.

'Economy Not Charity': Cheltenham National Kitchens and their menu for one week in February 1918. (By permission of Cheltenham Local and Family History Centre)

and independent to like anything communal.' The third kitchen was opened on Thursday, 14 February 1918 at the back of the Borough Laundry, St Georges Street, in premises formerly used as an armoury. The Women's Volunteer Reserve supplied the staff for the kitchen on Mondays and Fridays. Being situated in the St Paul's area, where most of the families had sent men to the war, the *Graphic* caption read: 'It will supply a great want in this neighbourhood.'

CONKERS FOR FLOUR, NUT SHELLS FOR MUNITIONS

The mayor appealed in the local newspapers on 4 September 1917 for horse chestnuts to be collected and taken to the Corporation Central Depot, St James' Square. The Ministry of Munitions and the Food Controller had asked local authorities to arrange for this collection to free grain for human consumption. Flour made from horse chestnuts could be used in certain industrial processes, essential to the war. It could also be ground into meal for horses, cattle and sheep and as a substitute in the manufacture of starch. For every ton of horse chestnuts, half a ton of grain could be saved. By 1 December, Cheltenham schoolchildren had collected 8 tons of horse chestnuts.

This wasn't the only contribution by Cheltenham's schoolchildren to the food economy drive. Five school gardens, albeit for the use of boys of the elementary schools, provided vegetables for Cheltenham General Hospital. By November 1917 the school gardens had grown over 18cwt of potatoes and large quantities of onions, carrots, beetroot and cabbages. Commenting on a scheme to set up more school gardens, proposed in January 1918, the *Chronicle*'s editorial considered: 'The boy who likes gardening will hardly develop that silliest and shallowest of modern swank tendencies which holds manual labour in contempt.'

'To the inhabitants of Cheltenham from Mr Rees Jones, the town's Mayor. Fruit stones and Nut Shells Wanted' – read the headline of the letter in the newspapers on 11 July 1918. An urgent appeal was made for stones and shells, the need for which was eluded to for some mysterious purpose, explained only as '… so urgent … and a constant supply will be required during the next few months … which will contribute to the safety of Soldiers at the Front.' The shells and stones, once collected, had to be dried in ovens or the sun and placed in a receptacle in the Municipal Offices' entrance hall. All was revealed in a subsequent letter from the Mayor's Parlour on 31 July, thanking the public and, in particular, the Boy Scouts of Gloucester Road School, who deposited two large sacks full of stones and nut shells, which he felt was proof of patriotic spirit. The mayor then explained, 'these stones and shells … can now be made into a valuable preparation to be utilised as a protection against the poisonous gases of a treacherous enemy.'

The Gloucestershire Education Committee was asked in August 1918 by the Ministry of Food to organise the collection of blackberries for making jam for the navy and army, the blackberry quota for the county being 5,000 tons. Advertisements placed in the Cheltenham newspapers asked schoolchildren and adults to bring the blackberries to their local schools where the teachers would weigh the crop and pay 3d per pound. The fruit was packed in Cheltenham and sent to the government-controlled jam factories. Children from 312 Gloucestershire schools gathered a total of 313 tons of blackberries. The county Education Committee minutes recorded that the scheme was so thoroughly organised by schools that the authorities had more blackberries than they knew what to do with.

ONE LUMP OR TWO?

Householders applied to the Cheltenham Food Office for sugar cards and grocers registered their intention to sell rationed sugar on 1 October 1917. When the cards were issued the householder chose a grocer to register with where she would have to buy her whole supply of sugar for the week, at one visit, at only that supplier. The grocer's own supplies were then based on the number of customers who had registered with him. Sugar cards came into force on 30 December 1917. A letter to the *Echo*'s editor suggested that sweetshops should whiten their windows so that people were not induced to buy sweets, which it was considered they would not desire if kept out of their sight! In teashops, as people were not trusted to have bowls of sugar cubes left on tables, the waitress now showed the sugar bowl to the customers and asked 'one lump or two?' Ice cream manufacturers stopped production in January 1918 and ice-lollies were thereby 'invented', made of fruit cordials and no sugar. By March 1918, Cheltenham's mayoral teas had to cease, due to rationing.

'RAYTIONS' OR 'RAHTIONS'?

A letter to the *Echo* editor of 18 March 1918 posed the question: 'It sounds rather odd to hear two people in tramcars discussing the inevitable rationing and pronouncing the word differently. Is it "ray" or "rah"? I prefer to take this as my guide:

God Bless the Squire and his rich relations
And keep us in our proper stations
And may the Food Controller
Ne'er reduce our rations!'

Lord Rhondda brought in Sir Arthur Yapp of the YMCA, a man of ingenuity, ideas and energy, to boost public acceptance of voluntary food economy. Yapp set up the League of National Safety to appeal to the masses, with emotive slogans such as 'Food Savers are Ship Savers'. People were asked to enrol in the League by signing pledges which stated: 'I promise to abide by the new scale of voluntary rations. I realise that economy in the use of all food and the checking of all waste helps my country to complete victory.' On Mayoral Sunday, 11 November 1917, the mayor, Cheltenham Borough Council and most of the congregation at the parish church signed up for Yapp's Food Economy Pledges after coming out of the church. It had even been suggested that local clergymen should visit all of their parishioners to persuade them to economise. The League issued leaflets such as '34 ways of using potatoes' whilst another organisation, the National Food Economy League, issued leaflets aimed at a more specific audience – 'Patriotic Food Economy for the Well-To-Do' and 'War Time Recipes for Households where servants are employed'. Sadly, neither schemes were a success in spite of the King and Queen being shown 'growing' potatoes at Windsor and Lloyd George planting a kitchen garden at his home at Walton Heath. The Food Economy Campaign came to an end in February 1918 and Yapp returned to his work at the YMCA.

PIG FOOD

In Cheltenham, as part of the food economy drive, a collection of waste food to be fed to pigs was trialled successfully in parts of Leckhampton. It was expected to realise 1 ton of food waste per week if collected in the whole of Cheltenham. By September 1917, the plan was implemented. A council advertisement appeared in the newspapers explaining that householders were to keep any food scraps suitable for pig food in a separate covered pail near the dustbin when it would be collected on the ashman's weekly visit, along with the waste paper. Some of the waste paper was used for munitions, for example charger cases could be made out of old sweet boxes and an explosive tube firer from half an envelope or a couple of tram tickets. Cheltenham was one of the first towns in the country to set up a scheme for the collection of waste paper and food scraps for pigs. Mr Pickering, Cheltenham's borough surveyor, wrote a letter to the *CLO* on 13 December 1917 to inform readers that 'another tangible proof of the economy which is being practised lies in the eloquent testimony of the dustbin'. Since people had been reducing the amount they threw away, the quantity collected from dustbins had now been reduced by upwards of 1,000 tons a year.

Pickering assured the readers that none of the food fed to pigs was suitable for being fed to humans. By July 1918, the Corporation was also collecting with the dustbins, bones, tins, bottles, jars, old carpeting, rags and scrap metal.

SUGAR AND MARGARINE BUT NO PUD

England had only eight weeks' supply of sugar left and in May had only four days' worth in the whole country, claimed Sir Charles Bathurst at a meeting in Cheltenham in December 1917. He was the Chairman of the Royal Commission on Sugar Supply and told the meeting that 300,000 tons of sugar had been ordered from Java, but it was a three-month journey away. Christmas 1917 was the bleakest of Christmases, especially in the Cheltenham Workhouse, which served jam roll in place of plum pudding on Christmas Day.

The High Street, showing Home and Colonial and Liptons grocers in the High Street. The Maypole was on the opposite side of the street. (*Cheltenham Chronicle and Gloucestershire Graphic*, 28 July 1917)

The Cheltenham Food Control Committee had commandeered margarine destined for the High Street grocers in December 1917 and distributed the supply more evenly to shops other than those in the High Street. This was in order to alleviate the long queues around the main High Street grocery shops of the Home and Colonial store and Liptons, next to each other near The Plough Hotel, and the Maypole on the opposite side at No. 119½ High Street. The uneven supplies meant that 2–3 tons could arrive in Cheltenham one day and no more would be delivered for three or four days.

School attendance was affected, as evidenced by the Gloucestershire County Council Attendance Officer's report on 5 January. He told the Committee that mothers were keeping many children out of school to send two or three of their children to take it in turns to wait in shop queues and he described it as 'a distressing spectacle'. Women were taking time off from work, without permission, to queue for food. They had mouths to feed but jeopardized their jobs to prioritise.

On 13 January 1918, a gathering of trades union leaders, organised by the Works Committee of the Gloucestershire Aircraft Factory, based in Cheltenham, met at The Hippodrome in Albion Street to discuss the food problem as it affected Cheltenham workers. Two local delegates, having attended the national conference, reported that a resolution had been passed stating that unless the government tackled the food problem, workers of the country would down tools and there would be a national strike. Mr Creek of the aircraft company's Works Committee told the meeting that, in passing down the High Street, he didn't see any aristocrats or well-to-do outside the Maypole or the Home and Colonial – they were workers' wives. Mr Burge, representing the local Railwayman's Union, added: 'During the recent tea shortage, large quantities of tea had been going into the houses of the well-to-do in Cheltenham, notably at Pittville and Lansdown.' The *CLO* of 19 January refuted this allegation as 'utterly unfounded'.

In spite of the fact that distribution to other traders of a ton of margarine happened again on 19 January 1918, the longest queue ever to be seen in Cheltenham was formed outside the Maypole stores, as can be seen from the photo from the *Chronicle*. At 1.30 p.m. that Saturday, a railway van halted outside the shop and 15cwt of butter was unloaded. The queue stretched from the Maypole at No. 119½ High Street (near Pittville Street) to the Royal Hotel (John Lewis at Beechwood Shopping Centre) breaking at Winchcombe Street and forming up on the other side. The shop was open until 7 p.m. by which time around 2,000 customers had been served. The next morning, seven chests of tea arrived, containing about 700lb, and for this there was an equally eager demand. Also the same weekend, it was reported that 'Butchers' shops had very small supplies and there was a run on pork shops, many of which were totally besieged.'

Outside the Maypole at No. 119½ High Street; the longest food queues of the war on 19 January 1918. (*Cheltenham Chronicle and Gloucestershire Graphic*, 26 January 1918)

Nevertheless, the aircraft workers representatives agreed to send a deputation to the local Food Control Committee which met on Monday, 21 January and the event was reported in the paper thus: '… the point most strongly urged by the deputation was that all classes should share alike with a greater equality of distribution.'

That same day, 21 January 1918, their inability to control these excessive queues convinced the Cheltenham Food Control Committee that something more had to be done. The following day, a proposed local rationing scheme was sent to Lord Rhondda for approval. Cheltenham's Committee reported that, 'The working classes of the town would appear to be unanimous in demanding a rationing scheme.' The Committee also reported that as soon as the rationing plans were put in place, 'a canteen, we hear, will be provided at the Aircraft Factory, where the employees will have a Communal Kitchen of their own. This, to some extent, should relieve the position as far as the aircraft workers are concerned.' A solution was in place; the workers had been placated … for a while.

MEAT SHORTAGE

It wasn't long before the supply of meat was flagged up as desperately short. The working class knew that. The well-to-do ordered their meat on a Thursday or Friday whereas the working man or woman drew their wages on a Saturday and had to do with what was left. There were those of the working class in Cheltenham, it was reported in the paper, who hadn't eaten meat for three weeks but survived mainly on bread. It was reported in the paper on 19 January 1918 that the government was cutting butchers' supplies down to half of that in October 1917 when the average meat sold was

1½lb per head per week. In future that would be reduced to 12oz. Cheltenham's Butchers' Association decided to close their shops all day Mondays, at 1 p.m. Tuesdays and all day Wednesdays. It was inevitable that meat would have to be rationed.

One enterprising pork butcher, Tarr & Son of No. 151 High Street, went to Ireland in February to buy animals and slaughtered them on the premises so as to avoid restrictions. The paper tells the tale on 23 February 1918 that, 'Tarr's appeared to have an inexhaustible supply of meat as they kept the queue going until night-time.' The Waghorne brothers, butchers in the High Street, had no meat to sell so helped Mr Tarr cope with the enormous queues for that day. At the end of March 1918, it was announced in the paper that, 'Owing to the scarcity of meat, the butchers of Cheltenham have decided to close from Saturday 30th March to Thursday 4th April'. A few days later, on 6 April, meat rationing was started in Cheltenham. This halted the immediate setting up of a National Kitchen in the town, as it was thought to be impossible to administer the collection of meat coupons from those attending, the meat quantities served being so small, but a way round this problem was found.

PROTEST BY ANGRY WORKERS

Cheltenham read the rules for food rationing in the *Echo* of 1 February 1918 with a notice from the Borough of Cheltenham that butter, margarine and tea would be rationed from 11 February. Customers could choose which grocer they registered with – either all items at one grocer or a different shop for each item. No inducement was to be offered by the retailer. The amount of the ration was set by Cheltenham Food Control Committee from week to week, dependent on supplies. Registration for ration cards started on 4 February but it quickly became apparent that the number of ration cards already applied for '… considerably exceeds the population obtaining supplies in Cheltenham. It is evident that many households have obtained more cards than are required.' Teachers in Cheltenham's elementary schools were asked to help parents filling up their registration forms. Overall, the administration was deemed successful, hence the Cheltenham scheme was subsequently adopted by Gloucester City Council.

The following week Cheltenham Food Control Committee forbade all shop-keepers in Cheltenham to sell any margarine, butter or tea on Thursday, Friday or Saturday. Stocks were so low this drastic measure was made in order to accumulate a store to begin the new rationing scheme on the Monday.

'The feeling of dissatisfaction that was produced by this announcement … mani-fested itself with unmistakeable force on Friday morning,' so reported the *Echo* of Friday, 8 February. Before 6 a.m. in the morning, several hundred Cheltenham women munitions workers from the Shell Filling Factory at Quedgeley Munitions,

left Lansdown station and proceeded in a body to the home of Mr A.E. Hudson,
Cheltenham's Food Controller, and 'called him up'. A letter was presented representing the demands of the deputation and Mr Hudson agreed to meet with
them at the Municipal Offices at 10.30 that morning. Eight of the protesters met
with Mr Hudson, the Town Clerk and Miss Alice Andrews of the Food Control
Committee whilst a large crowd of munitions workers waited outside.

The deputation was in entire agreement with the rationing scheme, recognising
that it would secure a greater equality of distribution, but protested again the ban.
As munitions workers, they explained, they could not be expected to work on nothing
other than dry bread, which many of them had been driven to in consequence of
the restricted supply. 'We want something to tide us over this week,' they demanded.
Unless they could purchase their supplies on Saturday they wouldn't be able to shop
during the week because, under their working arrangements, they couldn't return
from the factory until 7.45 p.m.

'Are you asking for a preference for Munition Workers?' asked the Town Clerk and
the reply was 'Yes' as they had to work but couldn't do it on dry bread. The deputation threatened, 'If we cannot get our supplies, then the only thing is to "down
tools".' Miss Andrews pointed out that the rationing scheme had been arranged
in the interests of all and asked the deputation if the workers would be satisfied if
they were allowed to draw their week's allowance on the Saturday on production
of munitions and registrations cards. The deputation left satisfied.

Immediately afterwards, another deputation consisting of workmen from the
aircraft factory, led by Mr Morris, demanded an audience with Mr Hudson. Their
deputation's demand was that the ban on supplies should be removed absolutely, not
just for the munitions workers. They intimated that they came not only on behalf
of the workers at the aircraft factory but as representatives also of the Cheltenham
public. On hearing of the decision for the munitions workers it was pointed out
that the proposed action was giving preferential treatment whilst there were a good
many soldiers' wives who were not munitions' workers. What the deputation asked
was that the ban should be entirely removed and the supplies rationed out to the
public on Saturday.

Mr Hudson emphasised that the present stock of margarine in Cheltenham was
so low at 17cwt and, in spite of supplies expected at some time on Saturday, it wasn't

known if this would be sufficient. At length, it was arranged that the rationing scheme of 3oz margarine or butter and 1½oz tea would begin on Saturday afternoon for all, but Mr Hudson urged Mr Morris to ask his workers not to buy any margarine if they already had some in their house.

THE GENTLEMAN WHO PAYS THE RENT

Traditionally this is how cottagers referred to pigs. Pig keeping had always been traditional in Cheltenham, especially in the poorer neighbourhoods, but now became a necessity. Cheltenham and District Pig Society was started to coordinate pig clubs that were being set up in the town, encouraged by inducements from the government. The lowering of swine fever restrictions, the sharing of the meat from the pigs without the need to surrender meat coupons or being charged with 'food hoarding' and subsidised insurance, made pig-keeping clubs an attractive enterprise. The Corporation sub-committee in charge of allotments made plans for a small

Shirer & Haddon, drapers and household furnishers. The staff reared 'six happy porkers' in the stables at the back of their store. (*Cheltenham Chronicle and Gloucestershire Graphic*, 2 March 1918)

piggery of six styes, with drainage to the sewer system, in April 1918, having been approached by Mr Beak of Kennedy Lodge, Keynsham Road, who instigated the setting up of the Society. These styes were to be in the allotments which adjoined each other in College Road called Tip, Turners and Waterworks fields. By July 1918 there were 114 pig clubs in Gloucestershire and in October the Society joined with Cheltenham Market Gardeners' Association, who were already running a highly successful fruit pulping and vegetable drying and canning operation in Cheltenham. Jointly, with nearly 1,000 members, they became a force to be reckoned with when negotiating with the Cheltenham Council to acquire the control of the running of Cheltenham Market.

Businesses also joined the pig-rearing enterprise. Pigs were fattened up in the stables of Shirer and Haddon's, the drapers in the town, where they kept six 'happy porkers'. A larger enterprise was at the unused stables at The Queen's Hotel, where there were forty-three Gloucester Old Spot pigs, fed with scraps from the hotel.

CURFEW ORDER

Taking effect on 2 April 1918 came further restrictions for the southern half of the country, which included Cheltenham. This time it was the Curfew Order, which forbade lights to be used in shop fronts, no gas or electricity to be used on a stage or place of entertainment after 10.30 p.m. and no hot meals to be served or cooked in hotels and restaurants after 9.30 at night. Furthermore, gas and electricity was rationed to householders to five sixths of their usage of one year previously.

MEAT RATIONING

On Saturday, 6 April, national meat rationing began. There were different allowances depending on the person, i.e. a larger allowance was given for boys 13–18 years of age and workers on heavy labouring. Of the four meat coupons to be used per week, two could be used for beef, mutton or pork and two for bacon, poultry or other meats. New to the British table came tinned tuna, fish not being rationed, and powdered soup. The administration of the rationing scheme wasn't without its problems. The paper forms for the special categories were not available so those people had to make do with ordinary rations, like everyone else. The scheme, in the opinion of the *Chronicle* '… leaves something to be desired'.

As the Food Controller knew what quantities of provisions were needed in Cheltenham, through householders registering for coupons, the central supply depots were able to calculate Cheltenham's weekly rations. These amounted to 32 cattle and 329 sheep per week, 15 tons of sugar and 9.5 tons of butter or margarine. However, Mrs How Martyn (suffragette and sister of the WVR captain Florence Earengey) informed the new Cheltenham Women's Council on 30 May 1918 that this week Cheltenham had received only 8 cattle and 125 sheep. The deficiency could be made up one way only – frozen meat – a commodity never previously experienced in Cheltenham. The town's Food Controller, Mr Hudson, had to apply for 32,000lb of frozen meat from the government supply and pointed out to those who grumbled that they should '… think of those who had sailed perilous waters to bring them the meat … and our boys at the front who had to put up with eating this meat and had no choice in the matter.' Mr Hudson's task wasn't an easy one; his Committee had to act under no fewer than 300 different government orders in two years and in July 1918 the ration cards were scrapped to be replaced with new books with spaces left for food that may be rationed later.

FUEL RATIONING

'The day of the darkening order', as it was described by the *Echo*, was 30 September 1918. The restriction stretched people's resilience in yet another direction, limiting the amount of coal, gas and electricity to be used in homes and businesses. This caused considerable debate amongst the traders of Cheltenham who considered that in view of the drastic nature of the restrictions they would have to close at 6 p.m. The bakers of one part of town said they were against 6 p.m. closing as the munitions workers, most of whom lived in the lower part of town, did not return from work until after 6 p.m. when it was their custom to call in for bread. Mr Bloodworth, Chairman of the Baker's Association, pointed out that the districts of the town were so varied in character that it would be difficult to get all into line. The compromise was all shops to close at 6.30 p.m. However, the *Echo* reported that the small shopkeepers of Cheltenham struggled as 75 per cent of their takings were from supplying 'the odds and ends which the housewife finds she needs at the last moment'.

Food restriction and rationing had stretched the patience and ingenuity of Cheltenham housewives as never before. What could possibly happen next?

CHAPTER 11

The End?

'In war, truth is the first casualty' – so said Aeschylus. It is not surprising, therefore, that the news of the impending end of the war was greeted, as Cheltenham's parish church rector, the Revd H.A. Wilson said, '… with dazzling suddenness'. Who knew what to believe? Osbert Sitwell, the author, remarked, 'Victory had rushed on us with the speed and impact of a comet.' All news was heavily censored to keep up morale on the home front. People were tired of war and its effects but townspeople heard contradictory stories from the soldiers home on leave and from the wounded in the hospitals in Cheltenham. This is the way the end of this story unfolded in the *Echo* day by day.

FRIDAY, 1 NOVEMBER 1918

Turkey was out of the war. At home, there was optimism as the Cheltenham Medical Officer of Health reported a remission from the influenza epidemic in the town. The number of deaths was half the previous two weeks' total. Norah Bessie Billings, the youngest daughter of A.C. Billings, the well-known Cheltenham builder, and sister-in-law of Cheltenham's first lady GP, Dr Grace Billings, died of influenza on Tuesday, 5 November 1918. A week later the disease didn't spare one of the 'Leckhampton Stalwarts' who fought for the right to walk over the Leckhampton Hill. Tailor 'Jack' Price of Great Norwood Street died leaving a widow and eight children – his youngest son was killed in action the previous year.

SATURDAY, 2 NOVEMBER 1918

It was reported that Austria-Hungary's army was in revolt. The last of Germany's props had collapsed. The *Echo*'s editor wrote: '… the forecasts published in certain newspapers this week have been dismissed as purely imaginative and ridiculous at that … the German armies have not yet been broken.'

Of the enemy monarchs, the German Kaiser was on the brink, the monarchs of Bulgaria had abdicated, Tino of Greece had been dethroned, Emperor Francis Joseph of Austria had been 'removed by death' as had the Sultan of Turkey and Emperor Charles of Austria was in flight. Germany was in a vice and had no hope but to surrender. The *Echo*'s editor was more optimistic: 'There are times when bare statements of occurrence are far more eloquent than any combat.' The next day the prime minister, David Lloyd George, said '... this is the last and decisive phase of the war.' That day, Andrew Bonar Law, now Chancellor of the Exchequer, wrote: 'There should be no slackening ... the final victory is not yet won ... our armies are still fighting.'

PEACE IN SIGHT!!

☞ ARE YOU READY FOR IT? ☜

OUT WITH YOUR BOY'S WARDROBE! OVERHAUL IT! SEE WHAT HE REQUIRES. HE WILL SOON BE HOME! HE HAS GROWN BIGGER!

SECURE WHAT YOU REQUIRE NOW!

DID IT EVER STRIKE YOU THAT 500 MILLIONS OF PEOPLE REQUIRE COTTON FOR CLOTHING PURPOSES! PRICES WILL RULE HIGHER RATHER THAN LOWER AFTER THE WAR. THEREFORE BUY NOW.

"THE FAMOUS"

TAILORS, HATTERS & CLOTHIERS,
350-351 HIGH STREET, CHELTENHAM.
Proprietor—A. N. COLE.   Close Wednesdays 1 o'clock.

'The Famous', the men's outfitters, heralded on the *Echo*'s front-page advertisement 'Peace in Sight!' and on page 4 of the *Echo* it was reported prematurely the Armistice had been signed on 7 November. (*Gloucestershire Echo*, 12 November 1918)

'Reuters Agency is informed that, according to official American information, the Armistice with Germany was signed at 2.30 today.'

'The End?' asked the *Echo*'s leader and the editor considered it was a wonderful thought that at the moment at which he was writing, the war may really be ended. No, it was not the end. The paper had to explain what had happened. 'The above message from Reuters was received at the "Echo" office at 4.45 p.m. today and a special stop-press edition was at once circulated widely throughout Cheltenham. Later, however, we received another message. "Suppress message of signing an armistice". The reason for the order to suppress was not given.' The premature announcement caused wild excitement in Cheltenham and the newspaper reported that once the special edition hit the streets it was absolutely impossible to overtake tidings for which everyone was waiting with so much anxiety. However, at the time of the false announcement the German delegates had not even reached the French lines. They didn't leave Berlin, 500 miles from the French meeting place, until Wednesday afternoon.

FRIDAY, 8 NOVEMBER 1918

The *Echo*'s leader read: 'We may take advantage of the breathing space before the dramatic news, which it is devoutly to be hoped will be real news and not unfounded rumour.' It was reported that Marshal Foch, representing the Allies, had sent a telegram informing the German High Command where to send their delegates. To allow the delegates the swiftest path, the German lines had been ordered to cease fire on the front from 3 p.m. Thursday. At 9 a.m. Friday morning, ten Germans were escorted to the meeting place, where they received the terms of the Armistice, at which they expressed astonishment at the severity of the terms, to be accepted or refused within 72 hours, expiring on Monday morning at 11 o'clock, French time. The German delegation asked for a provisional suspension of all hostilities, which was refused. Their courier, Captain von Helldorf, was to take the terms to Spa in Belgium where the Kaiser was waiting. Because of German fire, he had not been able to leave the French lines until Saturday.

SATURDAY, 9 NOVEMBER 1918

The Kaiser abdicates. The people of Cheltenham read the following report, which had arrived at the *Echo* offices at 4.45 p.m.: 'News transmitted through the wireless stations of the German Government states that the Kaiser and King has decided to renounce the throne.' At the Lord Mayor's Banquet in London that night Lloyd George announced: 'The issue is settled … the German Empire is Headless and Helpless.' At the same time the five German rulers and their heirs either abdicated or were deposed.

SUNDAY, 10 NOVEMBER 1918

The Kaiser reached the Dutch frontier at Eysden at 7.30 a.m. where the imperial train took him and his entourage to Arnhem in Holland. His new home was to be a castle, offered for his use by Count Bentinck. Whilst in Germany, all the twenty-six ports of the German seaboard were in the hands of the revolutionaries, as was most of the country, including the cities of Kiel, Hamburg, Bremen and Hanover.

MONDAY, 11 NOVEMBER 1918

At 10.40 a.m. news reached the *Echo* office by telephone that the Armistice had been signed at 5 a.m. that morning and came into force at 11 a.m. The discussions between the German delegates and the Allies had lasted all night. A special edition of the newspaper was immediately printed and distributed.

Stop Press in the *Echo*: 'From all parts of the country reports arrive of almost indescribable enthusiasm and public rejoicing.' The senior curate at Cheltenham's parish church declared that for four years life had been the hope of the moment of the Armistice but that it was strange how simple it was when it came. The Home Office announced that restrictions were withdrawn for one week on the use of fireworks, the pealing of church bells and the striking of public clocks. Within an hour of the news being broadcast, the hooters on the electrical works and the brewery sounded out – a warning of joy not of an impending raid, for which they had been intended.

In London, engineers hastened to reactivate the striking mechanism of Big Ben so that the bells of the big clock could ring at 11 a.m. for the first time since August 1914. At Buckingham Palace, the King waved at the chanting crowd outside and then ended his wartime abstinence by opening a bottle of brandy, originally laid down by the Prince Regent in 1815 to commemorate the victory at Waterloo. Sadly, it tasted 'very musty'.

Echo boy's banner on 11 November declares 'Armistice Decision Official'. (*Cheltenham Chronicle and Gloucestershire Graphic*, 16 November 1918)

'The Cheltonians are usually an indemonstrative folk: but today they have been letting themselves "go"! They are mildly mafficking! Armageddon over at last.' This was how the later edition of the *Echo* described Cheltenham on Monday, 11 November – Armistice Day. Several hundred cadets from the aeronautical school, billeted in Cheltenham, were the first to start the celebrations outside The Queen's Hotel, with a *feu de joie* – a celebratory rifle salute fired by rifles in rapid succession. They boarded lorries and careered around the streets waving flags and shouting for all they were worth. It was reported that, 'As everybody said, it was a godsend the cadets were there … for by ourselves we would have enthused feebly, instead we had infectious vitality.' The next day the cadets' impending departure from Cheltenham was announced. Soon the workers from various factories in town, allowed out by the bosses, joyfully downed tools and flocked into the streets. On the door of the Fruit Pulping Factory a notice had been posted: 'This factory will be closed until 6 a.m. tomorrow. We cannot work in these joyous times.'

Rich and poor, businesses and shops, all seem to have found a supply of Allies' flags and Union Jacks to parade with or drape outside their premises. The bars were thronged with people. One person cheekily asked Superintendent Hopkins of the police: 'May we buy you a drink?' He had had to decline; treating people to a drink was still banned under the Defence of the Realm Act.

Grammar school boys in their mortar boards liberated a large drum from the school band and marched with it up and down the 'High'. After morning school was over, a half-day holiday was declared and young Cheltenham added more music and colour. As the day wore on, people appeared on the streets with faces rouged and painted in 'horribly inflammatory shades'. All Cheltenham was out celebrating, it seemed. Even the mayor's buttonhole sported a flag. There were plenty of soldiers in Cheltenham, both able bodied and injured, to add to the throng. Every horse had at least one flag attached to its harness.

At 3.19 p.m. twelve bell ringers rang joyous peals in the grandsire method from St Mary's parish church – a peal of 5,040 changes, ending at 6.26 p.m. The bells had been muffled since 1914.

In the evening the volunteer band headed a procession from the Drill Hall in North Street. The first soldiers to leave town in August 1914, E and F companies of the 5 Battalion Gloucestershire Regiment, had headed out from here on 5 August 1914. This time the band was playing the 'National Airs of the Allies' and people joined the procession. The electrical company staff had removed the darkened globes over the powerful lights in the main streets so that, after years of gloom, the town was ablaze with an illumination more intense than peace time.

Grammar school boys and aeronautical school cadets celebrate Armistice, outside Cavendish House. (*Cheltenham Chronicle and Gloucestershire Graphic*, 16 November 1918)

Women from the aircraft factory at Sunningend Works and the Winter Gardens carrying aeroplane parts as they process jubilantly down the Promenade the day after the Armistice. (*Cheltenham Chronicle and Gloucestershire Graphic*, 16 November 1918)

TUESDAY, 12 NOVEMBER 1918

The rejoicing continued the next day with a giant, impromptu procession by 2,000 workers – many from H.H. Martyn's aeroplane factories at Sunningend, Lansdown and the Winter Gardens. The parade was headed by the work's band with several full-sized Bristol fighter planes on lorries, and workers, both male and female, carrying parts of the planes as trophies. Following them came decorated cars, festooned with flags and banners, a bugle band, a full brass band and ending with the work's firemen. The *Echo* commented: 'It was a wonderfully striking affair, for it gave a hint of the forces of vitality and patriotism especially of the women of our land, which converted the industrial energies into the weapons of war before which ultimately the Hun bit the dust.'

That evening at 7 p.m., a big torchlight procession, organised by the Sunningend workers and the aeronautical cadets, started out from the Midland railway station and travelled down Queen's Road, into Lansdown Place, Bath Road, the High Street and up the Promenade to The Queen's Hotel. The torches became a bonfire.

What a very different bonfire outside The Queen's Hotel on Tuesday, 12 November 1918 from that on the eve of war on 3 August 1914 at Stonewall Fields. What a very different Cheltenham.

OUR BOYS--
GOD BLESS THEM !

WE REJOICE IN THE NEWS OF PEACE.

THE BOYS ARE COMING HOME !

**"Ring out, ye Bells,—
Ring out the Old,
Ring in the New,
Ring out the False,
Ring in the True."**

HOME !

BACK TO OLD ENGLAND !

BACK TO CHELTENHAM !

Our Streets Will Soon Ring With the Tramp of Feet !

GIVE THEM A ROYAL WELCOME !

Build a Memorial to the Noble Dead !

Provide for the Widow and Fatherless.

Cheer the lot of Blinded and Broken Men.

Let even Business Go and Give the Boys the First Place.

"The Famous"

CLOTHING MARKET,
(UNDER THE TOWN CLOCK)

CHELTENHAM.

CLOSE WEDNESDAYS 1 O'CLOCK.

Proprietor—A. N. COLE.

In Cheltenham more than 1,600 families would be mourning their loss – ninety-one families lost two sons, seven families lost three or more men and two families had both father and son killed. One sister, distraught at losing two brothers, drowned herself. Queen Street, according to David Drinkwater, was the most tragic street in Cheltenham, with the loss of twenty men in a street of eighty houses.

In the words of the Rector of Cheltenham, in his sermon at the Thanksgiving service on that same day, Tuesday, 12 November 1918: 'It is a time in our history of such tremendous and bewildering import, we are so dazed by the wonder of it all, that to attempt a summing up is beyond the mind of man. The war is over.'

Postscript

CHELTENHAM'S FORGOTTEN WAR MEMORIAL PAINTING AND THE WINTERBOTHAM BROTHERS

There is a painting which has great significance to Cheltenham as it encapsulates and commemorates a part of Cheltenham's war. Cheltenham Corporation, in 1920, commissioned the war artist Fred Roe to paint, in oils, an official war picture for Cheltenham. Lieutenant Cyril Winterbotham, the principal figure in the picture, was killed in action on 27 August 1916. He was the youngest son of the late Alderman James Winterbotham and Mrs Winterbotham of Cranley Lodge, Wellington Square. Mrs Winterbotham lent Lisle House to the Red Cross for use as St Martin's Hospital and then a home for disabled soldiers. Cyril, born in Cheltenham and educated at Cheltenham College, was brother to a past and future town councillor at the time of the painting's subject in 1916. Just before he left for the war, Cyril had been accepted as the Liberal candidate for the Cirencester constituency.

This large picture, 40in × 60in, entitled 'A relieved platoon of the 1/5th Gloucesters, marching in from the trenches past headquarters at Hébuterne, 1916', was described in 1997 by James Brazier, editor of The Western Front Association's Bulletin, as 'Cheltenham's forgotten War Memorial painting'. It shows six officers of the Territorial Force battalion, an NCO and a group of soldiers, in a ruined village. Two of the officers in the painting, Major Noel Huxley Waller and Major J.F. Tarrant, commanded E and F companies of the 1/5th Battalion Gloucestershire Regiment (Territorial Force) – the first soldiers to leave the Drill Hall, North Street, Cheltenham on 5 August 1914 (see pp. 21–22). After the war Tarrant, by then a lieutenant colonel, resumed his role as secretary to the council of Cheltenham Ladies' College. Company Sergeant Major William Tibbles, the NCO in the picture, was born in Cheltenham and was awarded the Military Cross for his actions on 27 August 1916, having taken command when all of the officers, including Lieutenant Cyril Winterbotham, were killed. Tibbles suffered severe shell shock as a result.

Frederick Roe's painting 'The 1/5th Gloucesters at Hebuterne 1916'. (By permission of the Curator of Anne S.K. Brown Military Collection, Brown University Library, Providence, RI, USA)

Lieutenant Cyril Winterbotham was killed on 27 August 1916 in the vicinity of Skyline Trench, Orvillers, France in 'The Big Push' on the Somme. He was 29 years old. Described as one of the lesser-known war poets, by curious coincidence his poem 'The Cross of Wood' was published in the *Chronicle* the day before he died, as part of a report from the July issue of *The 5th Gloucester's Gazette*. In the same battalion, and also a copious contributor of poems to the gazette, was the well-known 'Gloucestershire Laureate' Lieutenant F.W. 'Will' Harvey, who had written a poem in the April issue about Major Noel Huxley Waller, later to be Colonel Waller. The Waller family architectural practice designed Cheltenham Town Hall.

Cheltenham Town Councillor, Captain James Percival Winterbotham, always known as Percy, was Cyril Winterbotham's elder brother and also appears in the picture, having served with him in the 1/5th Battalion of the Gloucesters as adjutant throughout the Battle of the Somme. Percy had played cricket for Gloucestershire in 1902, was a director of The Queen's Hotel, post-war becoming the hotel's Chairman and a Director of the Cheltenham Gas Company. He was a solicitor with his family's Cheltenham firm, Winterbotham, Gurney & Co., joining the army at the outbreak of war. Wounded by the splinter of a shell fragment at the Ypres Salient in June 1917, Percy was also 'slightly gassed' in August 1918. He died in Cheltenham at the age of 42 in 1925. Percy and Cyril Winterbotham's sister, Clara, served as a

Red Cross nurse in Cheltenham and was the first lady councillor, co-opted onto the council in 1918 in her brother's ward. In 1921 Clara Winterbotham became the first Lady Mayor of Cheltenham and later the second lady alderman.

A cross of wood was erected by the side of the trench where Winterbotham fell, listing his name and that of fourteen other men from his regiment who also died with him that day. One whose name is on the cross is Second Lieutenant Charles Brien, aged 23 years, an old Cheltenham Grammar School pupil, and, pre-war, a surveyor of taxes in Cheltenham. Two others named were from Cheltenham – Private Edward Keen and Private Ernest King. The wooden cross from the trench was brought back from France and placed in Cheltenham cemetery in October 1925.

The picture is on display at the Soldiers of Gloucestershire Museum in Gloucester, on loan from Cheltenham Art Gallery (now The Wilson) along with items from Winterbotham's family. Displayed with the picture is the original telegram sent to Cyril Winterbotham's widowed mother advising her that her son had been killed in action, along with his medals.

The *Echo* of 27 September 1920 hoped the picture '... set an example ... to encourage all who desire to see in Cheltenham a war memorial on a scale appropriate to the sacrifices of the town ...' The Cheltenham War Memorial was unveiled on 1 October 1921.

Lest we forget.

The Cross of Wood

God be with you and us who go our way,
And leave you dead upon the ground you won.
For you at last the long fatigue is done,
The hard march ended. You have rest today.

You were our friends. With you we watched the dawn
Gleam through the rain of the long winter night.
With you we laboured till the morning light
Broke on the village, shell-destroyed and torn.

Not now for you the glorious return
To steep Stroud Valleys to the Severn leas
By Tewkesbury and Gloucester, or the trees
Of Cheltenham under high Cotswold stern

For you no medals such as others wear
A cross of bronze for those approved brave.
To you is given, above a shallow grave,
The wooden cross that marks you resting there.

Rest you content. More honourable far
Than all the Orders is the cross of wood,
The symbol of self-sacrifice that stood
Bearing the God whose brethren you are.

Cyril Winterbotham, 1887–1916

Bibliography

Aldred, David H., *Cleeve Hill: The History of the Common and its People* (1990, Alan Sutton Publishing)

Beckett, Ian, *Homefront 1914-1918* (2006, no publisher given)

Benson, Derek, *Women's Suffrage Activism in Cheltenham* (2014, Kindle ebook)

Blake, Steven Blake, *A History of Cheltenham in 100 Objects* (2013, The History Press)

Bosanquet, Nick, *Our Land At War: Britain's Key First World War Sites* (2014, Spellmount)

Braybon, Gail, *Women Workers in the First World War* (1981, Croom Helm)

Brazier, James, 'Cheltenham's forgotten War Memorial painting: *The 1/5th Gloucesters at Hébuterne 1916 by Fred Roe*' by James Brazier from *The Western Front Association Bulletin* No. 49, October 1997

Brooks, Robin, *A Century of Cheltenham* (2001, Sutton Publishing; 2012, The History Press)

Brooks, Robin, *The Story of Cheltenham* (2003, Sutton Publishing Ltd)

Charman, Terry, *The First World War on the Home Front* (2014, Andre Deutsch/Imperial War Museum)

Cheltenham Ladies' College, *Cheltenham Ladies' College: A Chronicle of War Work 1914-1919* (1920 Chiswick Press, London)

Christian, Nick, *In the Shadow of the Lone Tree: The Ordeal of Gloucestershire Men at the Battle of Loos – 1915* (1996, Nick Christian)

Colchester-Wemyss, Maynard *Letters to the King of Siam 1903-1925* (Gloucestershire Archives D37/1/15 – D37/1/295)

Condell, Diana and Liddiard, Jean, *Working for Victory: Images of Women in the First World War* (1987, Routledge Kegan Paul)

DeGroot, Gerard, *Back in Blighty: The British at Home in World War 1* (1996, Longman; 2014, Vintage)

Devereux, Joseph and Sacker, Graham, *Leaving All That Was Dear: Cheltenham and the Great War* (1997, Promenade Publications, Cheltenham)

Dowen, Jack, *A Century of Continuous Scouting: History of the 10th Cheltenham All Saints' Scout Group 1910–2010*

Doyle, Peter, *First World War Britain* (2012, Shire Publications Ltd)

Edwards, Brian, *National Filling Factory No. 5, Quedgeley* (*Gloucestershire Society for Industrial Archaeology Journal* 1994, 33, pp. 32–52, www.gsia.org.uk/reprints/1994/gi199432.pdf)

Evans, David, *Be Proud that You're Fighting for England – Dursley 1914* (2008, Two Plus George Ltd, Barnham)

Faithfull, Lilian M. *In the House of My Pilgrimage* (1924, Chatto and Windus, London)

Faulkner-Aston, Harvey, *A Study of the Development and Present Day Conservation Issues Relating to Cheltenham's first Inter-War Housing Estate* (2004 MA in Architectural Conservation, Dissertation, University of Bristol. Gloucester Archives D13157)

Fountain, Nigel (ed.), *When the Lights Went Out: From Home Front to Battle Front Reporting the Great War* (2014, Guardian Books)

Gould, Jennifer, 'The Women's Corp: The Establishment of Women's Military Services in Britain' (1988 PhD thesis, University College London)

Hochschild, Adam, *To End All Wars* (2011, Macmillan)

Holman, Roger, *Cheltenham's Homes Fit for Heroes* (1981 Gloucestershire Community Council Local History Bulletin Autumn)

Jones, Anthea, *Cheltenham: A New History* (2010, Carnegie Publishing Ltd)

Lang, Seán, *First World War for Dummies* (2014, John Wiley & Sons Ltd)

MacDonagh, Michael, *In London, During the Great War* (1935, Eyre & Spottiswoode, London (quoted in Simkins))

Marwick, Arthur, *The Deluge: British Society and the First World War* (1965, Macmillan)

Miller, Eric, *Leckhampton Court: Manor House to Hospice* (2011, Matador Press)

Naunton Park Girls Council School Log Book (1 September 1907–31 August 1930. Gloucestershire Archives GA S78/9/2/1)

Newbould, Christopher and Beresford, Christine, *The Glosters: An Illustrated History of a County Regiment* (1993, Alan Sutton Publishing)

Nicholson, Juliet, *The Great Silence: 1918-1920 Living in the Shadow of the Great War* (2009 pb, John Murray).

Nicholson, Virginia, *Singled Out* (2007, Viking)

Owen, Barbara, *Wartime Letters of a Westbury Squire: Selected by Barbara Owen* (1992. Ref RR 328.21 16/212/2 Gloucestershire Archives)

Pakenham, Simona, *Cheltenham: A Biography* (1971, Macmillan, London)

Paxman, Jeremy, *Great Britain's Great War* (2013, Viking)

Rennison, John, *Wings over Gloucestershire* (1988, Picadilly Publishing; 2000 revised edition Aspect Publishing)

Rowbotham, Sue and Waller, Jill, *Cheltenham, A History* (2004, Phillimore & Co. Ltd)

Rowbotham, Sue, 'The Women's Suffrage Movement in Cheltenham 1871–1914' (*Journal of Cheltenham Local History Society* 2015, www.cheltlocalhist.btck.co.uk)

Rowe, Mark, *August 1914* (2013, Chaplin Books)

Simkins, Peter in association with the Imperial War Museum (1988) *Kitchener's Army: The Raising of the New Armies 1914-1916* (1988, 2007, Pen and Sword Books Ltd)

Taylor, A.J.P., *The First World War* (1974, Penguin Books)

Whitaker, John, *The Best: The History of H.H. Martyn & Company* (2nd Edition, 1998, Promenade Publications)

Whiting, Roger, *Cheltenham in Old Photographs – A Second Edition* (1988, Alan Sutton Publishing)

www.remembering.org.uk

Index

french lessons, 90, 138

Frodsham, Bishop, 122

Fruin, Mr, 45

fuel rationing, 178, 190

funeral, first, semi-military, 34

Gallipoli, 28

Gardiner, Mrs, 106

garments, 95, 97, 106, 108

Garrett, Dr, 156

gas, chlorine, 93

gas works, 43, 48

Geddes, Miss Ethel, 153, 167, 168

Gentlewoman, The, magazine, 106

George V, King, 8, 45, 53, 84, 74, 182, 194

George's, the Caterers, 50, *51*, 177

German residents, 53, 54

Gibbons, Mr J.S., Boddington Manor, 110

Gibbs, W.H., 106

Gilsmith, Cecil, The Hippodrome, 58,

girl gardeners, 125

Gloster Aircraft Co., The, 127, 128, 159

Gloucester County Association for Voluntary
Organisations, 96, *97*, 107

Gloucester, HMS, 99

Gloucester Old Spot pigs, 189

Gloucester Road, 38

Gloucester Road School, 154–156, 180

Gloucestershire Aircraft Co., 127

Gloucestershire Co-operative Society, 43

Gloucestershire County Council, 11, 42, 126,
161, 184

Gloucestershire County Cricket Club, 19, 26

Gloucestershire Education Committee, 181

Gloucestershire Regiments:

    1st Gloucestershire Royal Engineer
Volunteers, (GREV), 144

    3/4th, 3/5th, 3/6th Battations, 91

    5th Battalion, 16, 18–22, 27, 33, 95, 98,
100, 167, 200, 201

    7th Battalion, 103, 104

    8th Battalion, 27, 93

    9th Battalion, 37, 74–85, 91, 99

    10th Battalion, 75, 76, 79, 80, 82, 83, 86,
91-93

    11th Battalion, 34, 46, 118

    14th Battalion (Bantams), 142

    30th Railway Labour Battalion, 40

    'Cheltenham Territorial Cyclists' (of the
South Midland Cyclist Company), 139

    Royal Gloucestershire Hussars Yeomanry,
17, 19, 21, 38

Gloucestershire Surgical Appliance Co., 159

Glove Waistcoat Society, 176

Glyngarth School, 58

Goffinet, Baron C., 52

golf clubs:

    Cheltenham, 106

    Cotswold Hills, 32

Good Hope, HMS, 29

Gordon Boys, 38

Gordon Lamp, *37*, 38, 175

Gotha bombers, 129

Grace, W.G., 26, 27

Great Norwood Street, 156, 191

Green, E. (possibly Edwinson), 70

Green, Miss Molly, 100

'Greenfield', 58

Grey, Sir Edward, 18, 19

Grogan, Rear Admiral, 100

Guinness, Miss, 115

Gurney's, Mr, Private School, 58

Haddock, Councillor, 154

Haig, General Sir Douglas, 122

Hales Road, 71, 83

Hall, Joseph, 23

Hall, Marie, 70

Hall Road, 71

Hambourg, Mark, 62

Hanover Street, 55

Harker, Private George, 98

Harrods Department Store, 27

Harvey, Lt Lennox, steeplechase jockey, 110

Harward Buildings, 163

Haverfield, Hon. Mrs Evaline, 111

Healey, Gertrude, Pittville Lake, 125

Healing & Overbury, 163, 212, 214

Hearle Cole, Mrs, 95, 104, 145–147

Heath, Miss, 104

Heath's Nursery, College Road, 115, 171

Hébuterne, The 1/5th Gloucesters 1916, 201

war bonds, 166, 167

War Office, The, 68, 74, 78, 101, 129, 134, 140, 172

War Savings Committee,166, 174, 176–178

War Supply Department, Evening, 95, 108

War Supply Depots, 95, *107*, 108

Ward, Mrs Humphrey, 157

Warner, Sheppard & Wade, 110

Warwickshire Regiment, Royal, 91

Waterfield, Canon Reginald, 162

Wayre-Taylor, Miss, 115

Webb Bros (brickworks), 48

Webb, Mr, Cheltenham Window Cleaning Co., 126

Wellington Square, 200

Welstead, Mr, 48

Wesleyan School, Great Norwood Street, 156

West of England Munitions Committee, 69, 72

Westal Green, tank, 165

Western Counties War Exhibition, 62–64

Western Lodge, Western Road, 58, 64

Wethered, Miss Mina Ricketts, 87, 88, 95, *96*, 97, 106, 36, 138, 147, 153

Wethered, Mr E.B., 53

Wethered, Mrs, 88, 136

wheat, 169, 170, 173–176

whist drive, giant, 170

Whitcombe, Mrs and her dog Denis, 43

White Feather, The Order of the, 45, 46

White, Mr. A.J., 34

Wilde, Mrs. Helen Stanley, 115, 116

Willet & Co., Messrs, 54

Willett, William, 133

Williams, Joseph, 40

Williams, Mrs Gwatkin, 98

Willoughby, Edwin, 28, 48, 104

Winter Gardens, 60–64, 126, 128, 156, 163, 197

Wilson:

  Dr Edward, 15, 16, 52

  Mrs Edward, 113, 115

  Mrs Oriana, 15

Wilson, Revd H.A., 175, 191

Winterbotham:

  Alderman James, 200

Cyril, Lt, 200–203,

Cyril's 'The Cross of Wood' poem, 203

Miss Clara, 117, 167, 168, 201, 202

Mrs James, 159, 200

'Percy' (J.P.), 167, 201

Winterbotham, Gurney & Co., solicitors,

Winterbotham, Sir Henry, 36

Wixey, Lnce-Cpl Alfred, 103

Wolseley-Lewis, Revd T., 60, 61

women in men's jobs, 120–128

women voters, 167

women working in shops, 125

'Woodleigh', *90*, 172

Women of England's Active Service League, 45

Women Patrols, 89

Women's Emergency Corps, 111

women's enfranchisement, 111, 117, 120, 167

Women's Freedom League, 111

Women's Land Army Timber Section, Shab Hill, 142

Women's Right to Serve march, 120

Women's Royal Air Force (WRAF), 140, 155

Women's Social and Political Union (WSPU), 111

Women's Suffrage Declaration, 111

Women's Trade Union League, 105

Women's Volunteer Reserve, (WVR), 38, 111, *112*, 113, 137, 180

Women's War Club Committee, 100

Women's War Register, 68, 69

Worcestershire Regiment, 134

working classes, 12, 85, 87, 89, 119, 169, 170, 185

'Workman, Will', Will Dyson, 18

Wounded Soldiers' Club, 136

Wright, Fredk, 82, *83*, 87

Wright, Nellie, 142

Wright, Miss, *119*

Yapp, Sir Arthur, 18

YMCA, 87, 135, 137, 138, 182

YWCA, 140

Yonge, Miss Alice, 159

Zeppelin, Count Ferdinand von, 129

Zeppelins, 27, 36, 129–133, 159

Also from The History Press

GREAT WAR BRITAIN

Great War Britain is a unique new local series to mark the centenary of the Great War. In partnership with archives and museums across Great Britain, the series provides an evocative portrayal of life during this 'war to end all wars'. In a scrapbook style, and beautifully illustrated, it includes features such as personal memoirs, letters home, diary extracts, newspaper reports, photographs, postcards and other local First World War ephemera.

Find these titles and more at
www.thehistorypress.co.uk

The History Press

Also from The History Press

WAR IN THE SKIES

Also from The History Press

GLOUCESTERSHIRE

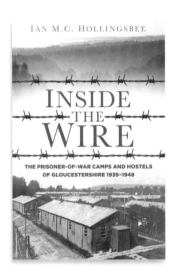

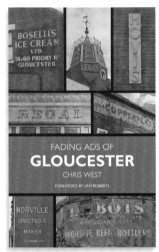

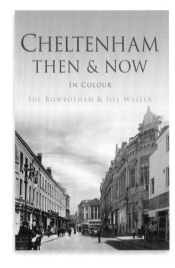

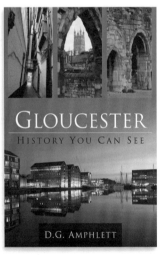

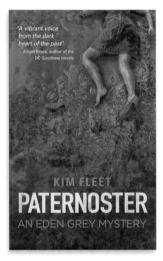

Find these titles and more at

www.thehistorypress.co.uk

Cheltenham Local History Society

Bringing Cheltenham History to Life

A society for those interested in learning about, researching and increasing public awareness of the history of Cheltenham.

- Talks - Monthly talks from September to May

- Walks and Visits – June to August

- Research Projects on Cheltenham

- Expert Advice - on your own historical research

- Publications - newsletters and annual journal

For more information or a membership application form please visit our website at

www.cheltlocalhistory.org.uk

Registered Charity No. 1056046